Get Out of Your Way!

How Law Firm Owners can Delegate, Empower their Team, and Thrive!

By Jay Ruane

DISCLAIMER

The attorney profiles and case studies presented in this book are composite fictional narratives created for illustrative purposes. While they draw upon the author's extensive experience coaching and consulting with attorneys over many years, the individuals portrayed are not real people. Any resemblance to actual persons, living or deceased, or to specific law firms is purely coincidental and unintended.

These fictionalized accounts represent common patterns, challenges, and situations that the author has observed across the criminal defense legal community, but they do not depict any particular individual's circumstances or practice. The stories have been crafted to protect the privacy and confidentiality of the many attorneys the author has had the privilege of working with throughout his career.

The strategies, insights, and recommendations contained in this book are based on real-world experience and proven methodologies, but readers should consult with their own professional advisors and use their own professional judgment before implementing any business, marketing, or operational changes in their practices.

Dedication

This book is dedicated to my wife Jill, who has always encouraged me to get out of my own way, and made everything I hold dear to me possible.

Table of Contents

Introduction 11
The Problem: You Are the Problem 12
Why This Happens in Legal Practice 13
The Unique Delegation Challenges in Law Firms 15
What Will Change When You Delegate Well 17
How to Use This Book 20
Quick-Start Guide for the Overwhelmed Attorney 20
The Journey Ahead 23

CHAPTER 1: Understanding the Bottleneck Syndrome 25
Why Law Firm Owners Tend to Micromanage 26
Common Mindset Traps 29
Symptoms: How to Know You're the Bottleneck 32
The Attorney-Specific Identity Crisis 36
Case Study: The Solo Practitioner Who Couldn't Take
Vacation 40
Recognizing Your Own Bottleneck Syndrome 43
Action Items for This Chapter: 44

CHAPTER 2: The Real Cost of Being the Bottleneck 47
Lost Time and Opportunity Cost 48
Financial Analysis: The True Cost of Your Time 52
Slower Growth, Reduced Scalability 55
Team Morale and Retention Issues 59
Stress, Burnout, and Reduced Focus on High-Value Work 62
Client Service Suffers When You're the Bottleneck 65
Malpractice Risk When You're Spread Too Thin 67
Case Study: The Firm That Lost Its Best Paralegal to
Burnout 70
The Hidden Costs Add Up 74
The Point of No Return 76
Calculating Your Personal Bottleneck Cost 77

The Choice Point.. 80

Action Items for This Chapter:.................................... 82

Before Moving to Chapter 3: 83

CHAPTER 3: The Law Firm Delegation Landscape........... 85

What Makes Legal Delegation Different from Other
Businesses 86

Professional Responsibility and Ethical Obligations 87

Malpractice Risk Management in Delegation 90

Client Confidentiality and Privilege Considerations................ 94

State Bar Rules on Supervision and Delegation...................... 98

Trust Accounting: What Can and Cannot Be Delegated........ 101

The Liability Framework You Must Understand.................. 106

Navigating the Landscape Safely..................................... 111

The Choice: Paralyzed by Fear or Guided by Knowledge 113

Action Items for This Chapter:.................................... 115

Before Moving to Chapter 4: 116

CHAPTER 4: What to Delegate and What to Keep 117

Categories of Work: The Core vs. Peripheral Framework..... 118

The "Zone of Genius" Concept 121

Examples of Tasks to Delegate 123

Guardrails: What Should Never Be Delegated 129

Delegating to Attorneys vs. Nonlawyer Staff 131

Building Your Personal Delegation Strategy 133

The Delegation Decision Tree...................................... 136

Different Practice Areas, Different Delegation Strategies 137

The 80/20 Goal Revisited... 139

Action Items for This Chapter:.................................... 141

Before Moving to Chapter 5: 142

CHAPTER 5: Finding the Right People 143

Personality Traits and Work Habits of Strong Delegates....... 144

Hiring for Initiative, Judgment, and Accountability 149

Sample Interview Questions for Delegation Readiness 152

Onboarding and Training for Delegation Success 158

Building a Team of Problem-Solvers, Not Task-Executors... 163

Special Considerations for Hiring Associates vs. Support
Staff.. 167
When the Right Person Isn't Available: Build vs. Hire.......... 170
Creating Career Pathways That Retain Delegation-Ready
People.. 172
The Ongoing Hiring Strategy 174
Finding the Right People: The Foundation of Delegation
Success 175
Action Items for This Chapter:... 177
Before Moving to Chapter 6:.. 178

CHAPTER 6:   The Client Relationship Challenge 179
Why Clients Resist Delegation.. 180
Setting Client Expectations From the Start 183
Introducing Team Members to Build Confidence.................. 186
Training Teams to Maintain Your Client Service Standards . 190
Maintaining Personal Touch While Delegating 193
Handling "I Want to Speak to the Attorney".......................... 196
Making Delegation Enhance Client Service........................... 201
The Virtual Assistant Dimension 205
Practice Area-Specific Delegation Approaches 213
Communication Protocols for Client-Facing Delegation 216
Karen's Client Relationship Breakthrough 219
Action Items for This Chapter... 222
Before Moving to Chapter 7.. 224

CHAPTER 7:   Mastering Deadlines and Tracking
Systems 227
Why Deadlines Matter in Delegation 228
The Components of Effective Deadline Management 229
How to Set Realistic Deadlines When Delegating................. 231
Communicating Deadlines Clearly 233
Milestone and Interim Deadlines 235
Tracking Systems That Work Without Micromanaging 237
When Deadlines Are Missed: Response Protocols 240
Technology Tools for Deadline Management......................... 243

Creating a Culture of Deadline Accountability 247

Marcus's Transformation: From Crisis to Confidence 251

Action Items for This Chapter 254

Before Moving to Chapter 10: 255

CHAPTER 8:   When Delegation Fails 257

Recognizing the Warning Signs 258

Diagnosing the Root Cause 261

The Pull-Back Decision: When to Reclaim Work 264

Course-Correcting Failed Delegation 268

Learning from Delegation Failures 271

Building Resilience Into Your Delegation Approach 274

Nicole's Hard-Won Wisdom 278

Action Items for This Chapter 282

Before Moving to Chapter 11: 283

CHAPTER 9:   The Client Relationship Challenge 285

Why Clients Resist Delegation 286

Setting Client Expectations From the Start 289

Introducing Team Members to Build Confidence 292

Training Teams to Maintain Your Client Service Standards . 296

Maintaining Personal Touch While Delegating 299

Handling "I Want to Speak to the Attorney" 302

Making Delegation Enhance Client Service 307

Practice Area-Specific Delegation Approaches 311

Communication Protocols for Client-Facing Delegation 314

Karen's Client Relationship Breakthrough 317

Action Items for This Chapter 320

Before Moving to Chapter 11 322

**CHAPTER 10:   Decision-Making Frameworks That
Empower 325**

Why Decision Delegation Matters 326

The 1-3-1 Framework: Structured Problem-Solving 327

The Eisenhower Matrix: Prioritization Decisions 330

RAPID: Clarifying Decision Roles 334

The OODA Loop: Fast Decision-Making Under
Uncertainty 336
Building Decision-Making Confidence 339
Maintaining Quality While Delegating Decisions 343
Daniel's Decision Delegation Transformation 346
Action Items for This Chapter 349
Before Moving to Chapter 13: 350

CHAPTER 11: Feedback, Coaching, and Accountability .. 351
The Feedback Avoidance Trap 352
The Elements of Effective Feedback 355
Creating Accountability Without Micromanagement 358
Coaching for Capability Development 361
Addressing Performance Issues Constructively 365
Creating a Feedback Culture 368
Rebecca's Feedback Transformation 372
Action Items for This Chapter 375
Before Moving to Chapter 14: 376

CHAPTER 12: Scaling Delegation as You Grow 377
The Scaling Inflection Points 378
Creating Organizational Structure for Scaled Delegation 380
Developing Managers Who Delegate 382
Building Systems That Scale Without You 385
Embedding Delegation in Culture 389
Measuring Delegation Effectiveness at Scale 392
Thomas's Scaling Success 395
Action Items for This Chapter 398
Conclusion: From Bottleneck to Builder 399

ABOUT THE AUTHOR 402

Introduction

It was 11:47 PM on a Tuesday when Sarah finally closed her laptop. Again.

She'd started her day at 7:30 AM, rushed through back-to-back client meetings, squeezed in two court appearances, returned forty-three emails, reviewed every document her paralegal had prepared, approved every social media post her marketing person had drafted, and personally handled an intake call that came in at 9:15 PM because "the client specifically asked for the attorney."

Sarah runs a successful criminal defense practice. Seven years in, she has three attorneys working for her, two paralegals, and an office manager. On paper, she should have plenty of support. Her revenue is strong. Her reputation is solid. Her Google reviews are stellar.

So why does she feel like she's drowning?

Why is she the last one in the office every night? Why does her phone buzz constantly with "quick questions" from her team? Why does every decision, every document, every client communication seem to need her personal review before it can move forward?

The answer is uncomfortable but liberating: **Sarah has become her own bottleneck.**

And if you picked up this book, there's a good chance you have too.

The Problem: You Are the Problem

Here's the truth that most law firm owners don't want to hear: the biggest obstacle to your firm's growth isn't the market, your competition, or even your budget.

It's you.

Not because you're incompetent. Not because you don't work hard enough. In fact, it's usually the opposite. You work too hard, you're too involved, and you've made yourself indispensable to every single process in your practice.

You've built a successful law practice, but you've also built a cage around yourself. Every decision flows through you. Every problem lands on your desk. Every client wants to speak with you personally. Your team has learned to wait for your approval before moving forward because, well, that's what you've trained them to do.

The irony? You hired people to help you, but somehow you're busier than ever.

You're working nights and weekends while your team goes home at 5 PM. You're the first one to arrive and the last to leave. You check email on vacation (if you even take vacation). You've missed your kid's soccer games, postponed date nights, and convinced yourself that this is just what it takes to run a successful practice.

But here's what keeps you up at night: you know this isn't sustainable. You know you can't scale yourself. You know that if you got hit by a bus tomorrow, your practice would struggle. You know that the firm you've built is entirely dependent on your personal involvement in nearly everything.

You are the bottleneck. And until you fix that, you'll never have the practice you truly want.

Why This Happens in Legal Practice

If you're feeling defensive right now, take a breath. You're not alone, and there are very good reasons why law firm owners struggle with delegation more than almost any other type of business owner.

The Weight of Professional Identity

For most attorneys, becoming a lawyer wasn't just a career choice— it was an identity. You spent three years in law school, passed the bar exam, built your reputation case by case, and earned the right to call yourself an attorney. Your professional identity is deeply tied to your personal competence.

When you delegate, it can feel like you're giving away the very thing that makes you valuable. The whisper in your head says: "If I'm not doing the work, am I even a real lawyer? If my team handles the client communication, will clients still see me as their attorney? If I'm not reviewing every motion, every brief, every email, am I shirking my professional responsibility?"

This identity crisis is unique to professionals. A restaurant owner doesn't question their identity when they hire a chef. A construction company owner doesn't worry they're not a "real" builder when they delegate framing to a crew. But lawyers? We tie our self-worth to our personal involvement in the work.

The Specter of Malpractice

Let's be honest: you went to law school, not business school. You were trained to spot issues, anticipate problems, and be personally accountable for outcomes. You were taught that the buck stops with you—because legally, it does.

Every time you think about delegating, your malpractice insurance premiums flash through your mind. What if your paralegal misses a filing deadline? What if your associate gives incorrect advice? What if a client sues because someone on your team dropped the ball?

The fear is real because the risk is real. You can be disciplined, sued, or disbarred for failures in supervision. So you tell yourself it's just safer to do it yourself. At least then you know it's done right.

Client Expectations and Relationships

Your clients hired you, not your firm. When they call, they want to talk to you. When they have a question, they expect you to answer it. When they're scared, stressed, or facing serious consequences, they want the person whose name is on the door.

You've probably experienced the awkwardness of a client saying, "I'd really prefer to speak with you directly" when your associate tries to handle their call. You've felt the pressure to personally attend every hearing, every meeting, every phone call because that's what your clients expect.

And you've probably internalized the belief that great client service means personal service from you. After all, isn't that what sets your firm apart from the competition?

The Perfectionism Trap

You've built your reputation on quality work. Your attention to detail is what wins cases. Your thoroughness is what clients pay for. You take pride in doing things right.

So when you look at the work your team produces, you see the gaps. The motion that's good but not quite as polished as you would have written it. The client email that's fine but doesn't quite capture your tone. The research that's adequate but missing that one case you would have found.

You tell yourself you're maintaining quality standards. But really, you're trapped by perfectionism. Nothing is ever quite good enough unless you do it yourself or heavily edit it. So you end up spending hours "reviewing" work that essentially becomes you redoing the work.

The Control Imperative

Here's the uncomfortable truth: some of us became law firm owners because we like being in control. We don't love being told what to do. We prefer to set our own direction, make our own decisions, and be accountable only to ourselves.

That desire for control served you well when you were building your practice. But now it's strangling your growth. Because the same instinct that drove you to start your own firm is now preventing you from building a firm that doesn't revolve entirely around you.

Letting go feels like losing control. Delegating feels risky. Empowering your team to make decisions feels like chaos waiting to happen.

But real control doesn't mean making every decision yourself. Real control means building systems and teams that work the way you want them to work, even when you're not in the room.

The Unique Delegation Challenges in Law Firms

Law firms aren't like other businesses. The challenges you face in delegation are compounded by factors that don't exist in most industries.

Ethics and Professional Responsibility

You can't just delegate anything to anyone. State bar rules govern what tasks can be performed by non-lawyers, how you must supervise your team, and when you must personally review work product. You have an ethical duty of competent representation that means you can't simply hand off work and hope for the best.

Trust accounting rules mean you can't delegate certain financial functions. Client confidentiality rules mean you must carefully control who has access to what information. Conflicts checks must be thorough. Engagement letters must be clear.

Every delegation decision comes wrapped in ethical considerations that most business owners never face.

The Malpractice Minefield

One mistake by someone on your team can result in a malpractice claim that costs you hundreds of thousands of dollars and damages your reputation. Missed deadlines, incorrect advice, failed communication—these aren't just "learning opportunities" in a law practice. They're potential disasters.

You're not just worried about business outcomes; you're worried about professional survival.

Client Relationships Are Personal

Unlike many businesses where customers interact with a brand, legal clients form personal relationships with their attorneys. They're trusting you with their freedom, their money, their family, their business. That trust doesn't automatically transfer to your team members.

Building client confidence in your team while maintaining your relationships requires intentional strategy. It's not enough to hire good people and hope clients accept them. You need systems, communication protocols, and careful transition plans.

You Can't Scale Your Brain

In many businesses, scaling means doing more of the same thing. In law, every case is different. Every client has unique needs. Every situation requires professional judgment.

You can't just create a widget-making process and replicate it. Legal work requires analysis, judgment, and expertise. Finding people who can make good decisions and training them to think like you do is genuinely difficult.

So you end up being the brain of the operation for everything, and brains don't scale.

What Will Change When You Delegate Well

Now for the good news. When you break through these barriers and learn to delegate effectively, everything changes.

Your Practice Will Actually Grow

Right now, your revenue is capped by how much you personally can handle. You might have people working for you, but if every matter still requires your involvement, you've just raised the ceiling slightly. You haven't actually removed it.

When you delegate well, your practice can grow beyond your personal capacity. Cases move forward when you're in court on another matter. Client communication happens without your involvement in every email. New business gets developed even when you're focused on trial preparation.

Growth isn't just possible—it's inevitable. Because you're no longer the limiting factor.

You'll Stop Burning Out

The perpetual exhaustion you feel isn't because you're weak or lazy. It's because you're trying to do the impossible: be personally involved in everything happening in your practice.

When you delegate effectively, you'll leave the office at reasonable hours. You'll take vacations without your laptop. You'll have mental energy left over for your family, your hobbies, and your health.

You'll stop waking up at 3 AM running through your mental checklist of everything that needs your attention. You'll stop feeling guilty about taking time off. You'll stop resenting your practice for consuming your entire life.

Your Team Will Become Actually Valuable

Right now, your team might feel like they're generating more work for you, not less. You spend time answering their questions, reviewing their work, and fixing their mistakes. Sometimes you wonder if it would be faster to just do it yourself.

That's because you haven't actually delegated. You've just created more people who depend on you for every decision.

When you delegate well, your team transforms from order-takers to problem-solvers. They start making good decisions without you. They start catching problems before they reach your desk. They start adding genuine value instead of just checking tasks off a list.

You'll actually get the leverage you hired them to provide.

You'll Build Real Equity in Your Practice

A practice that depends entirely on you isn't worth much to anyone else. If you decided to sell, transition to of-counsel status, or retire, what exactly would a buyer be purchasing? The right to work as hard as you've been working?

When you build systems, delegate effectively, and develop a team that can operate without your constant involvement, you're building a real asset. Something with value beyond your personal hours.

Even if you never plan to sell, you're creating options. Options to slow down. Options to pivot to appellate work or consulting. Options to take a sabbatical. Options to pursue other interests while your practice continues generating income.

Real freedom comes from building something that doesn't completely depend on you.

You'll Actually Enjoy Your Practice Again

Remember why you went to law school? It probably wasn't because you dreamed of managing email, reviewing every document three times, and attending administrative meetings.

You wanted to practice law. To solve complex problems. To advocate for clients. To do the work that energized you.

When you delegate effectively, you get to spend your time on the work you actually want to do. The high-level strategy. The complex legal issues. The client relationships. The courtroom advocacy.

You'll rediscover why you became a lawyer in the first place.

You'll Build a Sustainable Practice

The practice you have right now might be successful, but is it sustainable? Can you maintain this pace for another five years? Ten years? Twenty years?

Or are you on a path toward burnout, health problems, damaged relationships, and resentment about the career you once loved?

Effective delegation isn't just about business growth. It's about building a practice you can sustain for the long term. A practice that energizes you instead of draining you. A practice that supports your life instead of consuming it.

How to Use This Book

You don't have to read this book cover to cover (though you certainly can). Here's how to get the most value:

If you're overwhelmed and need relief now: Skip directly to the Quick-Start Guide at the end of this introduction. Implement those five actions this week, then come back to read the full book.

If you're a systematic learner: Read straight through from beginning to end. Complete the worksheets and exercises as you go. Build your delegation system methodically.

If you have a specific problem: Use the table of contents to jump to the section that addresses your current challenge. Come back to other sections as you progress.

If you're skeptical: Start with Part One to see if the problems I describe match what you're experiencing. If they do, you'll be motivated to learn the solutions in later chapters.

If you learn by example: Focus on the case studies throughout the book. See how other attorneys have wrestled with and solved the same problems you're facing.

The key is to actually implement, not just read. Knowledge without action won't change anything about your practice. After each chapter, choose at least one thing to put into practice immediately.

Quick-Start Guide for the Overwhelmed Attorney

Can't wait to read the whole book? Start here. These five actions will give you immediate relief and start building your delegation muscle.

Action 1: The Five-Task Audit (15 minutes)

Right now, grab a piece of paper or open a document. List five tasks you did yesterday that someone else on your team could have done with proper training and authority.

Not five tasks you wish you could delegate someday. Five specific tasks from yesterday that didn't actually require your law degree or unique expertise.

Examples might include:

- Responding to a client's scheduling question
- Checking whether a document was filed
- Following up on a discovery request
- Drafting a routine motion
- Calling the court to get a hearing date

Now pick one of those five tasks. Just one. This week, delegate it to someone on your team with clear instructions about what a good outcome looks like and when you need it done.

Don't review their work unless they ask you to. Don't "quality check" it unless it's truly necessary. Just let them do it.

Action 2: The Email Pause (ongoing)

For the next week, add a two-hour delay before responding to any non-urgent email. When something hits your inbox, don't immediately reply.

This serves two purposes:

1. You'll discover that many "urgent" issues resolve themselves without your involvement
2. You'll create space for your team to handle issues instead of waiting for you

If someone needs an immediate response, they'll find another way to reach you. Most things that feel urgent aren't actually urgent.

Action 3: The Question Redirect (ongoing)

The next time someone on your team asks you a question, respond with: "What do you think we should do?"

Not in a sarcastic or dismissive way. With genuine curiosity about their thinking.

Listen to their answer. If it's reasonable (even if it's not exactly what you would have said), say: "That sounds good. Go ahead and do that."

Do this ten times this week. You're training your team to think through problems instead of immediately escalating to you.

Action 4: The Calendar Block (this week)

Block four hours on your calendar this week for high-value work only. The kind of work that only you can do. Strategy, complex legal analysis, business development, whatever is most valuable for your practice.

Protect these four hours fiercely. No meetings. No email. No "quick questions" from your team. If someone needs you, they can wait until after this block.

This is your first step toward reclaiming your time for work that actually matters.

Action 5: The Delegation Conversation (this week)

Schedule a 30-minute conversation with one person on your team. Tell them:

"I want to delegate more responsibility to you because I trust your judgment. I know I've been a bottleneck, and I want to change that. Here's one area where I'd like you to start making decisions without checking with me first: [name a specific type of decision]."

Then explain what guidelines or boundaries they should work within, and commit to letting them make those decisions without your pre-approval.

Have this conversation with at least one team member this week.

The Journey Ahead

Here's what I can promise you: learning to delegate effectively will be uncomfortable. You'll worry about losing control. You'll second-guess your team's decisions. You'll be tempted to jump back in and "fix" things when they don't go exactly as you would have done them.

But here's what I can also promise: on the other side of that discomfort is the practice you actually want. The freedom you crave. The sustainability you need. The growth you've been trying to achieve.

You didn't go to law school to become a perpetual bottleneck in your own practice. You went to be a great attorney. It's time to get out of your own damn way and build a practice that works for you instead of consuming you.

Let's begin.

CHAPTER 1:

Understanding the Bottleneck Syndrome

Michael had been practicing criminal defense for twelve years. He'd built a solid reputation, maintained a steady flow of clients, and earned a comfortable living. By most measures, he was successful.

But he hadn't taken a real vacation in seven years.

Oh, he'd tried. He'd book a week at the beach with his family, pack his bags, drive to the coast. But within twenty-four hours, his phone would start buzzing. A client with a question. His paralegal needed approval on a motion. The court clerk called about a scheduling conflict. An urgent email that "only he could handle."

By day two, he'd be working from the hotel room while his kids played in the sand without him. By day three, his wife would stop pretending not to be disappointed. By the end of the week, he'd return home more exhausted than when he left, having spent his "vacation" putting out fires remotely.

The worst part? Michael created this situation himself.

His paralegal was perfectly capable of handling routine motions. The client questions were rarely urgent. The scheduling conflicts could have waited. But Michael had spent years training everyone around him—his team, his clients, the courts—that he personally handled everything. He'd built a practice that couldn't function without his constant involvement.

Michael had become the bottleneck in his own firm.

If this sounds familiar, you're not alone. The bottleneck syndrome affects law firm owners at every level, from solo practitioners to managing partners of mid-sized firms. It's not a character flaw or a sign of incompetence. It's a predictable pattern that emerges from the way attorneys are trained, the nature of legal practice, and the specific challenges of building a professional services business.

Understanding why you've become a bottleneck is the first step toward freeing yourself.

Why Law Firm Owners Tend to Micromanage

Let's start with an uncomfortable question: Are you a micromanager?

If you bristled at that question, if you immediately thought "I'm not a micromanager, I just have high standards," then you probably are one.

Micromanagement isn't always the cartoonish boss standing over someone's shoulder criticizing every keystroke. In law firms, it's often more subtle:

- You review every document before it goes out, even routine correspondence
- You need to approve decisions your team should be able to make independently

- You rewrite emails your staff compose
- You're copied on every client communication
- Your team asks your permission for things that should be within their judgment
- You find yourself redoing work instead of accepting "good enough"

This isn't happening because you're a control freak (though that might be part of it). It's happening because of how you were trained and what you've been rewarded for throughout your legal career.

The Training Problem

Think about your path to becoming a lawyer. Law school taught you to spot every possible issue, anticipate every argument, and leave no stone unturned. You were rewarded for finding the obscure case, identifying the hidden problem, thinking three steps ahead.

Then you entered practice. If you worked at a firm, senior attorneys tore apart your work. They redlined your memos. They found the gaps in your research. They taught you that thoroughness and precision were everything.

You learned that mistakes were unacceptable. That "close enough" wasn't good enough. That your reputation depended on being right, being thorough, and being personally accountable for every detail.

This training served you well when you were learning. But now it's working against you.

Because when you look at your team's work, you can't help but see it through the lens of a supervising attorney who's supposed to find problems. You spot the issues, the gaps, the places where it could be stronger. Your training kicks in, and you start editing, revising, improving.

Before you know it, you've essentially rewritten the entire document. And your team learns that their work will never be quite good enough, so they might as well wait for you to do it or fix it.

The Reward Problem

Throughout your career, you've been rewarded for personal excellence. Clients hired you because of your skills. You won cases because of your preparation. You built your reputation through your individual performance.

Every win reinforced the message: your personal involvement makes the difference.

So when you delegate something and it doesn't go perfectly, your brain sounds the alarm. "See? This is why you need to do it yourself. This is why you can't trust others with important work."

But when you do something yourself and it goes well, you feel validated. "This is why I'm necessary. This is why the firm needs me to be involved."

You've created a mental reward system that punishes delegation and rewards personal involvement. Every time you step in and handle something yourself, you get a little hit of validation. Every time you delegate and something goes wrong, you get evidence that delegation is risky.

It's a self-reinforcing cycle that keeps you trapped in micromanagement.

The Expertise Problem

Here's another uncomfortable truth: you probably are better at most tasks than the people you've delegated them to. You have more experience, more knowledge, more context, and more skill.

This creates a genuine dilemma. When you review work and see ways to improve it, you're not imagining things. Your version probably would be better. Your edit probably does make the brief stronger. Your approach probably is more strategic.

But "better" is the enemy of "done." And "perfect" is the enemy of "scalable."

If the standard is "as good as I would do it," then you'll be personally involved in everything forever. Because by definition, no one else can do something exactly as you would do it. They don't have your experience, your instincts, or your brain.

The real question isn't "Is this as good as I could do it?" The real question is "Is this good enough to meet the client's needs and move the matter forward?"

Most of the time, the answer is yes. But your expertise makes it hard to see that, because you're always aware of how it could be better.

Common Mindset Traps

Beyond the structural issues of training, rewards, and expertise, there are specific mindset traps that keep law firm owners stuck in the bottleneck syndrome. See how many of these sound familiar.

Trap #1: "If I Want It Done Right, I Have to Do It Myself"

This is the classic perfectionist's trap, and it's particularly strong in attorneys because legal work genuinely has high stakes.

The flaw in this thinking is the assumption that "done right" means "done exactly as I would do it." But there are usually multiple ways to handle something effectively. Your way might be excellent, but that doesn't mean other approaches are wrong.

This trap keeps you doing work that others could handle competently, even if not identically to how you'd handle it. It prevents your team from developing their skills because they never get the chance to do work that really matters.

The reality check: Most tasks don't require perfection. They require competence. And competence can be achieved by people other than you.

Trap #2: "It's Faster to Do It Myself Than to Explain It"

In the moment, this is often true. It probably would take you fifteen minutes to explain a task and thirty minutes to do it yourself. So you do it yourself to save time.

But this trap ignores the investment principle. Yes, explanation takes time upfront. But that investment pays dividends forever.

If you spend thirty minutes explaining something once, that person can do it independently a hundred times in the future. You've traded thirty minutes now for countless hours later.

But if you always choose "faster to do it myself," you never make that investment. You're choosing short-term efficiency over long-term leverage.

The reality check: Training takes time, but it's time invested, not time wasted. The question isn't "Is it faster to do it myself?" It's "Do I want to do this task personally for the rest of my career?"

Trap #3: "No One Cares About This Case/Client as Much as I Do"

This one feels noble. You care deeply about your clients. You take their matters personally. You're invested in the outcomes.

And it's true—your team probably doesn't have the same emotional investment in each case that you do. They're not losing sleep over your clients' problems. They're not personally devastated when things don't go well.

But emotional investment isn't the same as competence or commitment. Your team can provide excellent service without being emotionally consumed by every case. In fact, a bit of professional distance often leads to clearer thinking and better judgment.

This trap keeps you personally handling things that don't require your emotional involvement—they just require competent execution.

The reality check: Professional care and personal emotional investment are different things. Your team can serve clients excellently without caring about them exactly the way you do.

Trap #4: "I'm Responsible, So I Have to Be Involved"

This is the trap of conflating legal responsibility with operational involvement.

Yes, you're ultimately responsible for your firm's work. Yes, your license is on the line. Yes, you could face malpractice claims or disciplinary action for your team's failures.

But responsibility doesn't require involvement in every task and every decision. You can be responsible for outcomes without being involved in every process.

In fact, this trap creates a false sense of security. Being personally involved in everything doesn't actually eliminate risk—it just spreads you so thin that you're more likely to miss real problems.

The reality check: You can maintain professional responsibility through systems, training, and strategic oversight. You don't have to personally touch every piece of work to fulfill your ethical obligations.

Trap #5: "They'll Do It Wrong and I'll Have to Fix It Anyway"

This is the pre-emptive disappointment trap. You're so convinced that delegation will fail that you don't really delegate—you just create more work for yourself to review and fix.

The insidious thing about this trap is that it becomes self-fulfilling. If you expect your team to fail and treat every delegation as something you'll need to fix, they'll sense your lack of confidence. They'll become tentative, over-check with you, and never develop the confidence to do quality work independently.

Your expectation of failure creates the failure you expected.

The reality check: People often rise or fall to the expectations set for them. If you expect competence and give them room to achieve it, you'll usually get competence. If you expect failure and hover waiting to fix things, you'll get dependence.

Symptoms: How to Know You're the Bottleneck

Still not sure if you're trapped in the bottleneck syndrome? Here are the telltale symptoms. The more of these you experience, the more likely you've become the obstacle to your own growth.

Symptom 1: Constant Interruptions

Your office door might as well be a revolving door. Throughout the day, people pop in with "quick questions." Your phone buzzes with texts. Slack messages pile up. Emails demand immediate attention.

Everyone needs something from you. A decision, an approval, an answer, your input, your review.

You can't focus on anything for more than twenty minutes without being interrupted. Complex work happens only early in the morning or late at night when everyone else is gone.

What this means: Your team has learned that you're the answer to every question and the solution to every problem. They're not resourceful or independent because you haven't required them to be.

Symptom 2: Email Inbox as Command Center

Your inbox has become the mission control center for your entire practice. Every email needs your personal attention. You're copied on everything "just so you know." Client communications flow through you. Team coordination happens via email threads that all include you.

You can't disconnect from email for more than an hour without anxiety. Vacation means checking your phone by the pool. Weekends mean catching up on the messages that piled up during the week.

Your inbox has 500+ messages because you're the only one who can decide what to do with most of them.

What this means: You've made yourself the central processor for all information and decisions. Nothing moves forward without flowing through you first.

Symptom 3: The Review Trap

Nothing leaves your firm without your review. Motions, letters, emails, social media posts, intake decisions—everything crosses your desk for approval.

You tell yourself this is quality control. But really, it's a trust issue. You don't trust your team to maintain standards without your oversight.

The result? You spend hours each day reviewing work that should be delegated fully. Your team waits for your approval on things they should be authorized to handle. Bottlenecks form because everyone's waiting for you to review their work.

What this means: You've positioned yourself as the quality gatekeeper, which means you're personally required for everything that happens in your practice.

Symptom 4: The Explanation Loop

When someone asks you a question, you answer it. Then they ask another question, and you answer that too. This continues until you've essentially walked them through the entire task.

At some point, you realize it would have been faster to just do it yourself. So next time, you do.

Or worse, you start doing things without being asked because you know the questions are coming and you'd rather just handle it yourself than go through the explanation loop again.

What this means: You haven't created systems, processes, or decision-making frameworks. Every situation is handled as a unique case requiring your personal judgment and explanation.

Symptom 5: The Rewrite Reflex

You ask someone to draft a letter. They do. You read it and immediately start rewriting it. Not because it's wrong, but because it's not quite how you would have said it.

The tone is slightly off. The structure could be better. That paragraph could be tighter. This section could be stronger.

By the time you're done "editing," you've essentially written a completely new letter. Your team member's work was just a rough draft for you to redo.

What this means: You're not willing to accept competent work that differs from how you'd personally do it. Your standards aren't "quality"—they're "exactly like I would do it," which is an impossible standard for anyone else to meet.

Symptom 6: First One In, Last One Out

You arrive at the office before everyone else and leave after everyone else has gone home. Weekends find you catching up on work. Evenings are spent answering emails and reviewing documents.

Meanwhile, your team keeps regular hours. They're not working nights and weekends. They're not stressed and overwhelmed.

Because all the work that can't be done during regular hours—the strategic thinking, the complex decisions, the important projects—lands on you.

What this means: You're doing two jobs: your actual leadership role and all the work you haven't successfully delegated. Your team has capacity you're not utilizing because you're handling things yourself.

Symptom 7: Nothing Moves Without You

Files sit waiting for your review. Decisions are postponed until you're available. Client issues remain unresolved because only you can handle them.

When you're in court all day, everything else stops. When you're out sick, the firm goes into holding pattern. When you take vacation (if you take vacation), you spend half of it working remotely because things can't wait.

What this means: You haven't built redundancy or empowered your team to keep things moving. You're a single point of failure for your entire operation.

Symptom 8: Volunteer Syndrome

You find yourself volunteering to handle things that your team should be doing. Someone mentions a task needs to get done, and you hear yourself saying "I'll take care of it" before anyone else can respond.

It's not that others aren't willing—you just don't give them the chance. You're so accustomed to being the solution that you automatically insert yourself.

What this means: You've developed a reflexive pattern of taking on work yourself rather than delegating it. You're not even consciously choosing to be the bottleneck—it's become automatic.

The Attorney-Specific Identity Crisis

For most professionals, work is something they do. For attorneys, work is often who they are.

Think about social situations. When someone asks "What do you do?" and you answer "I'm a lawyer," you're not describing a job—you're describing an identity.

This creates a unique challenge when it comes to delegation. Because if being a lawyer is who you are, and doing legal work is what validates that identity, then delegating legal work can feel like giving away pieces of yourself.

"If I'm Not Doing Everything, Am I Even Needed?"

This is the existential crisis at the heart of the bottleneck syndrome for law firm owners.

You built your firm through your personal effort and skill. Clients hired you for your expertise. Your reputation is based on your work product. Your value has always been tied to your direct involvement in the work.

So when you start delegating, a quiet voice asks: "If someone else can do this, what's my role? If my team handles client communication, case strategy, and legal work, what am I even here for?"

It's a real fear. And it's based on a fundamental misunderstanding of value and leadership.

The truth is, your value shifts as your firm grows. Early on, your value is in doing excellent legal work. As you grow, your value becomes:

- **Strategic vision:** Setting direction and identifying opportunities
- **System building:** Creating processes that produce consistent quality
- **Team development:** Growing people who can handle increasing complexity
- **Client relationships:** Maintaining key relationships and handling sophisticated matters
- **Business leadership:** Making decisions that affect the entire firm's success

You're not becoming less valuable when you delegate. You're becoming valuable in different, more leveraged ways.

But this requires an identity shift that many attorneys struggle with. You have to stop seeing yourself primarily as "the person who does the legal work" and start seeing yourself as "the person who builds the firm that does excellent legal work."

That's not a demotion. It's an evolution.

The Impostor Syndrome Connection

Here's a confession that many successful attorneys share privately: they sometimes feel like frauds.

Despite your success, despite your wins, despite your reputation, there's a voice that whispers "You're not as good as people think.

Eventually, they'll figure out you don't really know what you're doing."

This is impostor syndrome, and it's remarkably common among high-achieving professionals. The pressure to maintain an image of competence and expertise creates anxiety about being "exposed" as less capable than people believe.

Now add delegation to this mix.

If you already feel like you're not quite as competent as people think, delegating feels terrifying. What if your team does something poorly and it reflects on you? What if you give someone responsibility and they expose the fact that you didn't really have things as under control as everyone thought?

So you keep everything close. You handle things personally. You maintain the illusion of total competence by being directly involved in everything.

But here's the paradox: this approach actually makes you less competent. Because you spread yourself so thin that you can't do anything excellently. You're so busy doing everything adequately that you have no time to do anything masterfully.

The way out of this trap is to realize that:

1. **No one expects you to be personally excellent at everything.** Clients hire you for judgment, strategy, and leadership—not to personally perform every task.
2. **Building a capable team demonstrates competence, not weakness.** The ability to develop others and create systems shows greater expertise than doing everything yourself.
3. **Delegation actually reduces exposure risk.** When you're the bottleneck, you're more likely to make mistakes due to overload. When you have a well-trained team and good systems, quality and consistency improve.

Being Indispensable Is a Trap, Not a Goal

Many attorneys have internalized the idea that being indispensable is job security. If the firm can't function without you, you'll always be necessary. You'll always be valued. You'll always be safe.

But being indispensable is actually the opposite of security. It's a prison.

When you're indispensable:

- You can't take time off without everything falling apart
- You can't pursue new opportunities because you're trapped maintaining the current operation
- You can't sell or transition your practice because there's nothing to sell except your personal effort
- You can't slow down or semi-retire because everything depends on you
- You can't focus on what you love because you have to do everything

Real security comes from building something that works without you. Something with systems, trained people, and processes that produce results whether you're personally involved or not.

The goal isn't to make yourself indispensable. The goal is to make yourself optional.

That doesn't mean you become unnecessary or unimportant. It means you're free to focus on the work where you add the most value, rather than being consumed by everything that needs to get done.

Case Study: The Solo Practitioner Who Couldn't Take Vacation

Let's return to Michael, the criminal defense attorney we met at the beginning of this chapter.

Michael's path to becoming a bottleneck was gradual. When he started his practice, he did everything himself because he had to— he was a solo practitioner with no staff.

As he grew busier, he hired a part-time assistant. But he never really trained her to make decisions. He just gave her tasks to execute. File this motion. Send this letter. Call this client. Every task came with detailed instructions, and she was expected to check with him before doing anything outside those explicit instructions.

When he hired a paralegal a few years later, he fell into the same pattern. He'd give assignments, but he'd review everything before it went out. His paralegal learned that Michael would rewrite most of what she drafted, so she stopped trying to match his style and just created rough drafts for him to polish.

Clients got his cell phone number and texted him directly with questions. He always responded quickly because he prided himself on client service. His team never developed the ability to handle client communication because clients knew they could reach Michael directly.

Court clerks called his cell for scheduling issues. Opposing counsel emailed him directly rather than his staff. Everything flowed through Michael because that's how he'd set it up.

He told himself this was just the nature of a small practice. Someone had to be in charge. Someone had to make sure things were done right. Someone had to maintain quality and client service.

What he didn't realize was that he'd built a practice that was entirely dependent on his constant involvement. His team wasn't incompetent—they were untrained in decision-making and unempowered to act independently.

The vacation attempt was the wake-up call.

Sitting in that hotel room, fielding questions that his paralegal could have answered, reviewing a motion that didn't really need his review, Michael finally saw the truth: he'd created this situation. Every interruption, every "only you can handle this" moment, every crisis that required his personal attention—he'd trained everyone to behave this way.

His team wasn't bothering him on vacation because they were incompetent or inconsiderate. They were doing exactly what he'd taught them to do: check with Michael before making any decision, escalate any question to Michael, wait for Michael's approval before moving forward.

He'd spent years building a practice that couldn't function without him. And now he was trapped in it.

The Turning Point

The moment of clarity came on day three of his "vacation." His daughter asked if he wanted to build a sandcastle. He said "In a minute, honey, Daddy has to answer this email."

He watched her walk away, shoulders slumped. And he thought: "This email isn't actually urgent. My paralegal could handle this. But I've never empowered her to do so."

That night, after his kids were asleep, Michael made a decision. This pattern had to change. He couldn't keep being the bottleneck. He couldn't keep sacrificing his life to maintain a practice that had become a prison.

He didn't have all the answers. He didn't know exactly how to delegate effectively or build systems that worked without his constant involvement. But he knew the current situation was unsustainable.

When he returned from "vacation," he had a conversation with his paralegal.

"I need to change how we work together," he said. "I've been a bottleneck, and it's not fair to you or me. Starting next week, I want you to handle client questions about scheduling, status updates, and routine procedural issues without checking with me first. Here are the guidelines..."

It was a small step. Just one category of decisions. But it was the beginning of Michael reclaiming his practice—and his life.

The Results (Six Months Later)

Michael's transformation wasn't instant or perfect. He struggled with letting go. He had to resist the urge to jump in and "fix" things when his paralegal handled something differently than he would have.

But he stuck with it. He gradually expanded his paralegal's authority. He created simple decision-making frameworks. He built systems for common situations. He trained his team to think through problems instead of immediately escalating to him.

Six months later, Michael took another vacation. This time:

- His paralegal handled routine client questions without involving him
- His assistant managed scheduling conflicts independently
- Only genuinely urgent matters were escalated to him (and there were far fewer than he'd expected)
- He checked email once per day, usually finding that most issues had already been resolved

He actually spent time with his family. He relaxed. He came back refreshed rather than exhausted.

More importantly, he realized his practice hadn't fallen apart without his constant involvement. In fact, some things had improved. His paralegal had developed confidence and competence. His clients were still well-served. The work got done.

Michael was no longer indispensable. And that felt like freedom.

Recognizing Your Own Bottleneck Syndrome

As you read this chapter, you've probably recognized some of these patterns in your own practice. Maybe you saw yourself in Michael's story. Maybe certain symptoms hit uncomfortably close to home. Maybe you felt defensive about some of the mindset traps.

That's good. Recognition is the first step toward change.

But awareness alone won't solve the problem. Understanding why you've become a bottleneck doesn't automatically free you from it. In fact, some attorneys read chapters like this, nod along in recognition, and then continue doing exactly what they've always done.

The question isn't whether you recognize the bottleneck syndrome. The question is: are you ready to do something about it?

The following chapters will give you the tools, frameworks, and strategies to delegate effectively, empower your team, and build a practice that doesn't depend on your constant involvement.

But those tools only work if you're willing to confront the uncomfortable truth: the biggest obstacle to your firm's growth isn't your market, your budget, or your competition.

It's you.

And the good news? That's the one obstacle you have complete control over changing.

Action Items for This Chapter:

1. Complete the Bottleneck Self-Assessment

Answer these three questions honestly:

- How many hours per week do you spend on work that doesn't require your law degree or expertise?
- How many times this week has your team asked "What should I do?" for decisions they could make themselves?
- Can you take a week off without the practice struggling?

Hours on non-attorney work: _____

"What should I do?" questions this week: _____

Can take week off without struggle: Yes / No

2. Identify Your Top Three Bottleneck Behaviors

From the symptoms list in this chapter, identify the three bottleneck behaviors you engage in most frequently. Write them down and commit to addressing one this week.

Bottleneck behavior #1: _____

Bottleneck behavior #2: _____

Bottleneck behavior #3: _____

Which one will you address first: _____

3. Track One Day of Interruptions

For one full work day, track every time someone interrupts you with a question or decision request. Note whether each interruption was truly necessary or could have been handled by the team member.

Date of tracking: _____

Total interruptions: _____

Interruptions that were necessary: _____

Interruptions team could have handled: _____

Before Moving to Chapter 2:

Complete the Bottleneck Audit and identify at least three specific areas where you've become a bottleneck. Awareness of the specific problems in your practice will make the solutions in upcoming chapters more actionable and relevant to your situation.

CHAPTER 2:

The Real Cost of Being the Bottleneck

Rachel ran the numbers and couldn't make sense of what she was seeing.

Her trust and estate planning firm had grossed $1.2 million last year. Not bad for a five-person operation. She worked her tail off, billed solid hours, and brought in good clients. By most measures, she was successful.

But when she calculated her actual take-home after all expenses, paying her team, and covering overhead, she'd made $180,000. That's 15% of gross revenue.

She pulled up the benchmarking data from her practice management consultant. Similar firms her size were typically seeing owner compensation of 35-40% of gross revenue. If she were hitting that benchmark, she should have taken home $420,000 to $480,000.

Where was the other $240,000 to $300,000 going?

She spent the next week tracking her time obsessively. What she discovered was sobering.

Out of her 60-hour work week:

- 15 hours were spent on routine administrative tasks her assistant could handle
- 12 hours were spent reviewing documents her associate had drafted (and largely rewriting them)
- 8 hours were spent answering team questions and making decisions they should be empowered to make
- 6 hours were spent on client communications that her team could manage
- 4 hours were spent fixing mistakes or handling crises that better systems would prevent

That's 45 hours per week—three-quarters of her working time—spent on work that shouldn't require a lawyer earning $400+ per hour.

Only 15 hours per week were spent on high-value activities: case strategy, complex legal work, business development, and client relationship management.

Rachel had become an expensive bottleneck in her own firm. And it was costing her hundreds of thousands of dollars per year.

The real cost of being a bottleneck isn't just inconvenience or stress. It's measurable, quantifiable, and often shocking when you actually calculate it.

Lost Time and Opportunity Cost

Time is the only truly finite resource you have. You can make more money, hire more people, and expand your office. But you can't make more time.

When you spend your time on low-value activities, you're not just wasting that time. You're losing the opportunity to spend it on high-value activities that could transform your practice.

The Time Allocation Reality Check

Let's start with a brutal assessment. Pull out your calendar and time tracking from last week (if you don't track time, start this week and come back to this exercise).

Categorize every hour you worked into one of these buckets:

Ultra-High Value (Only You Can Do This)

- Complex legal strategy and analysis
- Sophisticated client relationship management
- Court appearances requiring your specific expertise
- Business development with referral sources or high-value prospects
- Strategic planning and firm leadership

High Value (You Should Do This)

- Attorney supervision and mentoring
- Case evaluation and matter acceptance decisions
- Key client communications on significant issues
- Writing or speaking that builds your reputation
- Financial oversight and major business decisions

Medium Value (Others Could Do With Training)

- Routine legal research and writing
- Standard client communications
- Document review that doesn't require judgment calls
- Team coordination and scheduling
- Basic case management tasks

Low Value (Should Be Delegated)

- Administrative tasks
- Routine emails and correspondence
- Scheduling and calendar management
- File organization and document management
- Data entry and system updates

No Value (Should Be Eliminated)

- Fixing preventable problems
- Redoing work others have done
- Searching for information that should be systematized
- Meetings that could be emails
- Interruptions that should be blocked

Now calculate what percentage of your time falls into each category.

If you're like most law firm owners stuck in the bottleneck syndrome, your breakdown probably looks something like this:

- Ultra-High Value: 10-20%
- High Value: 15-25%
- Medium Value: 25-35%
- Low Value: 20-30%
- No Value: 10-20%

That means 60-80% of your time is spent on work that either shouldn't require your involvement or shouldn't exist at all.

The Opportunity Cost Calculation

Here's the financial reality: every hour you spend on low-value work is an hour you can't spend on high-value work.

Let's say your effective hourly rate for high-value work (business development, complex legal work, strategic planning) is $500 per hour in terms of revenue generated or saved.

But you spend 20 hours per week on tasks worth $50-100 per hour (administrative work, routine emails, fixing preventable problems).

The opportunity cost isn't just the difference between $500 and $75 per hour. It's the compounding effect over time.

20 hours per week at $425 opportunity cost per hour = $8,500 per week $8,500 per week × 48 working weeks = $408,000 per year

That's not a theoretical number. That's real money you're leaving on the table by doing work that others could handle.

But it gets worse. Because those 20 hours per week aren't just costing you $408,000 in lost high-value work. They're also preventing you from building the systems and teams that would multiply your effectiveness even further.

The Compound Effect of Misallocated Time

When you spend your time on low-value work, you can't invest it in high-leverage activities like:

Building Systems: An hour spent creating a process that handles a recurring situation saves you that hour every time that situation arises. Do it once, benefit forever.

Training Your Team: An hour spent training someone to handle a category of work independently saves you hours every week that you would have spent doing or reviewing that work.

Business Development: An hour spent cultivating a referral relationship could bring you cases for years. An hour spent on content marketing could attract clients for the life of your practice.

Strategic Planning: An hour spent thinking about your business model, your positioning, or your growth strategy could identify opportunities worth hundreds of thousands of dollars.

These high-leverage activities don't just produce value in the moment. They compound over time, creating exponential returns.

But you'll never get to them if you're trapped doing routine work that shouldn't require your involvement.

Financial Analysis: The True Cost of Your Time

Most attorneys dramatically undervalue their time because they don't calculate it correctly.

You might think, "I bill at $400 per hour, so that's what my time is worth." But that's not even close to the full picture.

Calculating Your True Hourly Value

Here's how to calculate what your time is actually worth to your practice:

Step 1: Determine Your Annual Revenue Target

What do you want your practice to generate in revenue this year? Let's say $1.5 million.

Step 2: Calculate Available Working Hours

52 weeks per year

- 2 weeks vacation (you should take more, but let's be realistic)
- 10 federal holidays
- 5 sick/personal days = 45 working weeks

45 weeks × 40 hours per week = 1,800 working hours (If you work 50-60 hour weeks now, we're calculating what it should be, not what it currently is)

Step 3: Divide Revenue Target by Available Hours

$1,500,000 ÷ 1,800 hours = $833 per hour

That's your target revenue per hour worked.

But wait—you're not going to spend every hour on billable or revenue-generating work. You need time for business development, administration, team management, and strategic work.

Step 4: Adjust for Non-Revenue Time

A healthy law practice typically allocates time like this:

- 60% billable/revenue-generating work
- 20% business development and client relationships
- 20% firm management and administration

So if you have 1,800 working hours and 60% should be billable: $1,800 \times 0.60 = 1,080$ billable hours

Step 5: Calculate Your Required Billable Rate

$1,500,000 ÷ 1,080 billable hours = $1,389 per billable hour

That's what you need to generate per billable hour to hit your revenue target while maintaining a sustainable work-life balance.

The Bottleneck Tax

Now here's where being a bottleneck kills your economics.

When you spend your time on tasks worth $50-150 per hour, you're not just losing the difference between that and your target rate. You're paying what I call the "bottleneck tax"—a series of hidden costs that compound the problem:

Direct Loss: The difference between your target rate and the value of low-level work

- Your target: $1,389 per billable hour
- Value of administrative task: $75 per hour
- Direct loss: $1,314 per hour

Efficiency Loss: Low-value work takes longer than it should when you do it

- You spend 30 minutes scheduling a deposition
- Your assistant could do it in 15 minutes
- You've lost 15 minutes of your $1,389/hour time = $347

Opportunity Loss: While doing low-value work, you can't do high-value work

- Hour spent reviewing routine correspondence: -$1,389 in potential billable time
- Plus the administrative cost you should have delegated: -$75
- Total opportunity loss: $1,464 per hour

Growth Loss: Time spent on low-value work can't be invested in growth

- Hour spent on administrative work instead of business development
- Potential client worth $25,000 in lifetime value
- If one BD hour typically generates one new client per quarter
- Lost growth value: $25,000 ÷ 40 BD hours = $625 per hour

Total Bottleneck Tax per hour spent on low-value work: $2,436

That's not an exaggeration. That's the real cost when you account for direct loss, efficiency loss, opportunity loss, and growth loss.

The Million-Dollar Calculation

Let's bring this back to Rachel's situation.

She was spending 45 hours per week on work that shouldn't require her involvement. At $2,436 bottleneck tax per hour:

45 hours × $2,436 = $109,620 per week $109,620 × 48 weeks = $5,261,760 per year

Over five years, Rachel's bottleneck behavior will cost her practice over $26 million in lost value.

Even if we're conservative and cut those numbers in half to account for estimation errors, that's still $2.6 million per year or $13 million over five years.

Suddenly that $240,000-300,000 gap in her owner compensation doesn't seem like the full picture. The real cost is exponentially higher when you account for lost growth, lost opportunities, and lost efficiency.

Slower Growth, Reduced Scalability

Being a bottleneck doesn't just cost you money directly. It fundamentally limits your practice's ability to grow.

The Growth Ceiling

Your practice can only grow as fast as you can personally handle increased volume. If you're the bottleneck, then growth means more work for you personally.

Here's what this looks like in practice:

Year 1: You're billing 1,200 hours and managing everything personally. Revenue: $480,000

Year 2: You work harder, bill 1,400 hours, still manage everything personally. Revenue: $560,000

Year 3: You're maxed out at 1,500 billable hours (the human limit while still managing a practice). Revenue: $600,000

Year 4: You can't bill more hours. Growth stops. Revenue: $600,000

Year 5: You're burned out. Quality suffers. You might even see revenue decline.

This is the growth ceiling created by being a bottleneck. You might see initial growth as you max out your personal capacity, but then you hit a wall. Growth stops because you've reached your personal limits.

The Scalability Problem

Contrast this with a practice that has effective delegation and systems:

Year 1: You bill 1,000 hours, delegate effectively, hire good people. Revenue: $500,000

Year 2: You hire an associate, build systems, bill 900 hours. Revenue: $750,000

Year 3: Your associate is productive, you've delegated more, bill 800 hours. Revenue: $1,100,000

Year 4: You hire another associate, focus on high-value work, bill 700 hours. Revenue: $1,600,000

Year 5: Three associates, strong systems, you focus on strategy and BD, bill 600 hours. Revenue: $2,400,000

Notice what happened? As the firm grew, your personal billable hours decreased while revenue increased dramatically.

That's scalability. That's what becomes possible when you're not the bottleneck.

The Multiplication Factor

Here's the key principle: every hour you spend building systems and developing your team multiplies your capacity.

When you're the bottleneck, 1 hour of your time = 1 hour of output.

When you delegate effectively:

- 1 hour training an associate = 1,000+ hours of their future output
- 1 hour building a system = infinite hours of automated efficiency
- 1 hour developing a team member's judgment = years of autonomous decision-making

The bottleneck model is additive: your output equals your personal hours worked.

The delegation model is multiplicative: your output equals your hours worked × the number of people you've empowered × the efficiency of your systems.

This is why some solo practitioners earn $200,000 working 60-hour weeks while some firm owners earn $1,000,000+ working 35-hour weeks. It's not that they're smarter or work harder. They've built multiplication into their practice instead of being trapped in addition.

The Flat Fee and Contingency Reality

If you run a criminal defense, family law, or personal injury practice on flat fees or contingency, you might be thinking "This billable hour math doesn't apply to me."

You're right—the calculations are different. But the bottleneck cost is just as real, maybe even more painful.

For Flat Fee Practices (Criminal Defense, Immigration, Family Law):

Your revenue is capped by how many cases you can handle. If you're the bottleneck reviewing every motion, handling every client call, and making every decision, you can only take on so many cases before quality suffers or deadlines get missed.

Let's say you can personally handle 40 active cases at a time with an average fee of $5,000. That's $200,000 in potential revenue at any given moment. If you close and replace cases every 3 months, that's $800,000 annually.

But if you delegated effectively and empowered your team to handle routine work? You could oversee 80-100 cases because you're only personally involved in high-value activities. Same team size, same overhead, but now you're looking at $1.6-2 million in revenue.

The bottleneck isn't just costing you time—it's directly capping your earning potential at half of what's possible with the same resources.

For Contingency Practices (Personal Injury, Employment Law):

Your bottleneck behavior might be even more expensive because case value varies so dramatically.

If you're spending 10 hours per week on administrative tasks, client handholding that a paralegal could handle, and reviewing routine correspondence, that's 10 hours you can't spend on:

- Taking intake calls for potentially high-value cases
- Negotiating better settlements (each hour of skilled negotiation could mean $50,000-100,000+ more in settlement value)

- Developing referral relationships with medical providers or other attorneys
- Properly working up cases to maximize value

One missed high-value case because you were too busy with low-value work could cost you $100,000-500,000 in fees. One settlement you accept because you don't have time to push harder could cost you $50,000.

The bottleneck tax in contingency practices isn't theoretical—it's the six-figure case you didn't have time to take, the settlement you left on the table, or the referral relationship you couldn't cultivate because you were drowning in work your team could have handled.

Regardless of your billing model, being a bottleneck creates the same fundamental problem: your personal capacity becomes the ceiling for your practice's potential.

Team Morale and Retention Issues

Being a bottleneck doesn't just hurt you. It damages your team in ways that cost you talented people and make hiring even harder.

The Motivation Drain

Think about what it's like to work for a bottleneck owner:

You draft a motion. You spend three hours on it, research the cases, write it carefully, format it properly. You're proud of the work.

You send it to your boss for review.

Two days later, it comes back completely rewritten. Your structure is changed. Your language is replaced. Whole sections are redone. There's barely anything left of your original work.

The message you receive: "Your work isn't good enough. You can't be trusted to do this well."

How motivated are you to put in effort on the next motion? Why bother doing your best if it's just going to be rewritten anyway?

This is what happens to team members who work for bottleneck owners. They learn that their work will never be good enough, so they stop trying to make it excellent. They produce rough drafts knowing you'll redo everything anyway.

Your perfectionism and inability to delegate creates a team of people who have learned helplessness. They stop taking initiative because initiative is pointless when everything requires your approval and revision anyway.

The Development Dead End

Good employees want to grow. They want to develop skills, take on more responsibility, and advance in their careers.

But when you're the bottleneck, you can't provide growth opportunities because you don't trust your team with meaningful responsibility.

Your paralegal has been with you for five years. She's smart, capable, and committed. She wants to handle client communications independently, manage cases with minimal supervision, and make judgment calls on routine issues.

But you won't let her. You review all her work, approve all her decisions, and keep her in a support role that doesn't utilize her full capabilities.

Eventually, she gets frustrated. She sees peers at other firms being empowered to do substantive work. She realizes she's not developing because you won't delegate meaningfully.

So she leaves. And you lose your best team member because you couldn't get out of the way and let her grow.

The Retention Crisis

High turnover is expensive. Really expensive.

The cost of replacing an employee is typically 50-200% of their annual salary when you account for:

- Recruiting costs
- Training time
- Lost productivity during transition
- Knowledge loss
- Remaining team morale impact
- Client relationship disruption

If you lose a $60,000 paralegal and it costs 100% of salary to replace them, that's $60,000 in hard and soft costs.

If your bottleneck behavior causes you to lose one good employee per year, you're spending $60,000+ annually on preventable turnover.

But it's worse than that. Because the employees who leave are often your best people—the ones with initiative, capability, and ambition. They're the ones most frustrated by not being empowered.

The employees who stay are often the ones comfortable with learned helplessness. They're happy to wait for your direction, avoid responsibility, and just execute tasks.

So your bottleneck behavior drives away your best people and retains your most dependent people. Over time, you end up with a team that can't function independently because the ones who could have all left.

The Hiring Handicap

Word gets around. In legal communities, especially local ones, reputation matters.

When you burn through talented employees because you can't delegate, people talk. The good candidates hear that you're impossible to work for. They hear that you micromanage, that you don't trust your team, that there's no room for growth.

So when you post a job opening, you don't attract top talent. You attract people who can't get jobs at better-managed firms. Or people who are desperate. Or people who are just starting out and don't know better yet.

Your bottleneck behavior doesn't just cost you the team you have. It limits the team you can build in the future.

Stress, Burnout, and Reduced Focus on High-Value Work

The personal toll of being a bottleneck is often the hardest cost to measure, but it might be the most significant.

The Stress Spiral

Being a bottleneck creates a self-reinforcing stress cycle:

You're overwhelmed with work, so you work longer hours.

Working longer hours makes you tired and less efficient.

Being less efficient means work takes longer and quality suffers.

Lower quality creates more problems that require your attention.

More problems mean more work and more overwhelm.

The cycle continues, with stress compounding on itself.

You start making mistakes you wouldn't normally make. You miss deadlines you would have hit when you were fresh. You snap at team members who don't deserve it. You lose patience with clients who are reasonably asking for updates.

Your health suffers. You're not sleeping well. You're not exercising. You're eating poorly because you don't have time for real meals. Your relationships suffer because you're always working or thinking about work.

And through it all, you tell yourself "This is just what it takes to run a successful practice."

But it's not. It's what it takes to run a practice where you're the bottleneck.

The Burnout Reality

Burnout isn't just being tired. It's a state of emotional, physical, and mental exhaustion caused by prolonged stress.

The three hallmarks of burnout are:

1. Exhaustion: You're depleted, running on empty, with nothing left to give. Even after a weekend or vacation, you come back tired.

2. Cynicism: You've become detached and negative about your work. Clients seem like burdens. Your team seems incompetent. The work that once excited you now feels pointless.

3. Reduced Efficacy: You feel ineffective and unaccomplished. Despite working constantly, you feel like you're not making progress or making a difference.

Sound familiar?

Burnout doesn't happen because you work hard. Plenty of people work hard without burning out. Burnout happens when you work hard on things that don't matter while neglecting things that do.

When you're a bottleneck, you work constantly on low-value tasks (email, review, administrative work) while never getting to do the high-value work that actually energizes you (complex legal work, strategy, meaningful client relationships).

This is the perfect recipe for burnout. Maximum effort, minimum fulfillment.

The Focus Fragmentation

Human brains aren't designed to multitask or constantly switch contexts. Every time you're interrupted or switch tasks, there's a cognitive cost.

Research shows that it takes an average of 23 minutes to fully return to a task after an interruption. And if you're interrupted frequently, you never achieve deep focus at all.

When you're the bottleneck, interruptions are constant:

- Team members with questions
- Clients calling your cell
- Emails demanding immediate attention
- Fires that need to be put out

Your attention is fragmented across dozens of small tasks and issues. You're never able to focus deeply on anything.

This has serious consequences:

Quality suffers: Complex legal work requires sustained focus. You can't do your best strategic thinking in 15-minute chunks between interruptions.

Creativity dies: Novel solutions and innovative approaches come from deep thinking. Fragmented attention kills creativity.

Satisfaction disappears: The work that drew you to law—solving complex problems, crafting elegant arguments, helping clients through sophisticated issues—requires the very thing you can't access: sustained focus.

So you end up doing shallow work constantly (email, routine review, basic questions) while the deep work that would actually move your practice forward never gets done.

Client Service Suffers When You're the Bottleneck

Here's a paradox: you became a bottleneck because you care deeply about client service. You want to ensure every client gets excellent attention. But being a bottleneck actually damages the client experience.

The Response Time Problem

When you're the bottleneck, everything waits for you.

A client emails with a question. Your assistant sees it but knows you need to approve the response. The email sits for a day until you can get to it. You draft a response. Your assistant sends it.

Total response time: 24-36 hours for a question that your assistant could have answered in 30 minutes.

From the client's perspective, your firm is slow to respond. They don't know you're personally reviewing every communication. They just know they waited a day for a simple answer.

Meanwhile, your competitor who has empowered their team to handle routine communications gets back to clients in an hour. Who do you think the client perceives as providing better service?

The Availability Problem

You're in court all day on one case. Three other clients have questions or concerns. They call, email, text. But you're unavailable.

If you'd empowered your team to handle these situations, clients would get immediate attention from a well-trained team member who knows their case and can help them.

Instead, they get "He's in court, I'll have him call you back" from a team member who isn't empowered to do anything else.

The client feels unimportant. Their urgent issue (to them) isn't being addressed. And they're forced to wait for you, even though someone on your team could help them right now.

Your bottleneck behavior has created the perception that you're unavailable and unresponsive.

The Consistency Problem

When you're overwhelmed and spread thin, your client service becomes inconsistent.

Some clients get great attention because you happen to have time when they need you. Others get poor attention because you're buried when they reach out.

Some matters move forward quickly because you're focused on them. Others stall because you haven't gotten to them yet.

This inconsistency is confusing and frustrating for clients. They don't understand why they get excellent service one week and slow service the next. They don't see your workload—they just see unreliable responsiveness.

A well-delegated practice with good systems provides consistent service because it doesn't depend on your personal availability at any given moment.

The Escalation Problem

Here's something you might not have considered: some clients don't actually want to deal with the lawyer for routine issues.

They want to know their filing was completed. They want to confirm a court date. They want to ask a basic procedural question.

They don't need to speak with you—they need quick, accurate information.

But because you're the bottleneck, every issue gets escalated to you. Simple questions become complex because they have to wait for your availability.

If you'd trained and empowered your team, clients could get immediate answers to routine questions from knowledgeable staff. They'd only hear from you when there's actually something that requires attorney judgment or attention.

This would be better for everyone: clients get faster service, your team feels valuable, and you focus on matters that truly need your expertise.

Malpractice Risk When You're Spread Too Thin

Here's the cost that keeps you up at night: being a bottleneck doesn't just hurt your business—it increases your malpractice risk.

The Deadline Miss

You're juggling forty active matters. You're personally tracking deadlines because you don't fully trust your case management system or your team to flag important dates.

You've got a motion due on Friday. You're aware of it. You plan to draft it on Thursday.

But Tuesday, an emergency hearing comes up on another case. Wednesday, you're in trial. Thursday morning, a client crisis erupts that consumes your day.

Thursday at 8 PM, you remember the Friday motion. You stay up until 2 AM getting it done. It's not your best work—you're exhausted—but it's done.

You email it to your assistant to file first thing Friday morning. You crash into bed.

Friday at 11 AM, you wake up to your assistant calling. "I didn't see your email until just now—it went to spam. I haven't filed the motion yet. The deadline was 10 AM."

You've missed a filing deadline. A preventable, expensive mistake that happened because you're personally managing too many things.

If you'd had a proper deadline tracking system, delegated deadline management to your team, and built redundancy into your processes, this would never have happened.

The Supervision Failure

Your associate is handling a criminal case. It's a routine matter, nothing complex. You're letting her handle it to free up your time for more pressing issues.

But you're spread so thin that you haven't checked in on the case. You haven't reviewed her strategy. You haven't supervised her work.

She makes a decision that seems reasonable to her but is actually problematic. She misses a nuance in the law. She doesn't recognize an issue that you would have caught immediately.

The case goes badly. The client suffers consequences that could have been avoided.

This is a supervision failure. You're responsible because you're the supervising attorney, but you failed to supervise because you were too busy being a bottleneck on other matters.

The Exhaustion Error

You've been working 70-hour weeks for months. You're exhausted, running on caffeine and adrenaline.

You're reviewing a settlement agreement at 11 PM. You miss a critical clause. Something you would normally catch, but you're too tired to see it.

The agreement gets executed. Three months later, the problem emerges. Your client is harmed. You're facing a malpractice claim.

This is the exhaustion error. Your judgment was impaired by the very work pattern that made you a bottleneck. You were trying to maintain quality by reviewing everything personally, but you were too burned out to actually maintain quality.

The System Failure

You don't have robust systems because you don't have time to build them. You're too busy doing the work to create the processes that would prevent problems.

So you're relying on your memory, your personal attention, and your ability to keep track of everything.

But human memory is fallible. Attention is limited. And when you're managing too many things, mistakes are inevitable.

Something falls through the cracks. A client isn't updated. A deadline isn't calendared properly. A conflict isn't caught.

This is system failure caused by bottleneck behavior. You didn't have time to build proper systems because you were too busy doing everything yourself. And the lack of systems created the very risks you were trying to avoid.

The Paradox

Here's the ultimate paradox of bottleneck behavior:

You maintain tight control because you want to avoid mistakes and maintain quality.

But maintaining tight control spreads you so thin that you're more likely to make mistakes and quality suffers.

The very thing you're doing to prevent malpractice is increasing your malpractice risk.

Proper delegation, good systems, and well-trained teams actually reduce risk. They create redundancy, clear processes, and multiple people watching for issues.

But you can't build those safeguards when you're trapped being the bottleneck.

Case Study: The Firm That Lost Its Best Paralegal to Burnout

Jennifer had been a paralegal at Marcus's family law firm for six years. She was exceptional—organized, detail-oriented, great with clients, and increasingly capable of handling complex work.

Marcus valued Jennifer enormously. He paid her well, gave her bonuses, and told her frequently how much he appreciated her work.

But Marcus was a classic bottleneck owner. He reviewed everything Jennifer did. He made all decisions, even routine ones. He was copied on every email. He personally approved every document that went out.

Jennifer didn't mind at first. She was learning, and Marcus's attention to detail helped her develop her skills. But after a few years, it became frustrating.

She could handle client communications independently—she knew the cases, she knew the clients, she knew what to say. But she still had to wait for Marcus's approval before responding to even routine questions.

She could draft documents competently—she'd done hundreds of them. But Marcus would still rewrite significant portions, often changing things that didn't need changing, just because he'd phrase them differently.

She could make scheduling decisions and judgment calls on minor procedural issues. But Marcus insisted on being consulted on everything.

The Slow Burn

Over time, Jennifer began to feel less like a skilled professional and more like an extension of Marcus's hands. She wasn't using her judgment—she was just executing his decisions.

She started to feel devalued. If Marcus needed to review and revise everything she did, what was the point of her being there? She could have been replaced by someone with half her skill level and Marcus would still do the same amount of work.

She raised this with Marcus during her annual review. "I'd like more responsibility. I think I'm ready to handle client communications without approval, and to make certain case management decisions independently."

Marcus agreed in principle but did nothing to change the dynamic. He was too busy, too overwhelmed, too convinced that his personal involvement was necessary for quality control.

The Breaking Point

The breaking point came on a Friday evening.

Jennifer had been at the office since 7 AM. She'd managed three client crises, drafted four motions, coordinated with opposing counsel on six matters, and handled about forty client communications.

At 6 PM, she sent Marcus a routine email to a client confirming a hearing date. It was straightforward, nothing that needed review.

At 6:15 PM, she was packing up to leave when Marcus replied: "Let's revise this. I'd say it differently. See my edits."

Jennifer looked at the edits. He'd changed "Please confirm you can attend the hearing on June 15th at 2 PM" to "I want to confirm your availability for the hearing scheduled for June 15th at 2:00 PM."

The meaning was identical. The tone was nearly identical. This was not a substantive improvement—it was just Marcus's preference for slightly different phrasing.

Jennifer had to stay late to send the revised email because Marcus wanted the client to get it before the weekend.

She sat at her desk, looking at those meaningless edits, and something broke inside her.

Six years of being second-guessed. Six years of her judgment being overridden on matters that didn't matter. Six years of being treated as if she couldn't be trusted to send a basic email without supervision.

She was done.

The Resignation

Jennifer gave notice the following Monday. Two weeks later, she was gone.

Marcus was shocked. He'd thought Jennifer was happy. He paid her well. He appreciated her. What went wrong?

In the exit interview, Jennifer was direct: "I can't work for someone who docsn't trust me to do my job. I've proven myself for six years, but you still treat me like I started yesterday. I need to work somewhere that I can actually use my skills and judgment."

Marcus tried to convince her to stay. He offered more money. He promised to delegate more.

But Jennifer had already accepted a position at another firm—at the same salary, actually. The money wasn't the issue. The issue was being valued, trusted, and empowered to do the work she was capable of doing.

The Aftermath

Replacing Jennifer was expensive and painful.

The recruiting process took two months and cost $8,000 in agency fees.

The new paralegal, while competent, needed six months to get up to speed on the systems, clients, and Marcus's preferences.

During that transition, Marcus had to work even longer hours to cover the gap. He couldn't delegate as much to the new person, so he ended up doing more himself.

Client service suffered during the transition. Response times slowed. Some details fell through cracks. A few clients complained about inconsistency.

All told, losing Jennifer cost Marcus:

- $8,000 in direct recruiting costs
- $60,000 in lost productivity during the transition (his time and errors)
- $15,000 in overtime and temporary help
- Immeasurable damage to team morale and client relationships

But the biggest cost was opportunity. Jennifer had been ready to take on significant responsibility. With proper delegation, she could have managed entire cases independently, freeing Marcus to focus on business development and complex legal work.

Instead, Marcus spent six months recovering from her loss and training a replacement who might eventually reach the level Jennifer had already achieved—if that person didn't also burn out from working for a bottleneck owner.

The Wake-Up Call

Six months after Jennifer left, Marcus ran into her at a bar association event. She looked happy, relaxed. She told him about her new role.

"I'm managing complex cases independently now. My boss trusts me to make decisions. I communicate directly with clients. I feel like I'm actually practicing family law, not just assisting someone else who practices family law."

Then she said something that haunted Marcus: "You trained me well. I learned so much from you. But you could never let me actually use what you taught me. Working for you felt like being perpetually in training for a job I was never going to be allowed to do."

Marcus realized he'd created his own problem. His inability to delegate, his need to control everything, his bottleneck behavior—it hadn't protected quality. It had driven away his best person and trapped him in a cycle of training people who would eventually leave for firms that actually empowered them.

That conversation was the beginning of Marcus's journey out of bottleneck behavior. But it came too late to save his relationship with his best employee.

The Hidden Costs Add Up

When you tally the true cost of being a bottleneck, the numbers are staggering.

The financial bleeding is severe. Lost opportunity costs run $200,000-500,000+ annually. The bottleneck tax on misallocated time adds another $100,000-300,000+ each year. Every valued employee you lose to burnout or frustration costs $30,000-100,000+ to replace. And the lost growth from your inability to scale? That compounds into millions over time.

The operational damage is pervasive. Team morale and engagement deteriorate when people feel underutilized and untrusted. Top talent won't apply to work for a firm known for micromanagement. Client service suffers with slower response times and inconsistent quality. Productivity plummets from constant context switching. System failures and preventable errors multiply because you're spread too thin to build proper safeguards.

The personal toll is brutal. Chronic stress manifests in health problems. Burnout replaces the passion that once drove you. Relationships with family and friends suffer from your perpetual absence and distraction. The high-value work you actually enjoy— the reason you became a lawyer—gets crowded out by administrative minutiae. Freedom and flexibility become distant memories.

The risk exposure is frightening. Malpractice exposure increases exponentially when you're spread too thin. Supervision failures occur because you can't adequately oversee anyone when you're doing everything. Deadlines get missed and administrative errors pile up. Your entire practice becomes a house of cards with a single point of failure: you.

When you add it all up, being a bottleneck could easily cost you $500,000 to $1,000,000+ per year in direct and indirect costs.

Over a decade, that's $5-10 million in lost value.

Over a career, it's the difference between building a practice worth millions that supports the life you want and burning out in a job you created for yourself that you've come to resent.

The Point of No Return

There's a dangerous moment in every bottleneck owner's journey: the point where they've been doing everything for so long that they can't imagine any other way.

They know they're overwhelmed. They know they're leaving money on the table. They know they're risking burnout.

But the idea of changing seems impossible. "This is just how I run my practice. This is who I am. This is what my clients expect."

They've confused their current operational model with their identity. They believe that being personally involved in everything is what makes them a good lawyer, a good business owner, a good leader.

This is the point of no return—not because change is impossible, but because they've convinced themselves it is.

If you're reading this chapter and recognizing yourself in these costs, you're at a critical juncture.

You can continue on the current path. Keep being the bottleneck. Keep paying these costs—financial, operational, personal, and risk-related. Keep telling yourself "this is just what it takes" until you burn out or your practice plateaus or you lose another great employee.

Or you can decide that enough is enough.

The costs are too high. The risks are too great. The life you're living is not the life you want.

You can choose to learn how to delegate effectively, build systems, empower your team, and create a practice that doesn't depend on your constant involvement in everything.

The rest of this book will show you how. But first, you have to acknowledge the true cost of continuing as you are.

Calculating Your Personal Bottleneck Cost

It's time to get specific about what being a bottleneck is costing you personally.

Exercise: Your Annual Bottleneck Cost

Step 1: Calculate Your Time Misallocation Cost

From your time audit in Chapter 1, how many hours per week do you spend on work that shouldn't require your involvement?

_____ hours per week on low-value work

What is your target revenue per hour? (From the calculation earlier in this chapter)

$_____ per hour

Time misallocation cost per week: _____ hours × $_____ = $_____

Annual time misallocation cost: $_____ × 48 weeks = $_____

Step 2: Calculate Your Opportunity Cost

How many hours per week should you be spending on high-leverage activities (business development, strategic planning, complex legal work) but aren't because you're stuck on low-value work?

_____ hours per week lost

What is the value of one hour of high-leverage work in terms of revenue generated or saved?

$_____ per hour

Opportunity cost per week: _____ hours × $_____ = $_____

Annual opportunity cost: $_____ × 48 weeks = $_____

Step 3: Calculate Your Turnover Cost

How many valued employees have you lost in the past three years due to lack of empowerment or growth opportunities?

_____ employees

What is the average cost to replace an employee (50-200% of salary)?

$_____ per replacement

Total recent turnover cost: _____ employees × $_____ = $_____

Annualized turnover cost: $_____ ÷ 3 years = $_____

Step 4: Calculate Your Growth Loss Cost

What is your current annual revenue?

$_____

If you weren't a bottleneck, what growth rate would be reasonable? (15-25% annually is achievable with good delegation)

_____%

What would your revenue be at that growth rate?

Current revenue × (1 + growth rate) = $_____

Annual growth loss: Potential revenue - Current revenue = $_____

Step 5: Calculate Your Total Annual Bottleneck Cost

Time misallocation cost: $_____ Opportunity cost: $_____
Turnover cost: $_____ Growth loss cost: $_____

Total Annual Bottleneck Cost: $_____

Over 10 years at this rate: $_____ × 10 = $_____

Over your remaining career (20-30 years): $_____ × _____ years = $_____

The Reality Check

Look at those numbers. Really look at them.

That's not a theoretical cost. That's real money you're leaving on the table. Real growth you're preventing. Real stress you're enduring unnecessarily.

Now ask yourself: Is it worth it?

Is maintaining control over every task worth $500,000 per year?

Is personally reviewing every document worth missing your kid's activities and working weekends?

Is being indispensable worth the inability to take a real vacation?

Is doing it all yourself worth burning out the best employees you'll ever find?

The costs of being a bottleneck are real, measurable, and compounding. Every year you continue this pattern, the costs grow larger and the hole gets deeper.

But here's the good news: the moment you recognize these costs, you can start doing something about them.

The following chapters will give you the frameworks, systems, and strategies to delegate effectively, empower your team, and eliminate the bottleneck that's costing you so much.

But you have to be willing to change. You have to acknowledge that the current approach, no matter how comfortable or familiar, is not sustainable.

You have to decide that you're worth more than being a perpetual bottleneck in your own practice.

The Choice Point

Every law firm owner who reads this chapter will arrive at a choice point.

Some will recognize themselves in these costs, feel momentarily uncomfortable, and then rationalize why their situation is different. "My practice is unique. My clients need me personally. My team isn't capable of handling more responsibility."

These rationalizations are comfortable. They allow you to continue as you are without the discomfort of change.

But they're also expensive. Every rationalization costs you hundreds of thousands of dollars. Every excuse keeps you trapped in a pattern that's destroying your health, limiting your growth, and preventing you from building the practice you actually want.

Others will read this chapter and feel the weight of recognition. They'll see the true cost of their bottleneck behavior—not just in dollars, but in lost time, damaged relationships, missed opportunities, and diminished quality of life.

They'll realize that the path they're on leads nowhere good. More overwhelm, more burnout, more frustration, and ultimately either a plateau or a breakdown.

And they'll make a different choice.

They'll decide that the cost is too high. That the current pattern has to change. That learning to delegate, building systems, and empowering their team is not optional—it's essential.

If you're in this second group, you're ready for the next chapter.

If you're still in the first group, rationalizing and defending your current approach, I'd invite you to do one thing:

Share your bottleneck cost calculation with someone you trust. Your spouse, a friend, a mentor. Show them the numbers. Tell them honestly about your stress level, your work hours, your inability to disconnect.

And ask them: "Does this seem sustainable? Does this seem worth it?"

Sometimes we need someone else to reflect back to us what we can't see ourselves. Sometimes we need permission to admit that the way we're working isn't working.

Because here's the truth: you don't have to live this way.

You don't have to be the bottleneck.

You don't have to sacrifice your health, your relationships, and your sanity to run a successful practice.

There's a better way. And it starts with acknowledging the real cost of the current way.

Action Items for This Chapter:

1. Calculate Your True Hourly Value

Determine your effective hourly rate and identify how many hours weekly you spend on work below that rate. Calculate your annual opportunity cost.

Your annual target income: $_____

Your effective hourly rate: $_____ (annual income ÷ 2000)

Hours per week on below-rate work: _____

Annual opportunity cost: $_____ (hourly rate × weekly hours × 50)

2. Conduct Your Personal Time Audit

Track one full week of your time in 30-minute blocks. Categorize each block as either high-value (strategy, complex legal work, key relationships) or low-value (administrative, routine tasks, work others could do).

Week of: _____

High-value hours: _____

Low-value hours: _____

Percentage of time on high-value work: _____%

3. Identify Your Highest-Cost Bottleneck

From the costs discussed in this chapter (financial, growth, team, burnout, client service, malpractice risk), identify which one is hitting your practice hardest right now. Commit to addressing it first.

Highest-cost bottleneck area: _____

Specific impact on my practice: _____

First step to address it: _____

Before Moving to Chapter 3:

You should now have a clear, quantified understanding of what being a bottleneck is costing you. These aren't abstract concepts—they're real dollars, real stress, real risks, and real limitations on your life and practice.

The next section of the book moves into solutions. You'll learn exactly what to delegate, how to find the right people, and how to build the systems that eliminate bottleneck behavior.

But those solutions only work if you're genuinely committed to change. If you're still defending your current approach or minimizing the costs, the strategies in the following chapters won't help.

Take a moment right now to acknowledge the cost. Sit with it. Feel the weight of it.

Then make the decision: are you ready to change?

If the answer is yes, turn the page. The path out of bottleneck behavior starts in the next chapter.

CHAPTER 3:

The Law Firm Delegation Landscape

Tom had been running his family law practice for fifteen years when he hired his first associate attorney. Fresh out of law school, eager to learn, ready to take on responsibility.

Tom was excited. Finally, he'd have someone to share the workload. He could delegate cases, focus on business development, maybe even take a real vacation.

Three months later, Tom received a letter from the state bar. A complaint had been filed against him—not for anything he'd done personally, but for something his associate had done. Or more accurately, hadn't done.

The associate had missed a critical filing deadline on a custody matter. The client's case was severely damaged. And Tom, as the supervising attorney, was being held responsible for a failure he didn't even know had occurred until it was too late.

"But I hired a licensed attorney," Tom protested to his malpractice carrier. "He passed the bar. He's supposed to know how to handle these things."

The carrier's response was blunt: "You're still responsible for adequate supervision. Delegation doesn't eliminate your professional obligations—it changes how you fulfill them."

Tom had learned the hard way what many law firm owners eventually discover: delegation in a law practice isn't like delegation in other businesses. You can't simply hand off work and assume it's handled. The ethical rules, professional responsibility standards, and liability framework create unique challenges that don't exist when you're delegating at a restaurant, a construction company, or even a medical practice.

Understanding this landscape—the specific rules, risks, and responsibilities that govern legal delegation—is essential before you can delegate effectively and safely.

What Makes Legal Delegation Different from Other Businesses

In most businesses, delegation is straightforward. You hire someone with the necessary skills, train them on your processes, give them authority to make decisions, and hold them accountable for results.

If they make a mistake, you might lose money or a customer. It's a business problem with business consequences.

In a law practice, the stakes are fundamentally different.

First, you're dealing with someone else's life, liberty, property, or family. Your personal injury client is counting on you to secure their financial future after a devastating injury. Your criminal defense client could lose their freedom if you fail. Your estate planning client is trusting you to protect their life's work and

86

provide for their family. The consequences of mistakes aren't just business losses—they're life-altering disasters for real people.

Second, you're bound by a complex web of ethical rules that don't apply to other businesses. The ABA Model Rules of Professional Conduct (and your state's version of them) govern nearly every aspect of how you practice law, including how and what you can delegate. Violating these rules doesn't just create liability—it can cost you your license to practice.

Third, you remain personally responsible for work you delegate in ways that don't apply in other industries. A restaurant owner who hires a chef isn't personally liable if the chef burns a dish. But an attorney who delegates legal work remains professionally responsible for the quality and competence of that work, even when someone else performs it.

Fourth, you're dealing with confidential information that's legally protected. Client confidentiality isn't just a best practice— it's a mandatory ethical obligation with significant consequences for violations. You can't delegate work to just anyone, and you can't share client information freely even within your own organization.

Fifth, the work you're delegating often requires professional judgment that can't be reduced to a checklist or procedure. Legal analysis, case strategy, and client counseling involve nuanced thinking that's difficult to systematize or delegate without maintaining close oversight.

These differences mean that the delegation strategies that work brilliantly in other businesses can be dangerously inadequate in a law practice. You need to understand the specific legal landscape before you can navigate it safely.

Professional Responsibility and Ethical Obligations

The foundation of legal delegation is built on professional responsibility rules. In most jurisdictions, these are based on the

ABA Model Rules of Professional Conduct, though your state's specific version may vary in important ways.

The critical rule for delegation is Model Rule 5.1, which addresses the responsibilities of supervisory lawyers. This rule establishes that partners and lawyers with managerial authority must make reasonable efforts to ensure that all lawyers in the firm conform to the professional conduct rules. More importantly for delegation purposes, it makes supervising lawyers responsible for another lawyer's violation of the rules if they order or ratify the conduct, or if they know about the misconduct and fail to take reasonable remedial action.

In practical terms, this means you can't just delegate work to an associate and walk away. You remain responsible for ensuring that the work meets professional standards and complies with ethical rules.

Model Rule 5.3 extends this responsibility to nonlawyer assistants. You must make reasonable efforts to ensure that nonlawyer employees and contractors conduct themselves in ways that would be proper for a lawyer. This includes paralegals, legal assistants, investigators, and any other staff who work on client matters.

The rule specifically states that a lawyer is responsible for a nonlawyer's conduct if the lawyer orders or ratifies the conduct, or if the lawyer is a partner or has managerial authority and knows of the conduct at a time when its consequences can be avoided or mitigated but fails to take reasonable remedial action.

What does "reasonable supervision" actually mean? The rules don't provide a precise checklist, which creates anxiety for attorneys trying to delegate. But ethics opinions and case law have provided some guidance. Reasonable supervision generally includes providing adequate training, establishing clear procedures and guidelines, implementing systems to monitor work quality and deadlines, and being available for consultation when questions arise.

It does not mean you must personally review every document or approve every decision. In fact, overly restrictive supervision that prevents staff from developing competence and judgment can actually harm client service and firm efficiency.

The competence requirement (Model Rule 1.1) also affects delegation. You must provide competent representation, which requires the legal knowledge, skill, thoroughness, and preparation reasonably necessary for the representation. When you delegate work, you must ensure that the person performing it—whether another attorney or a supervised nonlawyer—has or can acquire the necessary competence.

This means you can't delegate complex appellate work to a first-year associate without adequate training and oversight. You can't hand a sophisticated estate plan to a paralegal and expect them to draft documents without attorney involvement in the substantive decisions. You must match the complexity of the delegated work to the competence of the person receiving it, and you must provide the training, resources, and supervision necessary to ensure quality results.

Client communication (Model Rule 1.4) presents another delegation challenge. You must keep clients reasonably informed about the status of their matters and promptly comply with reasonable requests for information. You must also explain matters to the extent reasonably necessary to permit clients to make informed decisions.

Many attorneys struggle with delegating client communication because they worry about maintaining these obligations. But the rule doesn't require that you personally handle every client interaction. It requires that clients receive adequate information and explanation. A well-trained paralegal or associate can often provide better, more timely communication than an overwhelmed attorney who responds three days late because they're buried in work.

The key is ensuring that whoever communicates with clients has accurate information, understands the matter sufficiently to explain it clearly, and knows when issues need to be escalated to you for attorney judgment or decision-making.

Your state's specific rules may vary from the Model Rules in important ways. Some states have more restrictive requirements for supervision of nonlawyers. Others have specific rules about fee splitting, referrals, or delegation that don't appear in the Model Rules. Some jurisdictions have ethics opinions that provide detailed guidance on delegation in specific practice areas.

Before implementing any delegation strategy, you must research your own state's professional responsibility rules. Don't assume that what's permissible under the Model Rules is automatically allowed in your jurisdiction. Check your state bar's website for ethics opinions on delegation and supervision. When in doubt, contact your state bar's ethics hotline for guidance.

The ethical rules aren't meant to prevent delegation—they're meant to ensure that delegation doesn't compromise client service or attorney accountability. Understanding these rules allows you to delegate confidently within the boundaries they establish.

Malpractice Risk Management in Delegation

Ethical violations can cost you your license. Malpractice can cost you everything else.

The intersection of delegation and malpractice risk is where many attorneys' fears become most acute. Every time you delegate, you're potentially introducing risk. But paradoxically, not delegating also creates risk by spreading you so thin that mistakes become inevitable.

The key is understanding how to manage malpractice risk in delegation rather than trying to eliminate it through total personal control.

Vicarious liability is your starting point. Under the doctrine of respondeat superior, you're liable for the negligent acts of your employees performed within the scope of their employment. This means that when your associate misses a statute of limitations, or your paralegal files documents in the wrong court, or your legal assistant gives a client incorrect information, you're legally responsible.

This is true whether you knew about the mistake or not. Whether you specifically approved the action or not. Whether you were even in the office that day or not. If it happened on your watch and within the scope of employment, you're liable.

This reality terrifies many attorneys into micromanagement. "If I'm liable anyway, I might as well do everything myself to ensure it's done right." But this reasoning is flawed for two reasons.

First, as we discussed in Chapter 2, doing everything yourself actually increases risk because you're spread too thin to do anything well. Exhausted attorneys make mistakes. Overwhelmed attorneys miss deadlines. When you're the bottleneck, you're more likely to commit malpractice, not less.

Second, proper delegation with good systems actually reduces risk more effectively than personal involvement in everything. A well-designed deadline management system catches more deadline issues than a solo attorney trying to remember everything. A competent, well-trained team spots more problems than an exhausted attorney working alone. Redundancy and systematic processes are more reliable than individual memory and effort.

The standard for malpractice in supervision cases focuses on reasonableness. Courts don't expect perfect supervision or error-free delegation. They expect reasonable systems, adequate training, and appropriate oversight given the complexity of the work and the experience of the person to whom it's delegated.

What's reasonable varies by circumstance. Delegating routine discovery responses to an experienced paralegal requires less oversight than delegating dispositive motion practice to a new associate. Allowing a senior attorney to handle settlement negotiations independently is reasonable; allowing a first-year associate to do so without review might not be.

Creating reasonable systems for delegation risk management typically includes several components. You need clear protocols for who can do what without approval. You need training programs that ensure people understand both the technical requirements and the judgment calls involved in their work. You need quality control mechanisms that catch errors before they harm clients—but these don't have to be you personally reviewing everything.

Peer review, where associates review each other's work before it goes out, can be highly effective. Checklists for complex procedures ensure critical steps aren't missed. Software systems that automatically flag approaching deadlines provide more reliable protection than personal calendaring. Regular file reviews on a sample basis catch systemic issues without requiring review of every action on every file.

Documentation becomes critical in delegation. When malpractice claims arise, you need to demonstrate that you provided reasonable supervision. This means documenting your training programs, your delegation protocols, your quality control systems, and your oversight activities.

It doesn't mean you need to document every conversation or supervision moment—that would be impossibly burdensome. It means you should have evidence that you've built reasonable systems and followed them consistently. Meeting notes showing regular case reviews with associates. Training materials and attendance records. Delegation policies in your office manual. System audit logs showing deadline monitoring.

This documentation serves two purposes. First, it actually improves your supervision by creating accountability and ensuring consistency. Second, it provides evidence of reasonable supervision if a claim arises.

Consider your malpractice insurance coverage in relation to delegation. Most policies cover employees acting within the scope of employment, but you should verify this. Some policies have specific requirements or exclusions related to supervision of other attorneys or nonlawyer staff. Some require you to notify the carrier when you hire additional attorneys or expand your practice areas.

Have a conversation with your malpractice carrier about your delegation practices. Ask about their risk management resources— many carriers offer training materials, checklists, and consultation on building proper supervision systems. They want to prevent claims, so they're usually happy to help you create effective delegation structures.

Certain types of delegation require special attention to malpractice risk. Delegating client intake decisions creates risk if the person making those decisions doesn't recognize conflicts or doesn't properly assess whether you're competent to handle the matter. Delegating trust accounting tasks creates risk if the person handling money doesn't understand IOLTA requirements. Delegating settlement authority creates risk if the person negotiating doesn't understand the client's goals or the reasonable value of the case.

For these high-risk delegation areas, you need enhanced systems. Dual approval for client intake decisions. Separate oversight for trust accounting from someone other than the person performing the tasks. Clear written authority and boundaries for anyone negotiating on behalf of clients.

The goal isn't zero risk—that's impossible. The goal is managing risk to a reasonable level while gaining the benefits of effective delegation. Proper systems, adequate training, appropriate oversight, and good documentation allow you to delegate confidently without exposing yourself to unreasonable malpractice risk.

And remember: the malpractice risk of being a bottleneck—making errors from exhaustion, missing deadlines from overload, providing inadequate service from being spread too thin—is often greater than the risk of well-managed delegation.

Client Confidentiality and Privilege Considerations

Client information is sacred in legal practice. The duty of confidentiality is broader than attorney-client privilege and applies to virtually everything related to a client's representation.

Understanding how confidentiality affects delegation is essential because you can't effectively delegate if you can't share client information with your team.

Model Rule 1.6 establishes the duty of confidentiality. A lawyer shall not reveal information relating to the representation of a client unless the client gives informed consent, the disclosure is impliedly authorized to carry out the representation, or the disclosure is permitted by specific exceptions in the rule.

The key phrase for delegation purposes is "impliedly authorized to carry out the representation." When you engage a team to represent a client, the client implicitly authorizes you to share information with that team to the extent necessary for the representation. You don't need separate consent forms for every piece of information you share with your paralegal or associate.

However, this implied authorization has limits. You can share information with team members working on the matter. You generally cannot share it with team members not involved in the representation, with outside contractors who aren't properly supervised, or with anyone outside your organization without explicit client consent.

Practical application in different practice areas requires different approaches. In a criminal defense practice working on flat fees, you might have case teams where the assigned attorney and paralegal have full access to all case information, while other attorneys and staff in the firm do not. In a contingency-based personal injury practice with larger cases, you might need to share information across multiple team members—attorneys, paralegals, investigators, medical experts—all of whom fall within the impliedly authorized circle.

In an estate planning practice billing hourly, you might have a primary attorney-client relationship but delegate drafting to a more junior attorney and administrative tasks to a paralegal, both of whom need access to sensitive financial and family information to perform their roles.

The distinction between delegation to employees and delegation to outside contractors matters for confidentiality. Your employees are generally considered part of your organization for confidentiality purposes. Outside contractors—freelance paralegals, contract attorneys, expert witnesses—require more careful handling.

When delegating to outside contractors, you must ensure they understand their confidentiality obligations. This typically means having them sign confidentiality agreements and, in many jurisdictions, ensuring clients consent to their involvement. The implied authorization to share information with your team doesn't automatically extend to outside contractors who aren't under your direct supervision and control.

Technology adds complexity to confidentiality in delegation. When you delegate work, you're often sharing information electronically—through email, practice management systems, cloud storage, or collaboration platforms. Model Rule 1.6(c) requires lawyers to make reasonable efforts to prevent inadvertent or unauthorized disclosure of client information.

This means you need to implement reasonable security measures for any systems used in delegation. Encrypted email for sensitive communications. Secure practice management systems with proper access controls. Password protection for shared documents. Clear policies about what can and cannot be discussed in public spaces or on unsecured devices.

What's "reasonable" depends on the sensitivity of the information and the available technology. You're not expected to implement NSA-level security for a routine traffic ticket case. But you should use widely available security measures appropriate to your practice and your clients' needs.

Attorney-client privilege creates an additional layer of consideration. While confidentiality is broad, privilege is more specific—it protects communications between attorney and client for the purpose of seeking or providing legal advice.

When you delegate work, you need to ensure that privileged communications remain protected. This generally means that communications between your team members about client matters are protected under the work product doctrine or as part of the attorney-client relationship. But careless communication practices can waive privilege.

For instance, if your associate discusses privileged strategy in an email that's inadvertently sent to opposing counsel, privilege might be waived. If your paralegal includes privileged information in a document that gets produced in discovery, you have a serious problem. Training your team to recognize privileged information and handle it appropriately is essential.

Conflicts of interest create special confidentiality challenges in delegation. Model Rule 1.7 prohibits representing clients with directly adverse interests or when there's a significant risk that representation will be materially limited by responsibilities to another client, former client, or third person.

When you delegate client intake or case acceptance decisions, the person making those decisions must understand how to run proper conflicts checks. They need access to information about current and former clients to identify potential conflicts, but they must maintain confidentiality about that information even while using it for conflicts screening.

Many firms use conflicts-check software that screens potential new clients against existing client databases without revealing unnecessary details. The person running the check sees only whether a conflict exists, not all the confidential information about existing clients. This protects confidentiality while enabling proper delegation of intake decisions.

Specific practice areas have specific confidentiality challenges. Criminal defense attorneys face particularly stringent confidentiality requirements, especially regarding potential evidence or witness information. Delegating investigative work or witness interviews requires careful attention to what information is shared and with whom.

Family law attorneys often deal with highly sensitive personal and financial information that clients may not want shared broadly, even within the firm. Personal injury attorneys working on contingency may receive medical records containing HIPAA-protected information that requires special handling. Estate planning attorneys working hourly often have access to complete financial pictures and family dynamics that must be carefully protected.

Regardless of practice area or billing model, the principle remains the same: you can delegate work and share information to the extent necessary for representation, but you must ensure that everyone with access to client information understands their confidentiality obligations and handles information appropriately.

When in doubt, get consent. If you're uncertain whether sharing particular information with a team member or contractor is impliedly authorized, ask the client. A simple conversation—"I'd like to have my paralegal work on this aspect of your case, which means sharing these details with her"—usually resolves any concern and provides explicit authorization.

Clients almost always consent when they understand that delegation improves their service. What upsets clients is discovering that information was shared without their knowledge or that people they didn't know were involved in their case. Transparency about your team approach and who will have access to their information prevents these problems.

State Bar Rules on Supervision and Delegation

While the ABA Model Rules provide a framework, the rules that actually govern your practice are your state's professional conduct rules. These vary significantly in their specifics about what can be delegated and how supervision must be maintained.

The unauthorized practice of law (UPL) is the line you cannot cross. Every state prohibits nonlawyers from practicing law, but states differ dramatically in where they draw that line. Some states have very restrictive definitions that limit what nonlawyers can do, even under attorney supervision. Others are more permissive, allowing extensive delegation as long as proper supervision exists.

Generally speaking, nonlawyers cannot give legal advice, represent clients in court proceedings (with some limited exceptions), or set fees. They can perform legal research, draft documents under attorney supervision, communicate with clients about factual matters and case status, and handle administrative tasks related to cases.

But the specifics vary. Some states allow paralegals to attend certain hearings or closings under supervision. Some prohibit nonlawyers from any client contact without attorney presence. Some have specific certification programs for paralegals that expand what they can do. Some have detailed ethics opinions on particular delegation scenarios.

Your state's specific rules on supervision may be more or less demanding than the Model Rules. Some states require direct supervision for any work performed by nonlawyers, meaning an attorney must be immediately available and reviewing work closely. Others allow more general supervision where the attorney maintains overall responsibility but isn't involved in every task or decision.

Some states have specific rules about supervision ratios—limiting the number of nonlawyers one attorney can supervise. Others have no such limits but expect supervision to be adequate to the workload and complexity.

Fee splitting and nonlawyer ownership rules affect some delegation decisions. Model Rule 5.4 generally prohibits sharing legal fees with nonlawyers and prohibits nonlawyer ownership or control of law firms. But some states have modified these rules to allow alternative business structures or different fee arrangements.

This affects how you can structure compensation for delegated work. Generally, you can pay nonlawyers salaries or hourly wages, and you can pay bonuses based on firm profitability. But you typically cannot pay them a percentage of fees from specific cases or give them ownership interests that would provide them control over professional judgment.

Some states have exceptions for paralegals, allowing certain profit-sharing arrangements. A few states have approved alternative business structures where nonlawyers can have ownership interests under specific conditions. You need to know your state's specific rules before implementing any compensation structure related to delegation.

Multijurisdictional practice creates delegation complexities if you practice across state lines. If you're licensed in State A but handle matters in State B, you need to comply with both states' rules regarding delegation and supervision. If you delegate work to an attorney licensed only in State B, you need to ensure that arrangement complies with both states' rules on supervision and multijurisdictional practice.

This is particularly relevant for attorneys in contingency practices who may take cases in multiple jurisdictions, or for attorneys in areas where state borders create overlapping practice areas. The rules about who can do what, and how supervision must be maintained, may differ between jurisdictions.

Research your state's specific requirements thoroughly. Start with your state bar's website, which should have your state's version of the professional conduct rules. Look for ethics opinions on delegation, supervision, and nonlawyer assistance—these often provide practical guidance on specific scenarios.

Many state bars have ethics hotlines where you can call with specific questions about delegation in your practice. Use this resource. The attorneys staffing these hotlines deal with delegation questions regularly and can provide guidance on your state's specific requirements and how they apply to your situation.

Consider joining your state bar's practice management or professional responsibility sections. These groups often provide CLE programs, written materials, and networking opportunities where you can learn how other attorneys in your state handle delegation within the rules.

Document your research and your delegation decisions. If you've researched your state's rules, consulted ethics opinions, and made delegation decisions based on that research, document it. Keep copies of the ethics opinions you relied on. Note the dates you called the ethics hotline and the guidance you received. If a question ever arises about whether your delegation practices comply with professional conduct rules, this documentation demonstrates that you made good faith efforts to comply.

The rules governing delegation aren't meant to be traps. They're meant to ensure that delegation enhances client service rather than compromising it. Understanding your state's specific requirements allows you to delegate confidently within proper boundaries.

Trust Accounting: What Can and Cannot Be Delegated

For many attorneys, trust accounting creates the greatest anxiety around delegation. The rules are strict, the consequences of violations are severe, and the work often seems too sensitive to delegate.

But running a law practice while personally handling every trust accounting transaction is neither practical nor necessary. You can delegate trust accounting work safely if you understand what must remain under attorney control and how to supervise delegated tasks properly.

The fundamental principle is that client funds must be safeguarded. Model Rule 1.15 requires lawyers to hold client property separate from the lawyer's own property, to appropriately safeguard property, to keep required records, and to promptly deliver funds or property that clients or third persons are entitled to receive.

These obligations cannot be delegated in the sense that you remain responsible for compliance even if someone else performs the tasks. But the actual work of trust accounting—recording transactions, writing checks, reconciling accounts, maintaining ledgers—can be delegated to properly supervised staff.

What typically can be delegated with appropriate supervision includes the mechanics of trust accounting. A trained bookkeeper or paralegal can record deposits and withdrawals, prepare trust account checks for your signature, reconcile bank statements, maintain client ledgers, and prepare regular reports on trust account status.

The key is "with appropriate supervision." You cannot simply hand over trust accounting to staff and never review it. You must implement oversight systems that ensure compliance and catch errors before they become serious problems.

What typically cannot be delegated includes decisions about when to deposit or disburse funds. The attorney must determine whether funds should go into the trust account, when earned fees can be transferred from trust to the operating account, how settlement proceeds should be distributed, and whether disputed funds should be held until the dispute is resolved.

Similarly, the attorney cannot delegate responsibility for ensuring compliance with trust accounting rules. While staff can perform the work, the attorney must verify that it's being done correctly and that all required records are being maintained.

Three-way reconciliation is the gold standard for trust accounting supervision. This means that each month, someone (often a delegated staff member) reconciles the bank statement balance to the trust account general ledger balance to the total of all client ledger balances. These three numbers must always match.

But here's the supervision component: while staff can perform the reconciliation, you should review it. At a minimum, you should review the monthly reconciliation report, confirm that the three balances match, review the list of client balances to ensure they seem appropriate, and investigate any unusual items.

Many attorneys delegate the monthly reconciliation work but reserve the first few days of each month for trust accounting review. Others delegate the reconciliation but have their CPA or bookkeeper provide a monthly certification that the reconciliation was completed properly. Some use trust accounting software that generates exception reports flagging unusual transactions for attorney review.

Signature authority on trust accounts should be carefully controlled. Many state bars require that only attorneys have signature authority on trust accounts. Even in states where nonlawyers can be signatories, best practice suggests limiting signature authority to attorneys who understand the trust accounting rules and the ethical implications of trust account transactions.

If you delegate check preparation to staff, they should prepare the checks but bring them to you for review and signature. This provides a critical control point where you verify that the disbursement is appropriate, properly documented, and accurately reflects the client ledger balance.

Technology can enable safe delegation of trust accounting. Modern practice management software with integrated trust accounting provides multiple safeguards. Software can prevent overdrawing client balances, require documentation before allowing disbursements, automatically perform three-way reconciliation, and generate exception reports for unusual transactions.

These technological controls don't eliminate your supervision obligation, but they reduce the risk that delegated trust accounting work will result in errors or violations. The software essentially builds some supervision into the process, though you still need to review reports and monitor compliance.

Different practice areas face different trust accounting challenges. Personal injury attorneys working on contingency often hold large settlement proceeds in trust and must properly calculate and disburse attorney fees, medical liens, and client portions. The delegation question is often whether staff can perform the settlement disbursement calculations or whether the attorney must personally verify every calculation.

Criminal defense attorneys working on flat fees may use trust accounts for unearned fee deposits. The question becomes who can determine when fees are earned and can be transferred from trust to the operating account. Estate planning attorneys billing hourly may hold retainers in trust and transfer funds as fees are earned—who can make the determination that fees are earned and process the transfer?

In all these scenarios, the answer is similar: staff can perform the mechanical work of calculations and transfers, but the attorney must review and approve the decisions about when and how much to transfer. The more standardized and systematic these decisions are (for example, a clear fee agreement specifying when flat fees are earned), the easier they are to delegate with appropriate review.

Separation of duties is a critical control for delegated trust accounting. The person who enters transactions should not be the same person who reconciles the account. The person who prepares disbursement checks should not be the person who signs them. The person who handles trust accounting should not be the only person who reviews it.

This separation creates natural checks and balances. Even in a small firm where one staff member handles most trust accounting work, the attorney should perform or review the monthly reconciliation. In larger firms, you might have one person handling deposits, another handling disbursements, and a third performing reconciliation, with attorney oversight of all three.

Documentation requirements for trust accounts are extensive and cannot be ignored. Model Rule 1.15 and state-specific rules typically require detailed records including deposit and disbursement receipts, bank statements, reconciliation reports, and individual client ledgers showing all receipts and disbursements.

These records must typically be maintained for a period specified by state rules, often five to seven years. While staff can maintain these records, you're responsible for ensuring that the requirements are met. This means having systems in place for record retention, knowing what records are required, and verifying periodically that proper records are being maintained.

Audit preparation can be substantially delegated. Many states conduct random trust account audits, and you may face an audit regardless of whether any problem has been identified. A well-organized staff member can prepare for an audit by gathering required records, organizing them logically, and ensuring that all documentation is available.

However, the attorney should review the audit preparation work and understand what will be presented to auditors. If the audit identifies issues, the attorney must be familiar enough with the trust accounting operation to respond knowledgeably and implement any required corrective measures.

When in doubt, consult your state's specific trust accounting rules. Many states have detailed trust account handbooks published by the state bar. Some states require trust account certifications or periodic reporting. Some have mandatory training for attorneys handling trust accounts.

These resources often provide specific guidance on what can be delegated and how supervision should be maintained. They may include sample forms, reconciliation templates, and checklists that make delegation safer and more systematic.

Your malpractice carrier may also have trust accounting resources and risk management guidance. Since trust accounting violations are a common source of both disciplinary actions and malpractice claims, carriers have strong incentives to help you get trust accounting right.

The goal is to delegate the work while maintaining control over the decisions. You can safely delegate trust account bookkeeping, reconciliation work, record maintenance, and other mechanical tasks. You cannot delegate the decisions about when to deposit or disburse funds, the responsibility for ensuring compliance, or the ultimate accountability for trust account management.

With proper systems, adequate training, appropriate supervision, and regular review, you can delegate trust accounting work effectively while maintaining compliance with professional responsibility rules and protecting client funds.

The Liability Framework You Must Understand

Understanding your liability exposure in delegation isn't about being paralyzed by fear—it's about making informed decisions about what to delegate, to whom, and with what safeguards.

The liability framework for law firm delegation has several layers, each with different implications for how you structure your delegation practices.

Personal professional liability as an attorney is the foundation. As discussed earlier, you're personally responsible for the professional conduct of lawyers you supervise and for ensuring that nonlawyer assistants comply with professional obligations. This responsibility exists regardless of your firm's structure.

Whether you're a solo practitioner, a partner in a partnership, or a shareholder in a professional corporation, you're personally liable for violations of professional conduct rules in matters you supervise. You can be disciplined, sued for malpractice, or both, based on the actions of people you've delegated work to.

This personal liability cannot be eliminated through insurance, indemnification agreements, or firm structure. It's inherent in being a licensed attorney with supervisory responsibility.

Malpractice liability layers on top of professional responsibility. Even if delegation doesn't violate ethical rules, it can create malpractice exposure if the delegated work is performed negligently and causes client harm.

As we discussed earlier, you're generally liable for the negligent acts of employees acting within the scope of employment. This is true whether the employee is another attorney, a paralegal, or administrative staff. The scope of employment is typically broad— if they were doing work for the firm related to client representation, it's within scope even if you didn't specifically authorize that particular action.

Firm entity structure affects but doesn't eliminate liability. Many attorneys practice through professional corporations or limited liability companies, hoping these structures provide protection from liability for delegated work.

The reality is more complicated. These structures may protect your personal assets from firm debts and obligations, and they may protect you from liability for other attorneys' malpractice in matters you weren't involved with. But they typically don't protect you from liability for your own malpractice or for malpractice in matters you supervised.

If you delegate work negligently—assigning a task to someone you know is incompetent, failing to provide necessary supervision, ignoring red flags that problems exist—your personal liability exists regardless of firm structure. The entity structure might affect whether firm assets or personal assets are at risk, but it doesn't eliminate the underlying liability.

Insurance is essential but not a complete solution. Professional liability insurance protects you from the financial consequences of malpractice claims, including claims arising from delegated work. But insurance has limits, both in coverage amount and in what's covered.

Most policies cover negligent acts but not intentional misconduct. They cover professional services but may not cover business operations or employment issues. They have dollar limits that could be exceeded by a catastrophic claim. And they typically have exclusions for certain types of claims or conduct.

Moreover, insurance doesn't protect your license. If delegation results in ethical violations, insurance might cover the malpractice claim but won't prevent disciplinary action. You could find yourself financially protected but professionally sanctioned or even disbarred.

The standard of care defines when liability attaches. In malpractice cases, the question is whether you met the standard of care that a reasonable attorney would meet in similar circumstances. For delegation, this means asking whether a reasonable attorney would have delegated this task to this person with this level of supervision.

Delegating routine discovery responses to an experienced paralegal with spot-check review meets the standard of care. Delegating complex dispositive motion practice to a first-year associate with no supervision likely doesn't. The standard considers the complexity of the work, the experience and competence of the person it's delegated to, and the supervision and oversight provided.

Causation matters for liability. Even if delegation was unreasonable, you're only liable if that unreasonable delegation caused harm to the client. If your associate makes an error in delegated work but you catch it before any client impact, there's no malpractice even though the delegation might have been questionable.

Conversely, if you delegate appropriately but something goes wrong through no fault in the delegation itself—for example, a client loses because of facts, not errors in your work—there's no liability even though delegation occurred. The client must prove that the negligent delegation caused actual harm.

Joint and several liability can multiply exposure in some situations. If you're practicing in a partnership or firm structure where multiple attorneys bear responsibility for client matters, you might be liable not just for your own delegation decisions but for other partners' delegation as well.

This is particularly relevant in firms where partners share management responsibility. If another partner delegates work negligently on a matter you're not involved with, you might still bear liability if you're in a management position and failed to implement adequate firm-wide supervision systems.

Indemnification and contribution among firm members create internal liability questions. Many firm partnership agreements or shareholder agreements include provisions about how liability is shared among firm members. These might specify that each attorney is responsible only for their own malpractice, or they might provide for sharing of liability based on ownership percentages.

These internal agreements affect how liability is ultimately borne among firm members, but they don't eliminate client-facing liability. A client can sue all responsible parties and collect from whoever has assets. The firm members then sort out contribution among themselves based on their internal agreements.

When delegating work that might involve other attorneys or when building firm-wide delegation systems, understand how your firm's internal agreements allocate liability. This affects how you structure oversight and supervision responsibilities.

Criminal liability is rare but possible in extreme cases. While most delegation problems result in professional discipline or civil malpractice liability, criminal liability can arise in egregious situations. Knowingly allowing a nonlawyer to practice law, participating in fraud through delegated work, or intentionally misappropriating client funds through delegated trust accounting can result in criminal charges.

These cases are rare and typically involve intentional misconduct, not ordinary negligence in delegation. But they represent the extreme end of the liability spectrum and underscore why some delegation decisions—particularly around trust accounting and client fund handling—require heightened caution.

Disciplinary consequences operate on a separate track from civil liability. You can face professional discipline even if no civil malpractice occurred, and you can face malpractice liability even if no ethical violation occurred. The standards and consequences are different.

Disciplinary actions can range from private reprimands to suspension or disbarment. These consequences affect your ability to practice law and earn a living, regardless of whether any client was actually harmed or whether malpractice insurance covers the financial consequences.

When making delegation decisions, consider both tracks of potential consequences. Ask not just "Could this result in a malpractice claim?" but also "Could this result in a disciplinary action?" The answers might differ, and both matter.

The timing of when liability attaches in delegation scenarios varies. In some cases, liability exists when you make an unreasonable delegation decision—assigning work to someone you know is incompetent. In others, liability exists when you fail to supervise adequately—not reviewing work or not implementing oversight systems. In still others, liability exists when you fail to remediate—discovering a problem and not fixing it.

This means you have multiple intervention points to prevent liability. You can make good delegation decisions initially. You can supervise adequately even if the initial delegation was questionable. You can remediate effectively even if supervision was initially inadequate. Liability is not inevitable just because you delegate—it results from a pattern of unreasonable decisions and failures across multiple stages.

Understanding vicarious liability versus direct liability matters for insurance and risk management. Vicarious liability is when you're held responsible for someone else's negligence because of your relationship with them. Direct liability is when you're held responsible for your own negligent acts.

In delegation, you face both types. You have vicarious liability for your employees' negligent acts within the scope of employment. You have direct liability for your own negligent supervision, training, or oversight.

Some malpractice insurance policies treat these differently or have different limits for each. Understanding this distinction helps you structure your insurance coverage appropriately and understand where your greatest exposures lie.

Navigating the Landscape Safely

The legal landscape of delegation is complex, but it's navigable. Thousands of law firms delegate effectively every day while maintaining compliance with ethical rules and managing liability exposure appropriately.

The key is approaching delegation thoughtfully rather than reactively. Don't delegate simply because you're overwhelmed. Don't avoid delegation simply because you're afraid. Instead, make deliberate decisions based on understanding the rules, the risks, and the safeguards available.

Start by knowing your state's specific rules. As emphasized throughout this chapter, the Model Rules provide a framework but your state's actual rules govern your practice. Research thoroughly, consult ethics opinions, use your state bar's resources, and when in doubt, seek guidance from ethics counsel or your state bar's ethics hotline.

Build systems that create natural safeguards. Good delegation systems don't just make work more efficient—they reduce risk. Clear protocols about who can do what without approval. Training programs that ensure competence before delegation. Quality control mechanisms that catch errors before client harm. Documentation systems that create accountability and provide evidence of reasonable supervision.

Match delegation to competence and provide training to close gaps. Don't delegate complex work to inexperienced people without adequate supervision and training. But also don't assume that anyone other than you is incapable of competent work. Most tasks can be delegated to people with appropriate skills and training. Your job is ensuring that the match between task complexity and delegate competence is reasonable, and that any gaps are filled through training and supervision.

Implement oversight that's proportional to risk. High-risk work—trust accounting, settlement negotiations, court filings with deadlines—requires closer oversight. Lower-risk work—routine correspondence, case status updates, discovery responses—can be delegated with lighter supervision. The key is proportionality, not uniformity.

You don't need to review every email your paralegal sends, but you should review settlement disbursement calculations. You don't need to approve every scheduling decision, but you should have systems that ensure court deadlines are tracked and met.

Document your delegation decisions and systems. Good documentation serves multiple purposes. It creates accountability and ensures consistency. It provides evidence of reasonable supervision if questions arise. It helps train new team members on how delegation works in your practice. And it allows you to refine and improve your systems over time.

Use technology to enhance compliance and reduce risk. Practice management software, trust accounting systems, deadline tracking tools, and document management platforms all provide safeguards that make delegation safer. They don't replace your judgment or eliminate your responsibility, but they create systematic protections that supplement human oversight.

Maintain appropriate insurance coverage and understand what it covers. Professional liability insurance is essential, but you need to understand its limits, exclusions, and requirements. Some policies require specific supervision practices or have limits on coverage for certain types of delegated work. Work with an insurance professional who understands law firm risks to ensure your coverage matches your delegation practices.

Create a culture of accountability and continuous improvement. The safest delegation occurs in environments where people take responsibility for their work, communicate openly about problems, and continuously work to improve quality and compliance. This culture can't be mandated—it must be built through leadership, systems, and consistent expectations.

Remember that the goal is client service, not risk elimination. The ethical rules and liability framework exist to protect clients, not to prevent all delegation. When you delegate effectively, you improve client service by providing more responsive communication, more thorough work product, and more consistent quality. The rules support this goal when delegation is done thoughtfully.

The Choice: Paralyzed by Fear or Guided by Knowledge

Many attorneys read about the ethical rules and liability exposure in delegation and conclude that it's too risky. They retreat into doing everything themselves, convinced that personal involvement is the only safe approach.

This reaction is understandable but wrong. As we've seen throughout this chapter, the legal landscape of delegation is complex but navigable. The risks are real but manageable. And the alternative—being the bottleneck—creates its own substantial risks to clients, to your practice, and to your professional standing.

The choice isn't between risky delegation and safe personal involvement. The choice is between thoughtful delegation with appropriate safeguards and risky bottleneck behavior that spreads you too thin to practice competently.

Tom, the family law attorney we met at the beginning of this chapter, learned this lesson through a painful experience. After his associate's error resulted in a bar complaint, he could have concluded that delegation was too dangerous. Instead, he concluded that he'd been delegating thoughtlessly.

He hadn't provided adequate training. He hadn't implemented oversight systems. He hadn't ensured that his associate understood how to handle the specific complexities of custody deadline calculations. His failure wasn't in delegating—it was in delegating without proper preparation and supervision.

Tom rebuilt his delegation practices on a foundation of knowledge rather than fear. He researched his state's rules on supervision. He implemented practice management software with deadline tracking. He created training protocols for new associates. He built oversight systems that caught problems before they harmed clients. And he documented everything to demonstrate reasonable supervision.

Three years later, his practice has grown dramatically. He has two associates, three paralegals, and an administrative staff of four. He delegates extensively—but thoughtfully, with systems and safeguards that protect both clients and his professional standing.

He still takes ultimate responsibility for all client work. He's still professionally liable for the work his team does. But he's managing that responsibility through effective systems rather than trying to do everything personally. And both his clients and his practice are better for it.

The legal landscape of delegation isn't a minefield to be feared. It's a framework to be understood and worked within. When you understand the rules, the risks, and the safeguards, you can delegate confidently and safely.

The next chapter will show you exactly what to delegate and what to keep, building on this foundation of understanding the legal landscape that governs your delegation decisions.

Action Items for This Chapter:

1. Research Your State's Specific Delegation Rules

Within the next week, research your jurisdiction's specific rules on delegation, supervision, and nonlawyer assistance. Document the key requirements that apply to your practice.

State: _____

Key delegation rules found: _____

Specific supervision requirements: _____

Date research completed: _____

2. Audit One Current Delegation for Compliance

Select one significant task you currently delegate. Evaluate it against the legal framework: Is supervision adequate? Is it appropriate for delegation? Are you meeting your professional responsibility obligations?

Task being audited: _____

Is this appropriate to delegate? Yes / No

Is supervision adequate? Yes / No

Changes needed: _____

3. Create Your Delegation Safety Checklist

Based on this chapter's guidance and your state's rules, create a simple checklist you'll use before delegating any legal work. Include: competence assessment, supervision plan, documentation requirements.

Checklist created: Yes / No

Key items on checklist:

1.

2.

3.

Before Moving to Chapter 4:

You should now understand the legal landscape that governs delegation in your practice. You know the ethical rules, the liability framework, and the specific requirements in your jurisdiction.

This knowledge isn't meant to paralyze you with fear—it's meant to empower you to delegate confidently within appropriate boundaries.

The next chapter builds on this foundation by showing you exactly what to delegate and what to keep. You'll learn how to categorize work, identify your zone of genius, and make strategic decisions about delegation that comply with the rules while freeing you from bottleneck behavior.

But those strategic decisions only work if they're built on the legal foundation you've established in this chapter. Take the time to complete the action items, research your state's specific rules, and build the compliance framework that will support effective delegation.

Knowledge of the legal landscape turns delegation from a risky leap into a calculated, strategic move that benefits you, your team, and your clients.

CHAPTER 4:

What to Delegate and What to Keep

David stared at the list he'd just made. Forty-three items. Forty-three different things he'd personally handled yesterday in his criminal defense practice.

Some made sense. He'd handled a suppression hearing that required his specific expertise. He'd counseled a client facing serious charges on whether to accept a plea offer. He'd negotiated with a prosecutor on a complex case.

But most of the list was different. He'd scheduled three client appointments. He'd drafted a routine discovery motion that followed a standard template. He'd responded to eight client emails asking about case status. He'd reviewed and approved a social media post. He'd personally filed documents at the courthouse because his paralegal wasn't sure about the procedure. He'd spent an hour searching for a file that was misfiled.

David circled the items only he could do. The hearing. The client counseling on the plea. The complex negotiation.

Three items. Out of forty-three.

The other forty tasks—representing about six hours of his day—could have been handled by his team if he'd properly delegated them.

This wasn't a unique day. This was every day. Six hours per day, thirty hours per week, 1,500 hours per year of David's time spent on work that didn't require his expertise, experience, or law degree.

At his effective rate of $450 per hour, that was $675,000 annually in misallocated time. Nearly three-quarters of a million dollars per year spent on work that could be delegated.

But here's what stopped David from delegating: he didn't know where to start. Which tasks should go first? Who should handle what? What must he keep? What are the rules? What's the system?

He was paralyzed by the enormity of the problem. So he kept doing everything himself, watching the hours pile up and the opportunities slip away.

The fundamental challenge of delegation isn't deciding whether to delegate—it's deciding what to delegate. Get this wrong, and you either delegate critical work that creates risk or keep routine work that perpetuates the bottleneck. Get it right, and you create a clear path to freedom.

Categories of Work: The Core vs. Peripheral Framework

The first step in determining what to delegate is understanding that not all work is created equal. Some work is core to your value as an attorney. Other work is peripheral—necessary for the practice but not requiring your specific expertise.

The mistake most attorneys make is treating everything as core work. Every task feels important. Every decision seems to need your judgment. Every document appears to require your review.

But this is an illusion created by habit, not an accurate assessment of value.

Core work is work that requires your unique combination of expertise, experience, and professional judgment. It's work where you add significant value that others in your practice cannot easily replicate. It's work that clients are specifically paying for when they hire you rather than someone else.

In a criminal defense practice, core work includes case strategy development, suppression hearing arguments, complex plea negotiations, trial advocacy, and high-stakes client counseling. It's the work where your years of experience, your courtroom skills, and your strategic judgment create real value.

In a personal injury practice working on contingency, core work includes case evaluation and acceptance decisions, settlement negotiations on significant cases, trial preparation and execution, complex legal research on novel issues, and strategic decisions about case development. It's the work where your ability to maximize case value and your litigation expertise matter most.

In an estate planning practice billing hourly, core work includes sophisticated estate plan design, complex tax planning, high-value client relationship management, and strategic advice on wealth transfer and asset protection. It's the work where your technical expertise and relationship skills create premium value.

Peripheral work is everything else. It's work that's necessary for running your practice and serving clients, but it doesn't specifically require your unique expertise. It's work that could be performed competently by someone with appropriate training and supervision.

Peripheral work includes routine legal research on established issues, document preparation following standard templates, client communication about case status and scheduling, administrative tasks related to case management, court filings and procedural work, discovery responses on routine matters, and coordination with courts, opposing counsel, and third parties.

This isn't unimportant work. It's essential to your practice. But it doesn't require your personal involvement to be done well.

The core vs. peripheral distinction isn't about complexity—it's about value creation. Some peripheral work is quite complex. A thorough discovery response in a personal injury case requires attention to detail and legal knowledge. A motion to suppress in a criminal case requires understanding of Fourth Amendment law. An estate planning document must comply with specific statutory requirements.

But these tasks, while complex, don't necessarily require your specific expertise if proper templates, training, and oversight exist. Someone else can perform them competently with the right support.

Conversely, some core work is deceptively simple. A two-minute conversation with a criminal defense client about whether to accept a plea offer might seem simple, but it requires judgment that only comes from years of experience. A quick assessment of whether to take a contingency case might take five minutes, but it requires evaluation skills that determine whether the case will be profitable.

Your goal is to spend at least 80% of your time on core work. If you're like most attorneys stuck in the bottleneck syndrome, you're probably spending 20-30% of your time on core work and 70-80% on peripheral work.

This inversion is killing your practice growth and your quality of life. The path to freedom is systematically moving peripheral work off your plate while protecting time for core work where you create real value.

The "Zone of Genius" Concept

Dan Sullivan, founder of Strategic Coach, popularized the concept of the "zone of genius"—the work where your unique abilities create extraordinary value. This concept provides a powerful lens for delegation decisions.

Your zone of genius is the intersection of what you're uniquely good at, what energizes you, and what creates the most value for your practice. It's not just work you can do—it's work where you excel in ways that others can't easily replicate.

For many attorneys, identifying the zone of genius requires honest self-assessment. You might be capable of doing many things competently, but only a few things extraordinarily well. Those few things are where you should focus your time.

The zone of genius in different practice areas looks different but follows similar patterns. In criminal defense, your zone of genius might be cross-examination and case theory development. You have a gift for finding the weaknesses in the prosecution's case and exposing them effectively. This is where you create value that justifies your fees and wins cases.

But you might not be uniquely gifted at legal research, document drafting, or client intake. You can do these things fine, but so can others with proper training. These tasks aren't in your zone of genius even though they're necessary for your practice.

In personal injury work, your zone of genius might be case evaluation and settlement negotiation. You have an intuitive sense for case value and a talent for negotiating maximum settlements. This ability directly drives your contingency fee revenue and makes you more profitable than competitors who settle for less.

But you might not be uniquely skilled at medical record review, demand letter drafting, or case coordination. These tasks don't leverage your specific talents even though they're essential to case success.

In estate planning, your zone of genius might be sophisticated tax planning and high-net-worth client relationships. You understand complex tax strategies and communicate them clearly to wealthy clients. This expertise commands premium hourly rates and attracts the best clients.

But you might not be uniquely talented at document assembly, routine client communications, or administrative coordination. These tasks, while necessary, don't utilize your highest-value skills.

The zone of genius test has three questions. For any task you're currently performing, ask: Am I uniquely good at this compared to others who could do it? Does this energize me or drain me? Does this create significant value for my practice or clients?

If the answer to all three is yes, it's in your zone of genius. Keep it.

If the answer to all three is no, it's definitely outside your zone of genius. Delegate it.

If the answers are mixed, consider the weight of each factor. Work that creates significant value but drains you might still be worth keeping if delegation would compromise quality. Work that energizes you but creates little value might be a hobby to pursue outside your practice.

Protecting your zone of genius time is the highest-leverage decision you can make. Every hour you spend outside your zone of genius is an hour you're not spending on work where you create extraordinary value. It's an hour of mediocre output instead of excellent output.

When you spend 30 hours per week on peripheral work outside your zone of genius, you're essentially telling your practice "I prefer to be mediocre at administrative tasks rather than excellent at the work I was trained to do."

The path to a more profitable, satisfying, and sustainable practice is ruthlessly eliminating work outside your zone of genius and protecting time for work within it.

Examples of Tasks to Delegate

Let's get specific. What exactly should you be delegating? Here's a comprehensive look at the types of work that can and should be delegated in most law practices, organized by category.

Administrative and Operational Tasks

These are the tasks that keep your practice running but have nothing to do with legal expertise. Almost all of this work should be delegated.

Scheduling and calendar management can be entirely delegated. Your assistant should handle appointment scheduling, court date calendaring, reminder systems, and coordination of your time. You should simply show up where your calendar tells you to be.

In a criminal defense practice, this means your assistant schedules client consultations, coordinates court appearances, manages attorney availability for hearings, and handles schedule conflicts with prosecutors and judges. In a personal injury practice working on contingency, your coordinator schedules depositions, mediations, client meetings, and medical appointments. In an estate planning practice billing hourly, your assistant manages client meetings, signing appointments, and coordination with financial advisors and accountants.

Document filing and court coordination should be delegated. Your team should handle electronic filing, physical document delivery to courts, obtaining hearing dates, coordinating with court clerks, and following up on filed documents.

This doesn't mean you're uninvolved in what gets filed—you still approve motions and pleadings. But the mechanical process of filing and the coordination with court personnel doesn't require your personal attention.

Client file management should be delegated. Someone else should organize files, maintain document management systems, ensure all documents are properly saved and indexed, handle conflict checks, and maintain file retention systems.

You should never spend time looking for documents, figuring out where something was saved, or organizing files. Your time is too valuable for work a competent administrator can handle.

Billing and invoicing should be delegated in hourly practices. Your bookkeeper or billing specialist should track time entries, generate invoices, send bills, follow up on outstanding payments, and handle payment processing.

In flat fee or contingency practices, someone else should track fee agreements, monitor payment schedules for flat fees, handle settlement disbursement calculations (with your review and approval), and manage client billing inquiries.

Vendor and technology coordination should be delegated. Someone else should manage relationships with office suppliers, coordinate with IT support, handle equipment maintenance, process vendor invoices, and manage subscriptions and software licenses.

Legal Research and Writing

Much legal research and writing can be delegated with appropriate review, freeing you to focus on strategy and complex analysis.

Routine legal research on established issues should be delegated. If the legal issue is well-settled and you just need cases and statutes, someone else can find them. Your associate or trained paralegal can research standard suppression issues in criminal defense, research routine liability questions in personal injury, or research established estate planning techniques.

You should reserve your research time for novel issues, complex legal questions, and cases where creative legal theories might make the difference.

First drafts of standard documents should be delegated. Routine motions, discovery responses, correspondence, and pleadings can be drafted by others using templates and your guidance. You review, refine, and approve, but you shouldn't be starting from a blank page on routine documents.

In criminal defense, associates or paralegals can draft discovery motions, routine suppression motions following standard fact patterns, and pretrial correspondence. In personal injury, team members can draft demand letters, routine discovery responses, and settlement correspondence. In estate planning, staff can draft standard wills and trusts, powers of attorney, and healthcare directives.

Case law summaries and research memos should be delegated. When you need to understand case law on a particular issue, someone else can read the cases, summarize the holdings, and prepare a memo explaining how the law applies to your facts. You review the memo and make strategic decisions based on it.

Document review and analysis in appropriate cases should be delegated. In personal injury cases with extensive medical records, a trained paralegal or nurse consultant can review records, create chronologies, and identify key medical facts. In criminal cases with voluminous discovery, associates can review and organize evidence, create summaries, and flag important documents for your attention.

Client Communication and Service

Client communication might feel like it must be attorney-only, but much of it can and should be delegated to create more responsive service.

Status updates and routine inquiries should be delegated. When clients want to know "what's happening with my case," a well-informed team member can provide that information. They can explain what's been done recently, what's coming next, and when the client should expect updates.

This actually improves client service because team members can respond same-day instead of clients waiting days for you to find time to call them back. Clients don't need to hear from you that their court date is next Tuesday—they just need accurate information promptly.

Scheduling communications should be delegated. Confirming appointments, rescheduling meetings, sending reminders, and coordinating client availability are administrative tasks that don't require attorney involvement.

Document collection and client coordination should be delegated. When you need documents from clients, tax returns for estate planning, medical records authorizations for personal injury, or discovery responses in criminal cases, someone else can request them, follow up, organize what's received, and notify you when everything is collected.

Intake screening and initial consultations can be partially delegated. In many practices, a trained intake specialist can conduct the initial information gathering, conflict check, and preliminary case assessment before you speak with the prospect. You then step in for the final evaluation and decision.

This allows you to spend fifteen minutes on qualified prospects instead of forty-five minutes on every person who calls, many of whom aren't a fit for your practice.

Client education and expectation setting can be delegated for routine matters. Explaining standard procedures, typical timelines, what clients should expect next, and how your process works doesn't require attorney involvement. Well-trained staff can handle this orientation, freeing you to focus on substantive legal advice.

Case Management and Coordination

The logistics of moving cases forward can be largely delegated, allowing you to focus on strategy and advocacy.

Discovery management in routine cases should be delegated. Your team can prepare routine interrogatories and requests for production, respond to routine discovery requests, schedule and coordinate depositions (you handle complex depositions personally), organize discovery responses from opposing parties, and maintain discovery tracking systems.

Expert witness coordination should be delegated. Someone else can research and identify potential experts, coordinate expert retention and engagement, manage expert document review and report preparation (though you direct what they should focus on), schedule expert depositions and trial preparation, and handle expert billing and payment.

Settlement coordination for routine matters can be delegated with your oversight. In personal injury practices, a settlement coordinator can calculate liens and obligations, prepare settlement disbursement spreadsheets (which you review and approve), coordinate with lien holders, prepare settlement documents, and handle settlement processing and distribution.

In criminal defense or other practices, staff can coordinate plea agreement logistics once you've negotiated the terms, prepare documentation, coordinate with clients, court, and prosecution, and handle administrative processing.

Trial preparation logistics should be delegated. Your team can organize exhibits and evidence, prepare witness lists and schedules, coordinate with court and opposing counsel on logistics, arrange for trial technology and demonstratives, and handle subpoena preparation and service.

You focus on strategy, witness preparation, and the substantive work of trial. You shouldn't be creating exhibit binders or coordinating with the court clerk about logistics.

Marketing and Business Development

Growing your practice requires marketing and business development, but much of this work can be delegated.

Content creation support should be delegated. While you might write key thought leadership pieces personally, someone else can handle routine blog posts, social media content, email newsletters, website updates, video editing and posting, and podcast production and distribution.

You provide the expertise and perhaps record short videos or outline blog topics. Your team handles the production, distribution, and technical work.

Relationship maintenance can be partially delegated. While you personally cultivate key referral relationships, your team can maintain your CRM database, send thank you notes and acknowledgments (you can personalize them), coordinate referral source events and gifts, track referrals and follow up, and handle routine relationship touchpoints.

Event coordination should be delegated. Whether you're speaking, attending conferences, or hosting events, someone else should handle registration and logistics, travel arrangements, material preparation, follow-up after events, and ROI tracking.

Website and online presence management should be delegated. Your team should handle website updates and maintenance, online review monitoring and response, directory listing management, social media scheduling and posting, and online advertising management (though you set strategy and budget).

Guardrails: What Should Never Be Delegated

Just as important as knowing what to delegate is knowing what must remain under your direct control. Certain work is so central to your professional responsibility, creates such significant risk, or requires such specific judgment that delegation is inappropriate or prohibited.

Professional judgment on substantive legal matters cannot be delegated. This includes determining legal strategy and case theory, advising clients on significant decisions (plea offers in criminal cases, settlement recommendations in civil cases, estate planning strategy), deciding what arguments to make and which to abandon, and evaluating risks and likely outcomes for client decision-making.

You can receive input from associates, research from team members, and analysis from paralegals. But the ultimate judgment calls about legal strategy and client advice must be yours.

Final case acceptance and conflict decisions must remain with you. While intake specialists can screen and gather information, you must make the final decision about whether to accept a case. This ensures you're competent to handle the matter, conflicts are properly considered, and the case fits your practice and resources.

In contingency practices, this is particularly critical because case selection directly drives profitability. In flat fee practices, proper case assessment prevents taking matters you can't handle competently. In hourly practices, thoughtful case acceptance ensures you can serve the client well and that the relationship will be productive.

Settlement and plea authority in significant matters must be yours or require your direct approval. While you might allow associates to handle routine settlements within clear parameters, significant decisions about resolving cases require your involvement.

A criminal defense client's decision about whether to accept a plea offer deserves your personal counsel based on your experience and judgment. A personal injury client's settlement decision on a major case requires your assessment of value and negotiation skills. These aren't moments to delegate.

Attorney-client privilege and confidentiality decisions require your judgment. Determining what information can be shared with whom, deciding when to assert or waive privilege, and assessing when confidentiality exceptions apply are legal judgments that require attorney expertise.

Your team can be trained to recognize privileged information and handle it appropriately, but close calls about privilege assertions or confidentiality boundaries need attorney decision-making.

Final trust accounting decisions cannot be delegated. While the mechanical work of trust accounting can be delegated as discussed in Chapter 3, the decisions about when to deposit funds, when fees are earned and can be transferred, how to disburse settlement proceeds, and how to handle disputed funds must be made by you or with your direct approval.

The ethical rules and the risk exposure make these decisions too important to delegate without your personal involvement.

Quality control and final review on high-stakes documents should not be fully delegated. For documents that go to court with your signature, that commit your client to significant obligations, or that create substantial risk if errors exist, you need to review them personally.

This doesn't mean reviewing every word of every document—that's not sustainable. But it means you review the key provisions, verify the critical facts, and ensure the document accomplishes what it's supposed to accomplish.

You might delegate the first draft, the research, and even the initial review to associates. But documents that go out with your name on them should have your eyes on them, particularly when stakes are high.

Ethical decisions and professional responsibility judgments require your involvement. When questions arise about what's ethically permissible, how to handle potential conflicts, whether to withdraw from representation, or how to address client requests that create ethical concerns, these require attorney judgment.

Your team should be trained to recognize ethical issues and escalate them to you. But the resolution of ethical questions must involve attorney decision-making.

Direct supervision of other attorneys cannot be fully delegated. While you might have a senior associate who mentors junior associates, you cannot completely delegate your responsibility to ensure associates are competent and complying with professional standards.

This means you need regular touchpoints with associates working on your cases, review of their work product on important matters, and oversight of their professional development and conduct.

Delegating to Attorneys vs. Nonlawyer Staff

The distinction between what you can delegate to other attorneys versus what you can delegate to nonlawyer staff affects how you structure your team and your delegation approach.

Attorneys can receive delegated work that requires legal judgment, analysis, and client counseling. They can make legal arguments, provide legal advice under your supervision, represent clients in court proceedings (in most jurisdictions), and handle complex legal research and strategy development.

This means associates can take on substantial responsibility for case management, including case strategy development (with your oversight), client counseling on routine matters, court appearances for motion practice and hearings, legal research and brief writing, and discovery and negotiation within established parameters.

The supervision requirement still applies—you're responsible for their work and must provide adequate oversight. But the range of work you can delegate to attorneys is broader than what you can delegate to nonlawyers.

Nonlawyer staff cannot provide legal advice, represent clients in most court proceedings, or make legal judgments. But within these constraints, they can handle extensive work that doesn't require attorney decision-making.

Paralegals and legal assistants can conduct factual research and investigation, draft documents based on templates and your direction, communicate with clients about factual matters and case status, manage case logistics and coordination, handle administrative and operational tasks, and prepare summaries and analysis for your review.

In many practices, highly skilled paralegals become essential team members who handle complex work independently within their scope of authority. They know when they need attorney input and when they can proceed on their own. This allows them to take significant workload off your plate while staying within ethical boundaries.

The cost difference between attorneys and nonlawyers affects delegation strategy. Associates command higher salaries than paralegals, often $70,000-120,000+ depending on experience and location. Skilled paralegals might earn $45,000-75,000. Administrative staff might earn $35,000-55,000.

This means you should delegate as much as possible to the lowest-cost team member who can handle it competently. Work that doesn't require legal judgment should go to paralegals, not associates. Work that doesn't require legal knowledge should go to administrative staff, not paralegals.

Many attorneys make the mistake of hiring only associates and then using them for tasks that paralegals could handle. This is expensive and inefficient. It also frustrates associates who went to law school to do legal work, not administrative tasks.

The sweet spot for most practices is a team structure with multiple levels. You might have one or two associates for work requiring legal judgment and representation. Several paralegals for sophisticated case management and document preparation. Administrative staff for scheduling, filing, client coordination, and operational tasks.

This allows you to delegate appropriately at each level, matching work complexity to team member capability and cost.

Building Your Personal Delegation Strategy

Now that you understand the categories of work, the zone of genius concept, and the guardrails around delegation, it's time to build your personal delegation strategy.

Start with a comprehensive task inventory. For one full week, track everything you do. Every phone call, every document you touch, every email you send, every decision you make. Create a complete list of how you're actually spending your time.

Be honest. Include the time spent searching for files, the interruptions you handle, the questions you answer. Don't just track the "important" work—track all of it.

Categorize each task using the frameworks from this chapter. For every task on your list, ask: Is this core or peripheral? Is this in my zone of genius? Could this be delegated to an associate? Could this be delegated to a paralegal? Could this be delegated to administrative staff? Must this remain with me?

You'll likely find that 60-80% of what you're doing could be delegated if proper systems and training existed.

Prioritize delegation opportunities based on impact. Not all delegation opportunities are equally valuable. Focus first on work that consumes significant time, doesn't require your unique expertise, and can be delegated without major systems changes.

Quick wins might include client scheduling (high time consumption, easy to delegate), routine discovery responses (moderate time consumption, clear templates exist), and status update calls (frequent occurrence, doesn't require attorney judgment).

Defer more complex delegation like case strategy development with associates or sophisticated settlement negotiations until you've built your delegation muscles with simpler tasks.

Create clear protocols for each delegated task. Don't just hand off work and hope for the best. For each task you delegate, document: Who is responsible for this task? What authority do they have (can they complete it independently, or do they need approval)? What quality standards must be met? When should they escalate to you?

These protocols prevent the confusion that causes people to keep coming back to you with questions instead of handling work independently.

Match delegation to your team's current capabilities. Don't delegate work your team isn't ready to handle. If your paralegal hasn't drafted motions before, start with simple templates and provide close review. If your associate hasn't handled client counseling, begin with routine matters and debrief after each interaction.

The gap between what you need to delegate and what your team can currently handle is filled by training, which we'll address in Chapter 5.

Implement delegation progressively, not all at once. Trying to delegate everything simultaneously creates chaos and increases the risk of failure. Instead, delegate one category of work at a time.

Start with administrative tasks that are easy to hand off. Once those are flowing smoothly, move to routine legal work with clear templates. Then tackle more complex delegation like case management or client communication.

Each successful delegation builds confidence—yours and your team's—and creates momentum for the next step.

Monitor results and refine your approach. After delegating a category of work, track what's working and what's not. Are tasks being completed competently? Are deadlines being met? Is quality acceptable? What problems are emerging?

Use this information to refine your delegation approach. Maybe you need clearer instructions. Maybe you need better training. Maybe you need different quality control systems. Maybe the work isn't ready to be fully delegated yet and needs more oversight.

Delegation is iterative. You won't get it perfect the first time. The goal is continuous improvement, not immediate perfection.

The Delegation Decision Tree

When you're uncertain whether to delegate a specific task, use this decision tree to guide your thinking:

First question: Is this task legally permissible to delegate? If it requires attorney judgment on substantive legal matters, final client advice on significant decisions, or involves ethical determinations that require attorney expertise, it probably can't be delegated. Keep it.

If it's work that can be performed under attorney supervision within your state's rules on unauthorized practice of law, proceed to the next question.

Second question: Is this in my zone of genius? If this is work where you excel uniquely, that energizes you, and that creates extraordinary value, keep it even if it could technically be delegated. This is where you should be spending your time.

If it's outside your zone of genius—work you're not uniquely good at, that drains you, or that creates ordinary rather than extraordinary value—proceed to the next question.

Third question: Is the task recurring or one-time? If it's recurring work that happens regularly, delegation creates ongoing leverage. The time invested in training and system-building pays off repeatedly.

If it's a one-time task, delegation might not be worth the training investment. It might be faster to just do it yourself this once. But consider whether this "one-time" task is really something that will come up again in different forms.

Fourth question: Do I have someone capable of handling this, or can they become capable with reasonable training? If you have a team member with the skills, or who can develop them with training you're willing to provide, delegate it.

If no one on your team could handle this competently even with training, you face a choice: hire someone with the right capabilities, develop the capability in your existing team through significant training, or keep the task yourself for now.

Fifth question: What's the cost of delegation failure vs. the cost of keeping it? Every delegation carries some risk. What happens if it's done poorly? How severe is the consequence? Can errors be caught and corrected before client harm?

Compare that risk to the opportunity cost of keeping the work yourself. What else could you be doing with that time? What value are you not creating because you're handling this task?

If the risk of delegation failure is low or manageable and the opportunity cost of keeping it is high, delegate.

If the risk is high and the opportunity cost of keeping it is relatively low, retain it for now and revisit once better systems or training can reduce the risk.

Different Practice Areas, Different Delegation Strategies

While the principles of delegation are universal, how they apply varies by practice area and business model.

Criminal defense practices working on flat fees often have standardized processes for common charges. A DUI case, a possession charge, a domestic violence case—these follow predictable patterns that allow extensive delegation.

Associates can handle routine court appearances and status conferences. Paralegals can draft standard motions and manage discovery. Intake specialists can screen potential clients using clear criteria. Administrative staff can coordinate with courts, prosecutors, and clients.

You focus on suppression hearings requiring sophisticated Fourth Amendment arguments, trial advocacy, complex plea negotiations, and high-stakes client counseling. The routine case management happens without your involvement, freeing you to deliver value where it matters most.

Personal injury practices on contingency need careful delegation of case evaluation and settlement negotiation since these directly impact your fee revenue. Poor case selection or weak settlement negotiation costs you money directly.

But medical record review, demand letter preparation, discovery management, and lien resolution can all be delegated to trained team members. Case managers can handle client communication and coordination. Paralegals can manage the case through settlement. Associates can handle depositions and motion practice.

You focus on case acceptance decisions (which cases to take), settlement negotiation on significant cases, trial preparation and execution on cases that don't settle, and strategic decisions about case development. Your judgment determines whether cases are profitable—the administrative work of managing them can be delegated.

Estate planning practices billing hourly can delegate extensive document preparation while keeping client relationship management and sophisticated planning strategies.

Paralegals can draft routine wills, trusts, and ancillary documents using established templates. Associates can handle moderately complex plans under your supervision. Administrative staff can coordinate signing appointments, manage document execution, and handle client communication about logistics.

You focus on sophisticated estate and tax planning strategy, high-net-worth client relationship management, complex trust design, and business succession planning. The document production happens efficiently without requiring your personal involvement in every detail.

Family law practices often require significant attorney involvement in client counseling given the emotional nature of the work, but discovery, financial affidavit preparation, and routine motion practice can be delegated effectively.

Corporate practices can delegate extensive contract review and drafting to associates and paralegals, while you focus on negotiation strategy and complex deal structures.

Litigation practices can delegate discovery management, document review, and routine motion practice while you handle depositions, complex motions, and trial work.

The key in every practice area is identifying the work where your specific expertise and judgment create value, and systematically moving everything else off your plate.

The 80/20 Goal Revisited

Remember the goal from earlier in this chapter: spend at least 80% of your time on core work in your zone of genius.

Most attorneys start at the opposite ratio—80% peripheral work, 20% core work. The path to an excellent practice is systematically flipping that ratio.

You don't have to achieve 80/20 immediately. Progress matters more than perfection.

If you're currently at 20% core work, getting to 40% core work doubles your time spent on high-value activities. That's a massive improvement even though you're not yet at the ideal ratio.

From 40% to 60%, then 60% to 80%, each step creates more leverage, more value, and more freedom.

Track your ratio monthly as you implement delegation. At the start of each month, estimate what percentage of your time was spent on core work versus peripheral work last month. As you delegate more effectively, watch this ratio shift.

When you hit 80%, you've achieved what most attorneys consider impossible: a practice where your time is spent almost entirely on work that only you can do, work that energizes you, and work that creates extraordinary value.

At that point, you're no longer trapped in your practice. You're leading it.

Action Items for This Chapter:

1. Complete Your Personal Task Inventory

Track everything you do for three full workdays. At the end, categorize each task as either core (requires your unique expertise) or peripheral (could be done by others with proper training).

Days tracked: _____

Core tasks identified: _____

Peripheral tasks identified: _____

Hours spent on peripheral work: _____

2. Delegate One Peripheral Task This Week

From your peripheral task list, select one task that you'll delegate completely this week. Choose something that appears regularly and would free up meaningful time.

Task to delegate: _____

Who will receive it: _____

Delegation conversation scheduled: _____

3. Calculate Your Delegation ROI

Using the 80/20 goal from this chapter, calculate the potential value of moving 80% of your time to core work.

Current % of time on core work: _____%

Target % of time on core work: 80%

Hours to reclaim: _____ (difference × weekly hours)

Annual value: $_____ (hours × your rate × 50)

Before Moving to Chapter 5:

You should now have a clear understanding of what work belongs on your plate and what should be delegated. You've categorized your current work, identified your zone of genius, and created a specific plan for what to delegate first.

But knowing what to delegate is only half the battle. The next challenge is finding and developing the right people to receive that delegated work.

Chapter 5 will show you how to identify the personality traits and work habits of people who excel at handling delegated responsibility, how to interview for delegation readiness, and how to onboard and train team members for delegation success.

Your delegation plan from this chapter will only succeed if you have the right people in place to execute it. The next chapter ensures you do.

One final action before moving on:

Share your delegation plan with at least one trusted advisor—your spouse, a business coach, a mentor attorney, or a peer who understands your practice. Ask them to hold you accountable to implementing it.

Accountability transforms plans into action. Without it, this chapter becomes interesting reading that produces no change. With it, you'll actually reclaim your time and transform your practice.

My accountability partner: _____

Date I will share my plan with them: _____

How they will hold me accountable: _____

Now you're ready to move forward. You know what to delegate. The next chapter shows you who should receive it and how to prepare them for success.

CHAPTER 5:

Finding the Right People

Lisa had finally accepted that she needed help. Her estate planning practice was drowning her in work she shouldn't be doing. She knew what to delegate—Chapter 4 had made that clear. Now she just needed someone to delegate to.

She posted a job listing for a paralegal. Within a week, she had fifty applications. On paper, they all looked qualified. Paralegal certificates. Relevant experience. Good references. Professional resumes.

She interviewed her top five candidates. All of them could answer her technical questions. They knew about estate planning documents, understood probate procedures, and had experience with the software she used.

Lisa hired the candidate with the most experience—eight years as an estate planning paralegal. Perfect, she thought.

Three months later, Lisa was more frustrated than ever.

Her new paralegal could do the work when Lisa told her exactly what to do. But that was the problem—Lisa had to tell her exactly what to do. Every task required detailed instructions. Every decision, no matter how small, required Lisa's approval. Every problem was escalated immediately rather than solved independently.

Lisa had hired someone who could execute tasks but not handle responsibility. Someone who could follow directions but not exercise judgment. Someone who had experience but lacked initiative.

She'd hired the wrong person. Not because the paralegal was incompetent—she was perfectly competent at task execution. But because Lisa needed someone who could think, decide, and act independently. She needed someone who thrived on responsibility rather than someone who avoided it.

Lisa had learned a hard lesson: when you're delegating, technical skills matter far less than personality traits and work habits. You can teach someone estate planning procedures. You can't teach someone to take ownership, exercise judgment, and solve problems independently.

Finding the right people for delegation isn't about finding the most experienced candidates. It's about finding people with the traits that make delegation successful.

Personality Traits and Work Habits of Strong Delegates

Before you can find the right people, you need to know what "right" looks like. The best delegation candidates share specific personality traits and work habits that make them excel at handling delegated responsibility.

These traits matter more than experience, education, or technical skills. You can train someone on your practice area, your software, and your procedures. You can't train fundamental personality traits.

Initiative is the foundation of successful delegation. The best delegation candidates don't wait to be told what to do—they identify what needs to be done and do it. When they encounter a problem, their first instinct is to solve it, not to immediately ask for help.

This doesn't mean they never ask questions or seek guidance. It means they try to solve problems first, and they ask for help when they've exhausted their own resources or when the stakes are high enough to warrant immediate escalation.

In interviews, you're looking for stories about times they saw something that needed to be done and did it without being asked. Times they encountered obstacles and found ways around them. Times they went beyond their job description because that's what the situation required.

A paralegal with initiative reviews a file and notices that a critical document is missing. Instead of just flagging it for you, they check the client portal, call the client to request it, follow up if it's not received, and only bring it to your attention if the client is unresponsive. You find out about the problem only after they've already solved it.

A legal assistant with initiative notices that the same question keeps coming up from clients. Instead of answering it individually each time, they draft a standard explanation, get your approval, and create a template response. They've turned a recurring problem into a systematized solution.

Judgment is what separates task executors from responsibility handlers. You need people who can make good decisions when you're not available to make them. This requires the ability to assess situations, weigh options, consider consequences, and choose appropriate courses of action.

Good judgment isn't about always making perfect decisions—it's about making reasonable decisions based on available information and knowing when a situation requires escalation to you.

In a criminal defense practice, a paralegal with good judgment knows when a prosecutor's discovery response requires immediate attorney attention versus when it's routine and can be processed normally. They understand the difference between "notify the attorney today" and "include in the weekly case update."

In a personal injury practice working on contingency, an intake coordinator with good judgment knows when a potential case is clearly worth pursuing, when it's clearly not a fit, and when it requires attorney evaluation before making a decision. They don't waste your time evaluating obvious rejects, but they don't turn away good cases by being overly restrictive.

In an estate planning practice billing hourly, an assistant with good judgment knows when a client's question requires attorney expertise and when they can provide the answer based on established procedures. They understand the line between helpful information and legal advice.

Accountability means taking ownership of outcomes, not just tasks. The best delegation candidates don't just complete assignments—they ensure that the intended result is achieved.

If they're responsible for filing a motion, they don't just prepare it and hand it to you. They ensure it gets filed on time, confirm that filing was successful, verify that all parties received notice, and check that it appears correctly in the court's system. They own the entire outcome, not just their piece of it.

When something goes wrong, people with high accountability look first at what they could have done differently. They focus on solving the problem and preventing recurrence rather than deflecting blame or making excuses.

You're looking for people who say "I'll make sure that gets done" instead of "I'll work on that." The former takes ownership of the outcome; the latter only commits to effort.

Resourcefulness is the ability to figure things out without constant guidance. The best delegation candidates don't immediately escalate every question or problem. They use available resources—documentation, past examples, internet research, consultation with peers—to find answers before asking you.

This doesn't mean they struggle in silence or waste time spinning their wheels. It means they make a reasonable effort to solve problems independently before seeking help. And when they do ask for help, they come with "Here's what I've tried and here's where I'm stuck" rather than "I don't know what to do."

A resourceful associate encounters an unfamiliar legal issue. Before asking you, they research case law, check practice guides, review past similar cases from your files, and consult with more experienced colleagues. When they come to you, it's with a summary of what they've learned and specific questions about how to apply it to the current case.

A resourceful paralegal needs to accomplish something they haven't done before. They find someone who has done it, review past examples, locate relevant procedures or checklists, and try to work through it. They only involve you when they hit a genuine barrier or need to confirm their approach on something high-stakes.

Communication skills matter enormously in delegation. You need people who can articulate clearly what they've done, what they're planning to do, what problems they've encountered, and what they need from you. Poor communication creates the need for constant checking in and status updates, which defeats the purpose of delegation.

Good communication includes knowing when to communicate. The best delegation candidates understand what you need to know immediately, what can wait for a regular update, and what you don't need to know at all because they've handled it.

They provide context when they communicate, not just facts. Instead of "The client called," they say "The client called asking about the court date. I checked the file, confirmed it's two weeks from Friday, and let them know. I also sent them a reminder about bringing the documents we discussed."

They document their work so others can follow what happened. They write clear emails that get to the point. They present information logically. They know how to escalate urgent matters effectively.

Reliability means you can trust them to follow through. When they say something will be done, it gets done. When they take responsibility for a task, it happens without your reminder or follow-up.

This seems basic, but it's surprisingly rare. Many people are good at starting tasks but poor at finishing them. Others are reliable on small things but drop the ball when workload increases. The best delegation candidates maintain reliability regardless of volume or pressure.

You're looking for patterns of follow-through in their work history. Projects they've managed from start to finish. Responsibilities they've maintained consistently over time. Situations where they delivered even when circumstances were challenging.

Coachability is the willingness and ability to receive feedback and improve. Even the best delegation candidates will make mistakes, especially as they take on new responsibilities. What matters is how they respond to feedback and whether they improve based on it.

People with high coachability receive critical feedback without defensiveness. They ask clarifying questions to understand what needs to change. They implement feedback and demonstrate improvement. They seek feedback proactively to continue developing.

People with low coachability make excuses when receiving feedback. They defend their approach rather than being open to alternatives. They might agree in the moment but don't actually change their behavior. They take feedback personally rather than professionally.

In interviews, you're listening for how candidates talk about past feedback or criticism. Do they acknowledge mistakes and growth? Do they credit others for their development? Do they show self-awareness about areas where they need to improve?

Emotional intelligence allows them to navigate client relationships and team dynamics. They can read situations, understand unstated needs, manage their own emotions under pressure, and interact effectively with diverse personalities.

In client-facing roles, this means recognizing when a client is anxious and needs reassurance versus when they're frustrated and need action. It means knowing when to be warm and empathetic versus when to be direct and professional.

In team settings, it means working effectively with colleagues, navigating disagreements constructively, and maintaining professionalism under stress. It means recognizing when to collaborate and when to work independently.

The best delegation candidates handle difficult clients with grace, de-escalate tense situations, build positive relationships across the team, and maintain composure when things go wrong.

Hiring for Initiative, Judgment, and Accountability

Traditional hiring focuses on credentials and experience. Delegation-focused hiring prioritizes traits over credentials. You're looking for people who will thrive with delegated responsibility, not just people who can perform tasks when told what to do.

This requires a different approach to job postings, resume screening, interviewing, and selection.

Your job posting should screen for delegation-ready traits from the start. Instead of listing tasks and required experience, describe the environment and expectations. You want to attract people who thrive on responsibility and repel people who prefer to simply follow instructions.

Your posting might include language like "You'll be expected to exercise independent judgment on routine matters," "Initiative and problem-solving skills are more important than industry experience," "You'll manage your own workload with minimal supervision," or "We're looking for someone who sees problems as puzzles to solve, not obstacles to escalate."

For a criminal defense practice, you might emphasize the fast-paced environment, the need for independent decision-making on case logistics, and the importance of client communication skills. For a personal injury practice on contingency, you might highlight case management responsibilities, the need to handle multiple deadlines independently, and the importance of attention to detail that affects case value. For an estate planning practice billing hourly, you might focus on client relationship management, document preparation ownership, and the need for initiative in identifying and resolving client issues.

Be explicit about what you value: "We'd rather hire someone with strong judgment and no legal experience than someone with years of experience who waits to be told what to do."

Resume screening should look for evidence of progressive responsibility and achievement. You're not just looking for job titles and tenure—you're looking for patterns that suggest initiative, judgment, and accountability.

Red flags include frequent job changes with no progression in responsibility, job descriptions that sound entirely task-focused with no indication of decision-making authority, lack of specific achievements or outcomes, or resumes that emphasize credentials over accomplishments.

Green flags include evidence of taking on increasing responsibility within roles, specific achievements that required initiative, descriptions that include words like "managed," "developed," "implemented," or "improved," volunteer leadership or community involvement that shows initiative, or career progression that shows growth and advancement.

A resume that says "Prepared legal documents as directed by attorneys" tells you someone can follow instructions. A resume that says "Identified inefficiencies in document preparation process and implemented template system that reduced drafting time by 40%" tells you someone takes initiative and delivers results.

Phone screens should quickly assess basic fit before investing in full interviews. In a 15-20 minute phone conversation, you can eliminate candidates who clearly won't thrive in a delegation-heavy environment.

Ask questions that reveal how they approach work: "Tell me about a time you identified a problem at work and solved it without being asked," "Describe a situation where you had to make a decision without your supervisor available," or "What do you do when you encounter something you don't know how to handle?"

Listen for responses that show initiative versus passivity. Strong candidates tell stories about seeing needs and filling them. Weak candidates talk about waiting for direction or escalating every decision.

If someone can't readily provide examples of independent problem-solving or decision-making, they're probably not delegation-ready regardless of their other qualifications.

Sample Interview Questions for Delegation Readiness

The interview is where you truly assess whether someone will excel at handling delegated responsibility. Traditional interview questions about skills and experience matter less than behavioral questions that reveal how someone actually works.

Questions that assess initiative:

"Tell me about a time when you saw something that needed to be done and did it without being asked. What was the situation, what did you do, and what was the result?"

Listen for: Specific examples where they took action independently. Evidence that they look for opportunities to add value beyond their assigned tasks. Results that show their initiative was effective.

Red flags: Struggling to think of examples. Stories where they asked for permission before acting on something routine. Examples that are more about following through on assigned work than taking true initiative.

"Describe a process or system you improved in a previous role. What prompted you to make the change, and how did you implement it?"

Listen for: Recognition of inefficiency without being told about it. Taking ownership of improvement rather than waiting for management to fix things. Practical implementation that shows follow-through.

Red flags: Changes that were suggested by others rather than identified by the candidate. Improvements that were never actually implemented. Inability to provide specific examples.

"What do you do when you have downtime at work? Walk me through a specific example."

Listen for: Using downtime productively without being directed. Looking for ways to help the team or improve processes. Initiative in organizing, learning, or getting ahead on work.

Red flags: Waiting for assignments rather than finding productive work. Using downtime for purely personal activities. Inability to identify productive uses of unstructured time.

Questions that assess judgment:

"Tell me about a time when you had to make a decision without your supervisor being available. What was the situation, how did you decide what to do, and what was the outcome?"

Listen for: Thoughtful decision-making process. Consideration of consequences and alternatives. Appropriate balance between acting independently and knowing when to escalate. Good outcome based on reasonable judgment.

Red flags: Inability to make decisions independently. Poor reasoning that led to predictable problems. Always escalating rather than deciding. Making impulsive decisions without considering consequences.

"Describe a situation where you made a mistake in judgment. What happened, what did you learn, and how has it affected your decision-making since?"

Listen for: Honest acknowledgment of a mistake. Learning from the experience. Changed behavior that shows growth. Self-awareness about judgment limitations.

Red flags: Inability to acknowledge mistakes. Blaming others for the outcome. No learning or behavior change. Defensive posture about past errors.

"How do you decide when to handle something yourself versus when to escalate it to your supervisor?"

Listen for: Clear criteria for escalation (stakes, complexity, novelty, risk). Bias toward solving problems independently when appropriate. Recognition of when expertise beyond their level is truly needed.

Red flags: Escalating everything to avoid responsibility. Never escalating even when clearly appropriate. Inability to articulate decision-making criteria.

Questions that assess accountability:

"Tell me about a project or responsibility you owned from start to finish. How did you ensure it was completed successfully?"

Listen for: True ownership that went beyond task completion to ensuring the outcome. Systems or approaches they used to track progress. Follow-through until results were achieved.

Red flags: Examples where they only handled part of something rather than owning the full outcome. Relying entirely on others to keep them on track. Lack of personal accountability for results.

"Describe a time when something you were responsible for went wrong. What was your role in the problem, and what did you do about it?"

Listen for: Taking appropriate responsibility rather than deflecting blame. Focus on solving the problem and preventing recurrence. Learning and improvement from the experience.

Red flags: Blaming others exclusively. Making excuses rather than acknowledging responsibility. No actions taken to prevent similar problems in the future.

"How do you handle competing priorities and ensure important deadlines aren't missed?"

Listen for: Personal systems for tracking and managing multiple responsibilities. Proactive communication when conflicts arise. Track record of meeting commitments despite competing demands.

Red flags: History of missing deadlines. Relying entirely on others to manage their priorities. Inability to describe personal accountability systems.

Questions that assess resourcefulness:

"Tell me about a time you had to figure out how to do something you'd never done before. How did you approach it?"

Listen for: Multiple strategies for finding answers (research, past examples, consulting resources, asking colleagues). Effort to solve independently before escalating. Successful outcome through their own resourcefulness.

Red flags: Immediately asking the supervisor rather than trying to figure it out. Giving up quickly when the answer isn't obvious. Inability to identify resources they could use to learn.

"Describe a situation where you encountered an obstacle that prevented you from completing a task as planned. What did you do?"

Listen for: Creative problem-solving. Persistence in finding alternatives. Ability to work around obstacles rather than being stopped by them.

Red flags: Giving up when the obvious approach doesn't work. Always needing someone else to solve problems. Inability to think creatively about alternatives.

Questions that assess communication:

"How do you keep your supervisor informed about your work? Give me a specific example of how you handled communication on a recent project."

Listen for: Appropriate level of communication (not too much, not too little). Clear, concise updates that provide necessary context. Understanding of what information is important to share.

Red flags: Over-communicating trivial details. Failing to communicate important information. Inability to provide context when sharing updates. Assuming supervisor knows things without being told.

"Tell me about a time you had to explain something complex to someone without a technical background. How did you approach it?"

Listen for: Ability to simplify without condescending. Checking for understanding. Adapting explanation based on audience needs.

Red flags: Using jargon inappropriately. Inability to gauge whether the listener understands. Impatience with questions or need for clarification.

Questions that assess reliability:

"Tell me about a time when you had a lot on your plate and tight deadlines. How did you ensure everything got done?"

Listen for: Systems for managing workload. Prioritization skills. Track record of delivery even under pressure.

Red flags: History of missing deadlines or dropping balls. Relying on others to rescue them. Poor planning that creates unnecessary crises.

"Describe a commitment you made that was difficult to keep. What made it difficult, and how did you ensure you followed through?"

Listen for: Determination to honor commitments despite obstacles. Problem-solving to overcome difficulties. Pattern of follow-through even when circumstances are challenging.

Red flags: Breaking commitments when things get hard. Inability to provide examples of difficult follow-through. Making commitments without thinking through feasibility.

Questions that assess coachability:

"Tell me about a piece of critical feedback you received from a supervisor. How did you respond, and what did you do with that feedback?"

Listen for: Non-defensive reception of feedback. Specific actions taken to improve. Demonstrable change in behavior. Appreciation for feedback as a growth tool.

Red flags: Defensiveness about feedback received. Making excuses rather than acknowledging the feedback. No actual behavior change despite agreeing with the feedback.

"What's an area where you know you need to improve? What are you doing about it?"

Listen for: Self-awareness about weaknesses. Active efforts to improve. Seeking feedback or learning opportunities. Growth mindset.

Red flags: Inability to identify any areas for improvement. Awareness of weaknesses but no action to address them. Blaming external factors for limitations.

The "tell me what I didn't ask" question:

End your interviews with an open-ended question: "What haven't I asked you that you think I should know about your ability to handle responsibility and work independently?"

Strong candidates use this opportunity to share relevant examples that showcase their delegation readiness. They might describe achievements, work style preferences, or experiences that demonstrate initiative and judgment.

Weak candidates struggle with open-ended questions, provide generic answers, or simply say "I think you covered everything."

This question reveals how someone thinks when not guided by specific prompts. It shows whether they can identify what's important and communicate it effectively.

Onboarding and Training for Delegation Success

Hiring delegation-ready people is essential, but it's only the first step. Even the best candidates need proper onboarding and training to succeed in a delegation-heavy environment.

Traditional onboarding focuses on policies, procedures, and systems. Delegation-focused onboarding emphasizes decision-making frameworks, authority levels, and cultural expectations about responsibility.

The first 90 days set the tone for the entire working relationship. How you onboard new team members determines whether they become independent contributors or dependent task-executors.

Many attorneys make the mistake of over-supervising during onboarding. They want to ensure quality, so they review everything, approve every decision, and provide detailed direction for every task. The new hire learns "I should check with the attorney before doing anything."

This creates learned helplessness from day one. The new hire might be naturally initiative-driven and judgment-oriented, but your onboarding process trains them to wait for direction and avoid independent action.

Better onboarding explicitly establishes expectations for independence while providing the support needed to meet those expectations.

Day one should include a clear conversation about delegation philosophy and expectations. Don't assume new hires understand what you mean by "taking initiative" or "exercising judgment." Be explicit.

You might say: "In this practice, we expect you to make decisions independently on matters within your authority. I'd rather you make a reasonable decision that turns out wrong than wait for me to decide everything. We'll define what's within your authority, and we'll train you on how to make good decisions. But the expectation is that you'll think, decide, and act."

Explain what kinds of decisions they can make independently, which ones require your approval, and which ones they should escalate immediately. Provide examples to make it concrete.

In a criminal defense practice, you might explain: "You can independently schedule client meetings, routine discovery, and most court appearances. You need my approval for significant motion strategy, plea negotiation approaches, and anything involving trial tactics. You escalate immediately anything involving ethical issues, potential conflicts, or emergency client situations."

In a personal injury practice on contingency, you might clarify: "You can independently manage case logistics, routine client communication, and standard discovery. You need my review before sending demand letters or settlement communications. You escalate immediately any liability questions, coverage issues, or situations where case value might be impacted."

In an estate planning practice billing hourly, you might establish: "You can independently prepare routine documents following our templates, schedule client meetings, and answer procedural questions. You need my review before anything goes to a client for signature. You escalate any unusual family situations, complex tax questions, or cases that don't fit our standard approaches."

The first 30 days should focus on learning systems and processes with gradually increasing independence. Start with close supervision on core tasks, but explicitly plan to reduce oversight as competence develops.

Create a structured progression: Week 1, they observe you performing key tasks. Week 2, they perform tasks with your real-time guidance. Week 3, they perform tasks independently with your review before completion. Week 4, they perform tasks independently and inform you when complete.

This progression should be explicit. Tell them: "This week, you'll watch me handle client intake calls and draft motions. Next week, you'll draft with me available for questions. Week three, you'll draft independently and I'll review before filing. By week four, you should be handling routine motions start to finish."

Create decision-making frameworks specific to your practice. Don't leave new hires to figure out how to make good decisions. Teach them your decision-making criteria for common situations.

For client communication, you might teach: "When a client asks a question, first determine: Is this a factual question about their case that you know the answer to? Is this a legal advice question that requires attorney judgment? Is this a procedural question about next steps? If it's factual or procedural and you're confident in the answer, respond directly. If it requires legal judgment or you're unsure, say 'That's an excellent question that requires attorney input. Let me discuss with the attorney and get back to you today.'"

For case management decisions, you might provide: "When deciding whether to escalate an issue to me, consider: Does this affect case strategy or client outcome? Is it novel or outside our standard procedures? Does it involve significant money or risk? If yes to any of these, escalate. If it's routine and follows our standard approach, handle it independently."

For quality decisions, you might establish: "When deciding if work is ready to go out, ask yourself: Have I followed the template or example? Have I verified all facts and dates? Have I proofread carefully? Would I be comfortable with my name on this? If yes to all, it's ready. If you're uncertain about any, request review."

Provide graduated authority that increases with demonstrated competence. Don't give new hires full authority immediately, but also don't keep them on training wheels indefinitely.

You might establish authority levels: Level 1 (first 30 days) - Complete tasks with review before finalization. Level 2 (30-60 days) - Complete routine tasks independently, inform when done. Level 3 (60-90 days) - Handle categories of work fully independently. Level 4 (90+ days) - Make judgment calls within defined parameters.

Make progression through levels explicit and based on demonstrated competence, not just time. "You'll move to Level 3 on discovery responses when you've completed 10 responses with minimal corrections needed. You'll move to Level 3 on client communications when you've handled 20 client interactions with appropriate judgment on escalation."

Build in regular feedback cycles that reinforce delegation expectations. Weekly check-ins during the first 90 days should focus not just on what work was completed, but on how decision-making and judgment are developing.

Ask questions like: "What decisions did you make independently this week? What was your thinking on each? Looking back, would you decide differently on any? What situations made you uncertain about whether to escalate to me? How did you resolve that uncertainty?"

This reinforces that you value independent thinking and good judgment, not just task completion. It helps them develop better decision-making skills by reflecting on their choices.

Provide specific feedback on their judgment and initiative: "I noticed you identified the missing document and obtained it from the client before I even knew it was an issue. That's exactly the kind of initiative I want to see" or "When the client asked about settlement value, you appropriately escalated to me rather than speculating. That shows good judgment about the line between information and advice."

Create a library of templates, examples, and resources that enable independent work. New hires can't exercise good judgment if they don't have models to follow.

Build a repository of past work product they can reference: Sample motions organized by type and jurisdiction. Template correspondence for common situations. Example case strategies with your annotations explaining the thinking. Decision trees for common scenarios.

For a criminal defense practice, this might include suppression motion templates for different fact patterns, sample plea negotiation approaches with notes on strategy, client communication scripts for common questions, and examples of how to analyze police reports for issues.

For a personal injury practice, this might include demand letter examples with annotations about valuation, settlement negotiation frameworks, medical record review templates, and sample case evaluation memos showing your analysis process.

For an estate planning practice, this might include document templates with drafting notes, client interview guides, estate plan design examples for different scenarios, and sample explanations of complex concepts for client education.

The goal is to provide enough structure that they can handle work independently while ensuring quality and consistency.

Explicitly address mistakes as learning opportunities, not failures. In the first 90 days, mistakes will happen as new hires learn to exercise judgment. How you respond determines whether they become more confident or more cautious.

When mistakes happen, focus on the learning: "You made a judgment call to proceed without consulting me, and it turned out we should have discussed it first. Let's talk about what factors should trigger consultation in situations like this. What will you look for next time?"

This is very different from: "You should have asked me before doing that." The first builds better judgment; the second trains people to avoid decisions.

Celebrate good judgment even when it leads to imperfect outcomes: "You decided to call the client proactively when you noticed the issue. That was the right call even though it turned out not to be as significant as we thought. I want you to keep making those judgment calls."

By day 90, new hires should understand your delegation philosophy, have demonstrated capacity to make good decisions independently, be operating with graduated authority appropriate to their competence, have access to resources and frameworks that enable independent work, and know when and how to escalate appropriately.

If a new hire reaches 90 days and is still checking with you before every decision, something went wrong in onboarding. Either you over-supervised and trained learned helplessness, or you hired someone who isn't delegation-ready despite what the interview suggested.

Building a Team of Problem-Solvers, Not Task-Executors

The distinction between problem-solvers and task-executors is fundamental to delegation success. Task-executors wait to be told what to do and how to do it. Problem-solvers identify what needs to be done and figure out how to do it.

Most law firms accidentally create teams of task-executors by rewarding compliance and punishing initiative. The attorneys who escape bottleneck syndrome build teams of problem-solvers by deliberately cultivating different behaviors.

Problem-solvers think about outcomes, not just tasks. When you assign work, frame it in terms of the result you need, not the steps to take.

Instead of: "Please prepare a discovery request for medical records following our standard template, send it to opposing counsel, and let me know when you receive their response."

Try: "We need the plaintiff's medical records to evaluate this case. Can you get those obtained?" This frames the outcome and trusts them to figure out the process.

A task-executor will follow your template mechanically. A problem-solver will consider whether the standard template is appropriate for this case, identify which specific records are most important, anticipate potential delays and plan for follow-up, and keep you informed of progress toward the outcome you actually need.

Problem-solvers take ownership of solutions, not just responsibilities. When they encounter obstacles, they find ways around them rather than simply reporting the problem.

A task-executor says: "I can't file the motion because the court's e-filing system is down."

A problem-solver says: "The e-filing system is down. I've checked and it should be back up by 3pm. If it's not, I can physically file at the courthouse before 4pm close to meet our deadline. I'll keep you posted."

The difference is ownership. The problem-solver takes responsibility for ensuring the outcome happens despite obstacles.

Cultivate this mindset by how you respond to problems. When team members bring you problems, ask "What do you think we should do?" before providing direction.

If they say "I don't know," respond with "I know you don't know for certain, but what are some options? What would you try if I weren't available?"

This forces them to think through solutions rather than simply escalating decisions. Over time, they'll start coming to you with "Here's a problem, here's what I think we should do, and here's where I need your input" instead of "Here's a problem, what should I do?"

Give them real problems to solve, not just tasks to complete. As they demonstrate competence, delegate outcomes and let them figure out the approach.

Instead of: "Please review these medical records and summarize the treatment history."

Try: "We need to understand whether the plaintiff's injuries were pre-existing or caused by this accident. What's your assessment based on the medical records?"

The first is a task. The second is a problem that requires analysis, judgment, and critical thinking. Problem-solvers thrive on the second type of assignment.

Celebrate resourcefulness and initiative even when the outcome isn't perfect. You want to reinforce the behavior of independent problem-solving, not just successful results.

When someone handles an unexpected situation independently and it works out well, acknowledge specifically what they did: "I love that you recognized the issue and handled it without needing my involvement. That's exactly what I need from this team."

When someone takes initiative and it doesn't work out perfectly, focus on the good judgment process: "You made a reasonable decision based on available information. The outcome wasn't what we hoped, but your thinking was sound. Keep making those kinds of calls."

This builds confidence in exercising judgment rather than training people to play it safe by always escalating.

Create systems that support problem-solving rather than requiring constant oversight. If your systems require your approval at every step, you're building task-executors. If your systems provide frameworks for independent decision-making, you're building problem-solvers.

Instead of: "Get my approval before responding to any client communication."

Try: "Here's our framework for client communication. Respond independently to questions in categories A and B. Consult me on questions in categories C and D. Escalate immediately on anything in category E."

This gives them clear guidance while enabling independent action within appropriate boundaries.

Hire for problem-solving orientation from the start. In interviews, ask about times they solved problems independently. Listen for candidates who light up when describing challenges they overcame versus candidates who seem most comfortable when given detailed instructions.

The difference between problem-solvers and task-executors often comes down to mindset. Task-executors see their job as doing what they're told. Problem-solvers see their job as achieving outcomes, with tasks as merely the means to that end.

You can develop problem-solving skills in people who have the right mindset. You can't create the mindset in people who fundamentally prefer to be told what to do.

Special Considerations for Hiring Associates vs. Support Staff

The considerations for hiring associates are somewhat different from hiring support staff, though both require focus on delegation readiness.

Associates carry different leverage potential and different risks. A strong associate can handle complete cases with supervision, provide legal analysis and strategy input, represent clients in court, and essentially function as a junior version of you. This creates enormous leverage when done well.

But associates also create higher risk. They can give legal advice, make court appearances, and take actions that create malpractice exposure. They need stronger judgment and more legal sophistication than support staff.

When hiring associates for a delegation-heavy practice, prioritize judgment and initiative over legal experience. A third-year associate with mediocre judgment is less valuable than a first-year associate with exceptional judgment and strong initiative.

Law school teaches legal analysis but rarely teaches practical judgment about case strategy, client management, or business decisions. You can teach an associate your practice area. You can't easily teach them to exercise good judgment under pressure.

Look for associates who clerked or worked during law school and took on real responsibility, not just research tasks. Ask about situations where they had to make decisions without senior attorney guidance. Explore how they handle ambiguity and uncertainty.

In a criminal defense practice, you need associates who can think strategically about case theory, make sound decisions about which issues to pursue, exercise judgment about client counseling approaches, and handle unexpected courtroom situations independently. Technical knowledge of criminal procedure can be taught; strategic judgment cannot.

In a personal injury practice on contingency, you need associates who can assess case value accurately, make sound settlement negotiation decisions, manage client expectations effectively, and identify issues that affect case outcomes. Understanding personal injury law can be learned; the instinct for case value and negotiation strategy is harder to teach.

In an estate planning practice billing hourly, you need associates who can understand client goals beyond just technical planning, make appropriate recommendations for plan structure, exercise judgment about complex family dynamics, and provide practical advice not just legal analysis. Estate planning technical knowledge is learnable; sophisticated client counseling requires maturity and judgment.

Support staff can often provide better ROI than associates if hired and developed properly. A highly skilled paralegal with ten years of experience might cost $65,000 but handle work that would otherwise require a $100,000 associate. They can't give legal advice or make court appearances, but they can manage cases, draft documents, communicate with clients on factual matters, and coordinate complex workflows.

The key is hiring support staff who can grow into sophisticated roles rather than remaining task-focused. Look for paralegals with a track record of increasing responsibility, evidence of independent case management, experience making decisions within appropriate scope, and strong client communication skills.

Career trajectory matters differently for associates versus support staff. Associates typically expect to develop toward partnership or senior attorney roles. Support staff may have different career goals—becoming senior paralegals, practice managers, or firm administrators.

Be clear about career paths when hiring. If you're looking for an associate to eventually handle cases independently and possibly become a partner, hire someone with those ambitions. If you need someone to be an excellent career paralegal, hire someone who sees that as their goal.

Mismatched expectations create turnover. An ambitious associate who wants to be in court won't stay long if you keep them doing research and drafting. A paralegal who loves case management won't thrive if you hire them expecting they'll eventually want to be a practice administrator.

Compensation structures differ and affect delegation dynamics. Associates often have higher base salaries but limited bonus potential unless they're on a partner track. Support staff may have lower base salaries but more potential for performance bonuses.

This affects how you structure delegation. Associates expect substantive legal work and professional development. Support staff expect fair compensation, clear responsibilities, and opportunities to excel within their role.

Neither is better or worse—they're different leverage points with different economics. The most effective delegation often uses both: associates for work requiring legal judgment and representation, support staff for sophisticated case management and client service.

Training needs differ significantly. Associates need legal reasoning development, professional responsibility guidance, and client counseling skills. Support staff need procedural expertise, decision-making frameworks within their authority, and clear boundaries around unauthorized practice.

Both need training in your delegation philosophy and decision-making frameworks, but the content is different. Associates learn how to make legal judgments independently within appropriate limits. Support staff learn how to manage cases and clients without crossing into legal advice.

When the Right Person Isn't Available: Build vs. Hire

Sometimes you can't find delegation-ready people in the market. You have three options: wait until you find them (which might be never), hire less-qualified people and build the skills (which requires investment), or continue being the bottleneck (which isn't really an option).

The build approach can work if you have the right raw material. Someone with strong initiative, good judgment, and high accountability can learn your practice area and develop sophistication. Someone without those foundational traits won't become delegation-ready no matter how much training you provide.

If you're going to build rather than hire ready-made talent, be realistic about the investment required. It might take six months to a year to develop a task-executor into a problem-solver. It might take two years to develop a new associate into someone who can handle cases independently.

This investment makes sense if you're committed to retaining the person long-term and if they have the foundational traits that enable development. It doesn't make sense if you're hoping to quickly fix your bottleneck problem or if the person lacks the basic traits needed for delegation success.

Consider adjacent industries as talent sources. Many skills that make someone delegation-ready are transferable from other fields. Someone who excelled at project management in another industry might become an excellent paralegal. Someone who handled complex client relationships in financial services might thrive as a legal assistant with client-facing responsibilities.

The advantage of adjacent industry hires is they often bring fresh perspectives and haven't been trained into the "that's not how law firms work" mindset. They may be more open to systems, processes, and ways of working that traditional legal professionals resist.

The challenge is they need training in your practice area and legal procedures. But if they have initiative, judgment, and accountability, that training is a worthwhile investment.

Law school isn't the only path to delegation-ready legal professionals. Many excellent paralegals don't have paralegal certificates. Many outstanding case managers don't have legal backgrounds. Focus on traits and abilities, not credentials.

Some of the best delegation success stories involve hiring smart, capable people from other fields and training them in legal work. They bring strong work habits, mature judgment, and problem-solving skills. The legal knowledge can be taught.

Create a development program if you're building rather than hiring ready talent. Don't just hope people will develop delegation readiness organically. Create structured development with clear milestones, regular feedback, graduated authority increases, and explicit training in judgment and decision-making.

Document the progression you expect: months 1-3 focus on procedures and technical knowledge, months 4-6 develop independent task completion, months 7-9 build decision-making within framework, months 10-12 demonstrate full delegation readiness.

Provide regular feedback specifically on delegation readiness: "You're mastering the technical work. Now I want to see more initiative in identifying what needs to be done before I ask. Here are situations where you could have taken that initiative this week..."

Be willing to make changes if development isn't happening. Some people simply aren't delegation-ready and won't become so despite your best efforts. If you've provided clear expectations, adequate training, and regular feedback, and someone is still operating as a task-executor after six months, they're probably not going to change.

Making a change is better than continuing to invest in someone who won't develop the traits you need. The longer you wait, the more you entrench the bottleneck pattern and the more you delay finding someone who can actually help free you from it.

Creating Career Pathways That Retain Delegation-Ready People

Once you find and develop delegation-ready people, you need to keep them. High performers with initiative and judgment have options. They won't stay long in environments that don't provide growth, recognition, and appropriate compensation.

Create clear advancement paths for different roles. Paralegals should see a path from junior to senior to lead paralegal or case manager. Associates should see a path from junior to senior to partner or senior counsel. Administrative staff should see a path from assistant to coordinator to practice manager.

These paths should include increasing responsibility, authority, and compensation. The best way to retain delegation-ready people is to keep giving them more to be responsible for and compensating them accordingly.

Recognition matters as much as compensation for high performers. People with initiative and judgment are often driven by impact and achievement, not just money. Recognize their contributions publicly, involve them in decisions that affect their work, seek their input on practice improvements, and give them credit for their achievements.

When a paralegal's initiative saves a case, acknowledge it. When an associate's judgment prevents a problem, celebrate it. When anyone takes ownership and delivers results, make sure they know you noticed and appreciated it.

Avoid the trap of punishing high performers with more work without more reward. It's tempting to keep delegating to your best people because you know it will get done well. But if they see more work without corresponding increases in compensation, authority, or title, they'll eventually leave.

The person who takes initiative gets rewarded with... more work? That's not a reward system that retains top talent.

Instead, reward initiative with increased authority, decision-making scope, compensation, and title. Show that taking ownership leads to career advancement, not just more responsibility without corresponding benefits.

Provide growth opportunities that keep them engaged. Delegation-ready people get bored with routine work. They need challenges, learning opportunities, and chances to expand their capabilities.

For associates, this might mean handling increasingly complex cases, taking on practice area specialization, developing new firm capabilities, or building toward partnership. For paralegals, this might mean managing complex cases independently, training junior staff, building systems and processes, or transitioning toward practice management roles.

Be transparent about where people stand and what's possible. Don't leave your best people guessing about their future with your firm. Have explicit conversations about career paths, what they need to do to advance, what opportunities exist, and what the timeline might be.

High performers appreciate clarity. They'd rather know that partnership isn't possible than wonder for years whether it might be. They'd rather know exactly what's required to advance than guess at what you're looking for.

Create ownership opportunities when possible. For attorneys, this might mean partnership or equity. For staff, this might mean profit-sharing, significant bonuses tied to firm performance, or phantom equity that provides financial benefits of ownership without actual ownership.

People who think like owners—taking initiative, exercising judgment, feeling accountable for outcomes—should be rewarded like owners when your ethical rules and business structure permit it.

The Ongoing Hiring Strategy

Finding the right people isn't a one-time event. It's an ongoing process as your practice grows and evolves.

Always be recruiting, even when you're not actively hiring. When you meet someone impressive in your network, at a conference, or even as opposing counsel's paralegal, make a note. Build relationships with potential future hires long before you need them.

The best hires often come from long-standing relationships, not job postings. You already know their work quality, their judgment, and their traits. They already know your practice and your standards.

Develop a reputation as a great place to work for delegation-ready people. Word spreads in legal communities. If your team members thrive on responsibility, exercise judgment, and grow their careers with you, talented people will want to join you.

Conversely, if you churn through people because you hire for tasks but treat them like task-executors, good candidates will avoid you.

Your retention and development of existing team members is your best recruiting tool for future team members.

Be willing to create positions for exceptional people. If you meet someone who has the traits you need but doesn't fit a current opening, consider creating a role for them. Exceptional delegation-ready people are rare enough that you shouldn't pass on them just because you didn't plan to hire right now.

You can always find work for someone with initiative, judgment, and accountability. You can't always find people with those traits when you happen to need them.

Continuously evaluate whether your team is delegation-ready. As your practice evolves and your delegation needs change, assess whether your current team can grow with you or whether you need different capabilities.

Someone who was delegation-ready for your practice three years ago might not be ready for where your practice is going. That's not a failure on their part—it's a natural evolution. Help them grow if possible, but recognize when a role has outgrown someone's current capabilities.

Finding the Right People: The Foundation of Delegation Success

Lisa, the estate planning attorney from the beginning of this chapter, eventually got it right. After her first hire failed to thrive in a delegation-heavy environment, she completely changed her hiring approach.

She rewrote her job posting to emphasize judgment and initiative over experience. She screened resumes for evidence of progressive responsibility, not just tenure. She conducted interviews focused entirely on behavioral questions about decision-making, problem-solving, and accountability.

She hired someone with less estate planning experience but demonstrated initiative in every previous role. Someone who lit up when describing problems she'd solved independently. Someone whose references emphasized her judgment and reliability, not just her technical skills.

The difference was dramatic. Within 60 days, her new paralegal was handling tasks that took Lisa six months to delegate to her first hire. Within 90 days, she was making judgment calls that her first hire never became comfortable making. Within six months, she was managing entire cases with minimal supervision.

Lisa had learned that finding the right people isn't about finding the most qualified people—it's about finding people with the traits that make delegation successful. Technical skills can be taught. Initiative, judgment, and accountability can't.

The foundation of delegation success is building a team of people who don't just execute tasks but take ownership of outcomes. People who don't just follow directions but exercise judgment. People who don't just complete assignments but solve problems.

Find those people, develop them properly, and retain them by providing growth opportunities. That's how you build a team that allows you to delegate effectively and escape the bottleneck.

Action Items for This Chapter:

1. Revise Your Next Job Description

For your next hire (or a current open position), rewrite the job description to emphasize delegation-readiness traits: initiative, judgment, problem-solving, and accountability over just technical skills.

Position: _____

New description emphasizes: _____

Updated posting: Yes / No

2. Create Your Behavioral Interview Questions

Develop 5-7 behavioral interview questions based on the examples in this chapter. Focus on initiative, decision-making, problem-solving, and learning from mistakes.

Questions created: Yes / No

Will use in next interview: _____

Sample question 1: _____

Sample question 2: _____

3. Assess One Current Team Member's Delegation Readiness

Select one current team member and honestly assess their readiness for more delegation using this chapter's framework. Create a development plan to build any missing capabilities.

Team member: _____

Delegation-ready now? Yes / No / Partially

Development needed: _____

Development plan created: Yes / No

Before Moving to Chapter 6:

You now understand what makes someone delegation-ready and how to find, hire, and onboard people who will thrive with delegated responsibility. You know the traits to look for, the questions to ask, and how to develop people who have the right foundation.

But hiring the right people is only valuable if you also build the right environment for them to succeed. Chapter 6 will show you how to handle the client relationship challenges that arise when you delegate client-facing work.

Your delegation-ready team can only deliver value if clients accept them, trust them, and work effectively with them. The next chapter ensures that happens.

One final action before moving on:

Schedule interviews for any open positions using your new delegation-focused approach. If you're not currently hiring, practice your behavioral interview questions with at least one person this week—either a current team member, a potential future hire, or a peer in a role-play scenario.

The best interview approach only helps if you actually use it. Practice turns knowledge into skill.

Practice interview scheduled for: _____ (date/time)

With: _____

Now you're ready to move forward with a clear understanding of how to build a delegation-ready team. The next chapter ensures your clients embrace that team as enthusiastically as you do.

CHAPTER 6:

The Client Relationship Challenge

The email arrived at 9:23 AM on a Tuesday. Karen, a successful estate planning attorney, read it with a sinking feeling.

"Dear Karen, I've been working with your paralegal Jessica on updating my estate plan, and while she seems nice, I really need to speak with you directly about some decisions. I hired you, not your assistant. When can we schedule a call? Best, Margaret."

Margaret was a good client. Sophisticated, reasonable, willing to pay appropriate fees. But she'd just articulated the fundamental challenge of delegating client-facing work: clients hire you, not your team. They want your expertise, your judgment, your personal attention. Delegation feels to them like bait and switch.

Karen had carefully delegated much of Margaret's estate plan update to Jessica. Jessica was highly competent, detail-oriented, and excellent with clients. The work was well within her capabilities.

But Margaret wanted Karen, and no amount of competent paralegal work would satisfy that expectation.

This wasn't unique to Margaret. Over the past month, three other clients had made similar requests. "I appreciate your team, but I really need to talk to you." "Can we schedule time with you directly?" "I'm sure your associate is capable, but I'd prefer you handle this."

Karen faced a dilemma that every attorney confronts when delegating client work. She needed to leverage her team to grow the practice and serve more clients effectively. But clients expected personal attorney attention and felt disappointed when they got team member attention instead.

If she gave in to every client request for personal attention, delegation failed and she remained the bottleneck. If she insisted on team member handling without client buy-in, client satisfaction suffered and retention decreased. She needed a middle path that preserved client relationships while enabling effective delegation.

This chapter shows you how to navigate the client relationship challenges inherent in delegation. You'll learn how to set expectations that make delegation acceptable to clients, introduce team members in ways that build client confidence, maintain the personal touch while delegating substantial work, handle the "I want to speak to the attorney" objection, and ensure client-facing delegation enhances rather than damages relationships.

Why Clients Resist Delegation

Understanding why clients resist delegation is the first step to overcoming that resistance. Client objections to delegation aren't irrational; they're based on legitimate concerns that deserve acknowledgment and thoughtful response.

The first reason clients resist delegation is the personal relationship they've built with you. They trust you because they know you, have worked with you, and feel confident in your judgment. Your paralegal or associate might be equally competent, but the client doesn't know that yet. The relationship is with you, not with your practice. Delegation asks them to extend trust to someone they don't know based only on your assurance that it's appropriate.

Margaret's resistance to working with Jessica stemmed partly from this relationship factor. Margaret had worked with Karen for five years. They'd developed rapport. Margaret knew Karen's communication style, understood how she thought about estate planning issues, and trusted her judgment completely. Jessica might be equally skilled, but Margaret would need time to develop similar trust.

The second reason is perceived value. Clients pay attorney rates for attorney expertise. When a paralegal handles their work, even if that's appropriate and efficient, clients sometimes feel they're not getting what they paid for. The billing rate logic doesn't matter—emotionally, they want the person they're paying premium rates for to do the work, not delegate it to someone with lower credentials.

This perception is especially strong in legal services because credentials matter so much. A J.D. and bar admission signal expertise in ways a paralegal certificate doesn't, even when the paralegal's skills for a specific task might be superior. Clients conflate credentials with competence and want the most credentialed person handling their matters.

The third reason is control and importance. Clients want to feel their matter is important enough to merit the attorney's personal attention. When work is delegated, some clients interpret it as "my matter isn't important enough for the attorney to handle personally." This isn't about actual quality of service; it's about feeling valued and prioritized.

The fourth reason is concern about quality and accountability. Clients worry that delegated work might not meet the same standards as attorney work. They wonder if the team member has adequate knowledge, whether mistakes might be made, and whether there's proper oversight. These are legitimate concerns about quality control in the delegation process.

The fifth reason is communication preferences. Some clients simply communicate better with attorneys than with other team members. They speak the same professional language. They understand attorney communication style. They worry that working with support staff will involve translation inefficiencies or communication breakdowns.

The sixth reason is past bad experiences. Many clients have had experiences with delegation gone wrong—work delegated to incompetent team members, matters handled by people without adequate knowledge, poor communication from non-attorney staff, or errors made because work was delegated inappropriately. These experiences create understandable skepticism about delegation.

Karen realized that Margaret's resistance likely stemmed from several of these factors. Margaret valued her relationship with Karen specifically. She equated Karen's personal involvement with quality and importance. And she'd mentioned once that a prior attorney had delegated work to an incompetent paralegal who made costly errors.

Understanding these root causes shaped Karen's response. She couldn't just insist that Jessica was competent and expect Margaret to accept it. She needed to address the underlying concerns: relationship building with Jessica, demonstrating value despite delegation, ensuring Margaret felt important, providing quality assurance, facilitating good communication, and acknowledging past bad experiences while distinguishing this situation.

The key insight is that client resistance to delegation is rarely about stubborn unreasonableness. It's about legitimate concerns that deserve respectful attention. When you understand what's driving resistance, you can respond in ways that address root concerns rather than just pushing back against surface objections.

Setting Client Expectations From the Start

The easiest client relationship challenges to solve are the ones you prevent. Setting appropriate expectations from the beginning of the client relationship makes delegation feel normal rather than unexpected.

The intake conversation is your first opportunity to establish delegation expectations. Before the client signs on, explain how your practice works. Describe your team structure. Explain what work you handle personally and what work team members handle. Make delegation part of the value proposition, not a secret to be revealed later.

Karen revised her intake approach based on lessons learned. She now explained: "I lead an experienced team that includes two senior paralegals and an associate attorney. For your estate planning work, I'll personally handle all strategic decisions about your plan structure, meet with you for key planning conversations, and review all final documents. My senior paralegal Jessica will handle document preparation, routine updates, and day-to-day communication. This team approach allows us to be more responsive and thorough than if I tried to do everything myself."

This framing accomplished several things. It described the team as an asset, not a liability. It specified exactly what work Karen would handle personally, giving the client certainty about her involvement. It explained the benefits of the team approach in terms the client cared about—responsiveness and thoroughness. And it set expectations before the client formed assumptions about how the engagement would work.

The engagement letter should reinforce these expectations in writing. Include language about team-based service delivery. Specify which team members may work on the matter and their roles. Explain billing rates for different team members and why the team approach creates value.

Karen's engagement letters now included: "Your matter will be handled by our estate planning team, led by Attorney Karen Mitchell and including Senior Paralegal Jessica Thompson. Karen will personally handle all strategic planning, complex legal issues, and final document review. Jessica will prepare documents, coordinate execution, and serve as your primary point of contact for routine questions and updates. This collaborative approach ensures you receive expert attention at each stage while maintaining efficiency and responsiveness."

The language in engagement letters matters because it creates the framework for the entire relationship. If the letter says "Attorney Karen Mitchell will handle your matter" with no mention of a team, clients reasonably expect that Karen will personally do all the work. If it explains a team approach upfront, delegation aligns with stated expectations.

Introduce team members early and personally. Don't just mention that others will be involved; make personal introductions that build confidence. In the first client meeting, introduce the paralegal or associate who will work on the matter. Explain their background, expertise, and role. Create a personal connection, not just an announcement that others exist.

Karen started bringing Jessica into initial client meetings for ten minutes. She'd introduce Jessica, have Jessica explain her background and experience, and then Jessica would ask a few questions about the client's goals. This personal introduction made Jessica real to the client rather than just a name on an email.

Set specific communication expectations. Explain who the client should contact for different types of issues. Make it clear that the team member is the appropriate first contact for routine matters, with you available for complex issues or upon request. This guidance helps clients know when to expect your personal involvement and when team member involvement is normal.

Karen told clients: "For routine questions about document preparation, timeline updates, or scheduling, reach out to Jessica directly. She's fully equipped to help you and will respond more quickly than I can. For complex planning questions, strategy discussions, or if you ever just want to connect with me directly, contact me anytime. Jessica and I communicate constantly, so we're always aligned on your matter."

Explain the quality control process. Clients worry about quality when work is delegated. Address that concern proactively by explaining how you ensure quality. Describe your review process. Explain how team member work is supervised. Make quality assurance visible.

Karen explained: "All documents Jessica prepares go through my review before you see them. I personally check every detail to ensure accuracy and alignment with your goals. Jessica's work is excellent, and my review adds an additional quality check. You get the benefit of Jessica's meticulous preparation and my oversight."

Build in personal touchpoints throughout the engagement. Even when substantial work is delegated, create moments of personal attorney contact. These touchpoints reassure clients that you're engaged and aware, even if you're not doing all the work yourself.

Karen scheduled three personal touchpoints for estate planning clients: initial strategy session, mid-point check-in after documents are drafted, and final review before execution. These touchpoints were Karen's personal involvement, while Jessica handled the work in between. Clients felt appropriately attended to without requiring Karen's involvement in every detail.

Use language that emphasizes "we" rather than delegation. Instead of "I'm delegating this to Jessica," say "We'll be working on this together, with Jessica handling preparation and me providing oversight and strategic direction." The "we" framing emphasizes collaboration rather than handoff.

The goal of expectation setting is to make the team approach feel like a feature, not a bug. Clients should understand from the beginning that they're getting a team's collective expertise, not just one attorney's time. They should know what work you'll handle personally and what work team members will handle. And they should feel confident that the team approach benefits them through better responsiveness, more attention to detail, and appropriate deployment of expensive attorney time on the work that truly requires it.

When expectations are set well from the start, delegation doesn't feel like a disappointment. It feels like exactly what the client signed up for.

Introducing Team Members to Build Confidence

Even when expectations are set appropriately, clients need to develop confidence in team members. The way you introduce and position team members determines whether clients embrace them or resist working with them.

The introduction should highlight expertise, not apologize for non-attorney status. Don't say "My paralegal will help with this." Say "Jessica, our senior estate planning paralegal with twelve years of experience, will prepare your documents." Lead with competence, credentials, and experience that build confidence.

Karen learned to introduce Jessica with specific expertise signals: "Jessica is our senior paralegal and she's been with the practice for eight years. She's prepared over a thousand estate planning documents and has deep knowledge of both simple and complex planning strategies. Frankly, she knows the technical details of document preparation better than I do. She's also fantastic with clients—patient, detail-oriented, and great at explaining complex issues in clear terms."

This introduction accomplished several things. It established Jessica's extensive experience. It specified her expertise area. It positioned her knowledge as potentially superior to Karen's in certain respects, which is credible and builds confidence. And it highlighted client service skills that matter to clients.

Introduce team members in person when possible, not just via email. Personal introduction creates connection that email cannot. The client sees the team member, hears their voice, observes their professionalism, and begins forming a relationship. Email introductions are functional but don't build the same rapport.

When in-person isn't possible, use video introduction. A brief video call where you introduce the team member, they explain their role and background, and the client can ask questions creates much stronger connection than email alone.

Have team members explain their own experience and approach, not just you vouching for them. When Jessica speaks about her background, experience, and how she works with clients, it's more powerful than Karen describing the same things. Let team members showcase their own competence.

In introduction meetings, Karen would ask Jessica questions that allowed her to demonstrate expertise: "Jessica, could you explain to Margaret how we'll handle the trust funding process?" Jessica's knowledgeable response built confidence more effectively than Karen's assurance that Jessica was competent.

Address the "what work will each of us do" question explicitly. Clients want to understand the division of labor. Walk them through a typical matter and explain who does what at each stage. This transparency removes uncertainty about roles.

Karen would explain: "Here's how we'll work together on your estate plan. First, you and I will meet to discuss your goals, family situation, and planning priorities—that's the strategic foundation. Then Jessica will prepare initial draft documents based on our discussion. I'll review those drafts to ensure they perfectly match your goals. You'll review them with Jessica, who will explain each provision and answer your questions. Any complex legal questions that come up, Jessica will bring me in. We'll make any needed revisions together. Then I'll do a final review before you sign. At the signing, Jessica will walk you through execution, and I'll be available if needed."

This detailed walkthrough showed exactly when the client would interact with each team member and what each person's role was at each stage. It removed mystery and created appropriate expectations.

Use collaborative language that emphasizes the team working together. Instead of positioning team members as substitutes for you, position them as specialists working alongside you. "Jessica and I" rather than "Jessica instead of me."

Share stories of past client successes involving the team member. "Jessica recently worked with a client whose estate plan was similar to yours in complexity. The client specifically mentioned how helpful Jessica's explanations were and how much they appreciated her attention to detail." Third-party validation builds confidence.

Create opportunities for the client to experience the team member's competence directly. After introduction, delegate a small, low-stakes task to the team member where the client will directly experience their capability. Success on that small task builds confidence for larger delegation.

Karen would have Jessica handle a simple initial task after introduction—perhaps gathering information about assets or explaining how certain documents work. Margaret's positive experience with Jessica on this small task built trust for more significant involvement later.

Demonstrate your confidence in team members through your own behavior. If you constantly second-guess their work in front of clients, you undermine their credibility. If you show confidence in their abilities and judgment, clients mirror that confidence.

Karen was careful never to undercut Jessica in client interactions. If a client asked a question Jessica could answer, Karen would let her answer or defer to her: "Jessica, you've handled this exact situation before. Can you explain how we typically approach it?" This deference signaled Karen's trust in Jessica's knowledge.

Acknowledge that developing comfort with team members takes time. Some clients will immediately embrace working with your team. Others need time to develop trust. Acknowledge that reality and give permission for the relationship to develop gradually.

Karen would sometimes say: "I know you hired me specifically and want to work with me. As you get to know Jessica, I think you'll find she's excellent to work with. But I'm always available if you need me. Over time, many clients find they're very comfortable working directly with Jessica for most matters, but there's no pressure. We'll work together in whatever way feels right to you."

This acknowledgment of the client's preference, combined with patience about relationship development and assurance of your continued availability, often helps clients relax and give team members a genuine chance.

Finally, create feedback loops where clients can express any concerns about working with team members. "How has your experience working with Jessica been so far?" asked genuinely and with openness to honest feedback, helps surface and address issues before they become serious problems.

The goal is clients who see your team members as trusted advisors in their own right, not just as intermediaries to you. That level of confidence doesn't come from a single introduction. It comes from thoughtful positioning, demonstrated competence, successful experiences, and time to develop trust.

Training Teams to Maintain Your Client Service Standards

Delegating to capable people isn't enough. They need to represent your practice in a way that maintains your standards and reflects your approach to client service.

Start by defining what "your standard" actually means. Many attorneys have an intuitive sense of good client service but have never articulated what that looks like. Your team can't replicate what you haven't defined.

Document your client service standards:

- Response time expectations (same-day for urgent, 24 hours for routine)
- Tone and manner of communication (professional but warm, empathetic but not overly familiar)
- Information clients should always receive (proactive updates on key developments, explanation of next steps)
- How to handle different emotional states (anxious clients need reassurance, frustrated clients need action plans, grieving clients need patience)

A criminal defense practice might define standards as: "Clients are often scared and sometimes feel judged. We never judge. We explain clearly without legal jargon. We respond to calls within 4 hours. We proactively update clients before court dates."

A personal injury practice might establish: "Clients are often in pain and financially stressed. We acknowledge their hardship. We explain the timeline early so they know what to expect. We return calls same-day. We never promise outcomes we can't guarantee."

An estate planning practice might set: "Clients are trusting us with deeply personal family and financial information. We maintain strict confidentiality. We explain complex concepts in plain English. We're patient with questions. We respect family dynamics without taking sides."

Create frameworks, not rigid scripts. You don't want team members to sound robotic, but you do want consistency in how common situations are handled.

For common client questions, provide language frameworks. Not word-for-word scripts (which sound fake), but approaches and key phrases to include.

For "When will my case settle?" in a personal injury practice:

- Framework: Acknowledge the question, explain the variables, give a realistic range if possible, commit to updates
- Key phrases: "That's the question every client asks, and I understand why..." "Several factors affect timing..." "Based on similar cases..." "I'll keep you updated as we learn more..."

For "What are my chances?" in a criminal defense practice:

- Framework: Explain why we can't guarantee outcomes, discuss strengths and challenges, focus on process and preparation
- Key phrases: "I can't make promises about outcomes..." "Here's what we know in your favor..." "Here are the challenges we'll address..." "I can promise we'll prepare thoroughly and fight hard..."

For "Is this normal?" in an estate planning practice:

- Framework: Validate their concern, explain what's typical, address any legitimate issues, reassure where appropriate
- Key phrases: "That's a common question..." "In estate planning, it's typical to..." "Let me explain why we do it this way..." "I'll make sure the attorney reviews this with you..."

Role-play difficult scenarios in team training. Talking about how to handle upset clients is different from actually doing it. Practice builds confidence and competence.

Create realistic scenarios based on actual situations:

- The client who calls angry that their case isn't moving faster
- The client who's scared after reading something online about their situation
- The client who wants guarantees you can't provide
- The client who's difficult to reach but complains about not being updated

Have team members practice responses. Provide feedback on what worked and what didn't. This builds muscle memory for handling tough conversations.

The Escalation Decision Tree

Teach the escalation decision tree explicitly. Team members need crystal-clear criteria for when to handle something themselves versus when to involve you.

Create a simple framework:

Green light (handle independently):

- Routine questions with established answers
- Scheduling and administrative matters
- Status updates on cases proceeding normally
- Client concerns that can be addressed with information

Yellow light (consult before responding):

- Questions about case strategy or legal advice
- Client concerns about outcomes or timelines
- New developments that might affect the case
- Situations where the client seems particularly upset or the issue is sensitive

Red light (immediate escalation):

- Ethical issues or conflicts

- Potential malpractice situations
- Client threatening to fire you or file a complaint
- Emergency situations affecting the client or case
- Anything involving media or public attention

Monitor and provide feedback on actual client interactions. Training doesn't end after onboarding. Regular feedback on real interactions helps team members improve.

Listen to recorded calls (with appropriate consent). Review email exchanges. Ask clients about their experience with team members. Provide specific, actionable feedback:

"When that client was upset about the delay, you did a great job acknowledging their frustration. Next time, also give them a specific timeline for next steps so they know what to expect."

Celebrate excellent client service. When a team member handles a difficult situation well, acknowledge it publicly. This reinforces your standards and shows others what excellent looks like.

Maintaining Personal Touch While Delegating

The biggest fear in delegating client-facing work is losing the personal connection that drives client relationships. But delegation and personal touch aren't mutually exclusive. You can delegate substantial work while maintaining the relationship equity that matters to clients.

The key is strategic personal involvement—identifying the moments that matter most to clients and preserving your personal involvement in those moments while delegating surrounding work.

Certain interactions carry disproportionate relationship weight. Initial consultations, strategy sessions, difficult conversations, major decisions, and problem resolution are high-impact client interactions. Your personal involvement in these moments preserves the relationship even when routine work is delegated.

Karen identified four high-impact moments in estate planning: initial goal-setting conversation, reviewing the first draft to confirm it matches expectations, addressing any family complexity or difficult decisions, and the final pre-signing review. She personally handled these four touchpoints even when Jessica handled all the work in between.

Clients who experienced Karen's personal involvement at these critical moments felt well-served even though Jessica handled 70% of the total work. The strategic touchpoints created perception of high personal engagement despite extensive delegation.

Routine communications can be delegated; personalized communications should come from you. Status updates, scheduling coordination, and information requests can come from team members. But acknowledgment of milestones, responses to client concerns, or celebration of successes should include your personal touch.

When Margaret's estate plan was completed, the routine "your documents are ready for signing" email came from Jessica. But Karen sent a separate personal note: "Margaret, I've reviewed your completed estate plan and it beautifully accomplishes your goals for your family. I'm confident you'll have peace of mind knowing your affairs are properly arranged. Looking forward to seeing you at the signing."

That personal note took Karen two minutes to write but created relationship value far exceeding the time invested. It showed personal attention and care that delegation alone might not convey.

Create personal contact even when delegating the work. After delegating a matter to an associate, call the client yourself to confirm the associate has everything they need and ask if there are any questions or concerns they want to discuss with you. This call takes five minutes but reinforces your engagement.

Use personal outreach when team members report concerns. If Jessica mentioned that Margaret seemed uncertain about a trust provision, Karen would personally call Margaret to discuss it. This converts a potential weakness of delegation into a relationship strength—the client gets team member attention for routine matters and attorney attention immediately when questions or concerns arise.

Share team member successes with clients in a way that reflects well on you. "Jessica caught an important detail in your asset list that we need to address" positions you as the leader of a sharp team, not as someone who's checked out. You get credit for building and leading a team that serves clients well.

Maintain visibility through check-ins even when delegating execution. "I know Jessica is handling the day-to-day work on your matter, but I wanted to check in personally to make sure everything is going smoothly and you're getting what you need." This check-in reassures the client while respecting the delegation to Jessica.

Personalize your involvement based on client preferences. Some clients are happy with efficient team-based service. Others want more personal attorney contact. Flexibility in adapting your involvement level to individual client preferences maintains satisfaction across different client types.

Karen learned that some clients thrived with heavy delegation to Jessica and minimal attorney contact. Others needed more of Karen's personal involvement to feel comfortable. She adjusted her approach based on individual client preferences rather than applying a rigid formula to everyone.

Use technology to scale personal touch. Personalized video messages, voice memos, or short personal emails don't require much time but create strong perception of personal attention. A 90-second video message from you explaining a complex issue feels highly personal even though it's more efficient than a phone call.

Create exclusive value in your personal interactions. When you do engage with clients personally, bring insights, expertise, or perspective that team members can't provide. Make it clear why your personal involvement adds value beyond what capable team members deliver.

When Karen met with Margaret for strategy sessions, she brought sophisticated planning insights, creative solutions to complex family situations, and nuanced judgment about trade-offs between different approaches. Margaret left those meetings appreciating why Karen's personal involvement mattered, even though Jessica could handle the technical execution.

Remember that relationship maintenance happens in small moments, not just big ones. A personal response to a client email, a quick call to check on them during a difficult time, or remembering and asking about something important in their life builds relationship equity that makes delegation more acceptable.

The goal isn't constant personal attention, which isn't scalable. The goal is strategic personal attention at moments that matter, combined with excellent team-based service for everything else. When clients feel personally cared for even while much of the work is delegated, you've achieved the right balance.

Handling "I Want to Speak to the Attorney"

Despite your best efforts at expectation-setting and team building, you'll still hear "I want to speak to the attorney." How you respond to this request determines whether it derails delegation or becomes an opportunity to strengthen both the client relationship and team dynamics.

The first principle is never dismissing or minimizing the request. "My paralegal can handle this" or "This doesn't require an attorney" might be factually accurate but feels dismissive to clients. They've expressed a preference. Honor it, even if you ultimately provide context that shapes how it's fulfilled.

When Margaret emailed requesting to speak with Karen directly, Karen didn't respond "Jessica is fully capable of helping you with this" even though that was true. Instead she responded "Absolutely, I'm happy to talk with you. I'll call you this afternoon. In the meantime, I want to make sure we're addressing your specific concerns. What questions or issues would you like to discuss?"

This response did several things. It immediately honored the request, showing respect for Margaret's preference. It created a specific plan rather than a vague promise. And it gathered information about what was driving the request, which helped Karen prepare and potentially address some concerns before the call.

Understanding what's driving the "I want the attorney" request is crucial. Sometimes it's about a specific complex issue that genuinely requires attorney involvement. Sometimes it's about relationship preferences—the client simply communicates better with you. Sometimes it's about control or importance. Each driver requires a different response.

On the call with Margaret, Karen discovered the issue was actually complex—Margaret had questions about tax implications that were beyond Jessica's scope. This was a legitimate need for attorney involvement. Karen addressed the tax questions, then explained: "These tax issues are exactly the kind of thing I should handle personally. Jessica knows to flag these for me, and I'm glad you raised them. For questions like this, I'm always your right contact. For document details, timeline, or execution logistics, Jessica is actually more knowledgeable than I am because she focuses on that daily."

This response validated Margaret's instinct to reach out to Karen while also reinforcing that Jessica was the right contact for other

197

issues. It educated about appropriate division of labor without making Margaret feel wrong for wanting attorney contact.

Sometimes the request is driven by lack of confidence in the team member. The client might have had a communication breakdown, received a confusing answer, or simply not connected well with the team member. In these cases, address the underlying issue rather than just providing your attention.

If Margaret had said "Jessica's answers just confused me more," Karen's response would be different: "I'm sorry Jessica's explanation wasn't clear. Let's make sure you get answers that make sense. I'll walk through this with you now. And let's also figure out how Jessica can communicate with you more effectively going forward. She's excellent at what she does, but everyone has different communication styles."

This addresses the immediate need while also working to improve the team member relationship rather than bypassing it.

The Warm Handoff Technique

Use "I want the attorney" requests as opportunities to strengthen team member credibility. After addressing the client's concern personally, you can often create opportunities for team members to demonstrate capability on related issues.

After discussing tax implications with Margaret, Karen might say: "Now that we've resolved the tax questions, Jessica will prepare revised documents reflecting our discussion. She'll walk you through exactly how the changes address the tax issues we discussed. If any new tax questions come up, bring me back in. But Jessica is excellent at explaining how the documents implement planning decisions."

This gives Jessica an opportunity to demonstrate her competence in explaining documents, potentially building Margaret's confidence for future delegation.

The warm handoff technique is particularly powerful for building trust:

Instead of: "My paralegal can help you with that" (which feels like a brush-off).

Try: "Let me connect you with Maria right now. She's our case manager and knows your file inside and out. She'll have the information you need and can help you immediately. I'll stay on the line to introduce you."

Then: "Maria, this is John Smith calling about his settlement timeline. I know you've been working on his case and can give him a complete update. John, Maria has all the details and can answer your questions. I'll let you two talk. John, if you need me for anything after talking with Maria, just let her know and I'll call you back."

This shows the client you're not abandoning them—you're connecting them with someone competent who can help them faster.

Sometimes clients need permission to work with team members. The "I want the attorney" request might really mean "I'm not sure if the paralegal is adequate for this." Giving explicit permission helps: "This is exactly the kind of thing Jessica handles regularly, and she's genuinely better at it than I am because she does it every day. You're in great hands with her. But I'm always here if you need me or prefer to work with me directly."

Create a path back to the team member after addressing the client's request. "I'm glad we had this conversation. Going forward, Jessica can handle updates on this issue—she and I will be aligned. But anytime something comes up that you want to discuss with me, just let me know."

This satisfies the immediate request while creating expectations that routine future contact on the issue can go through the team member.

Be honest about efficiency and responsiveness trade-offs when appropriate. Some clients are highly responsive to understanding the practical implications of their preferences: "I'm always happy to speak with you personally. I do want you to know that Jessica typically responds within an hour or two, while I might take a day to respond because of court schedule and other demands. For time-sensitive questions, Jessica will actually get you answers faster. But it's completely up to you—whatever works better for you is fine with me."

This gives clients information to make informed choices without pressuring them. Many clients, when they understand the responsiveness difference, become comfortable with team member contact.

Train your team on how to respond when clients request attorney involvement. Team members should never be defensive or take it personally. They should facilitate the connection: "Absolutely, I'll have Karen call you today. In the meantime, can you tell me what specific questions you have so I can give her context?"

Jessica learned to handle Margaret's attorney requests smoothly, providing Karen with background on the client's questions so Karen could prepare. This made attorney responses more effective and also sometimes revealed that Jessica could actually address the issue if she understood it better.

Track patterns in "I want the attorney" requests. If many clients ask for you specifically, that might indicate team members need additional training, your expectation-setting needs improvement, or your client base has legitimately higher needs for attorney involvement. If only certain clients make this request, you can adjust your approach with those specific clients.

Karen noticed that sophisticated business owner clients tended to request her involvement more frequently than individual clients with straightforward estates. This pattern led her to adjust her approach with business owners, providing more direct attorney involvement upfront because that's what the client segment valued.

Remember that some delegation isn't worth the relationship cost. If a particular client really wants your personal involvement and resists delegation despite your best efforts, it might be more valuable to provide that involvement than to insist on delegation. High-value clients or complex relationships might warrant less delegation than your standard approach.

Karen had one ultra-high-net-worth client who simply wouldn't work with anyone but her. Rather than fight it, she accepted it and billed accordingly. That one client's fees justified the personal attention even though it was inefficient by her normal delegation standards.

The goal isn't to eliminate "I want the attorney" requests. The goal is to respond to them in ways that address client needs, maintain relationships, strengthen team member credibility where possible, and educate clients about when attorney involvement is most valuable. Handle these requests skillfully and they become opportunities rather than obstacles.

Making Delegation Enhance Client Service

The ultimate goal is making delegation a client service enhancement rather than a necessary evil. When done well, team-based service delivers better outcomes than solo attorney service. Making that reality visible to clients transforms delegation from something they tolerate to something they value.

The first way delegation enhances service is through responsiveness. A well-trained paralegal or associate who responds within hours is more valuable to clients than an attorney who takes days to respond. Make this advantage explicit to clients.

Karen started framing it this way: "Jessica checks email constantly throughout the day and typically responds within an hour or two.

My court schedule and client meetings mean my responses often take longer. By working with Jessica on routine matters, you'll get faster answers and quicker turnaround. That's better service for you."

Framed as a service advantage rather than an accommodation to attorney workload, delegation becomes attractive. Clients prefer quick responses to credentialed responses when the quality is equivalent.

The second way delegation enhances service is through specialized expertise. Team members who focus on specific tasks often develop deeper knowledge in those areas than attorneys who split attention across many different tasks. Highlight this specialization.

"Jessica prepares trust documents every day. She knows every technical requirement, every potential issue, and every detail that matters. My practice is broader—estate planning, probate, business succession. In the specific area of trust document preparation, Jessica's focused expertise means fewer errors and more attention to detail than if I prepared everything myself."

This honest acknowledgment of specialized expertise builds team member credibility while also explaining why delegation serves clients better.

The third way delegation enhances service is through thoroughness. Team members with more bandwidth can spend more time on matters than overwhelmed attorneys can. That additional time often produces better work product.

"If I personally handled every aspect of your estate plan, I'd be rushing because I have twenty other clients competing for attention. With Jessica handling document preparation, she can give your documents the meticulous attention they deserve. She'll catch details I might miss when I'm juggling too much. That thoroughness protects you."

The fourth way delegation enhances service is through continuity. Team members who aren't in court, at trials, or juggling emergencies provide more consistent availability and follow-through. Emphasize this reliability.

"Jessica is always available to answer questions or address concerns. I'm sometimes in court all day or handling urgent matters. By working with Jessica for routine issues, you have a reliable contact who's always accessible. For complex issues or major decisions, you get me. You're getting the best of both—consistent daily support from Jessica and specialized attorney attention when it matters most."

The fifth way delegation enhances service is through multiple perspectives. When both an attorney and team member work on a matter, different perspectives catch different issues. Position this as quality enhancement.

"Jessica prepares the documents and I review them. This two-person approach means four eyes on everything, with different types of expertise. Jessica catches technical details and execution issues. I catch strategic and legal concerns. You benefit from both perspectives, which produces better results than either of us working alone."

The sixth way delegation enhances service is through appropriate cost management. Clients appreciate getting value for fees paid. Delegation allows attorney time to focus on high-value work while team members handle routine work at lower rates.

"By having Jessica handle document preparation at her rate and me focusing on strategy and complex legal issues at my rate, we're managing your costs effectively. You're paying for attorney expertise where it matters and paralegal support where that's sufficient. This approach keeps your total fees lower than if I personally handled everything."

This transparent discussion of cost efficiency positions delegation as client-focused rather than practice-focused.

Create feedback loops that demonstrate service quality from delegation. Ask clients specifically about their experience working with team members. When feedback is positive, it reinforces that delegation is working.

Karen would ask: "How has your experience working with Jessica been? Is she giving you the service and support you need?" When Margaret responded positively, as she usually did, it reinforced that delegation was serving her well.

When feedback identifies issues, address them immediately. If a client reports that a team member was slow to respond, unresponsive to concerns, or failed to meet commitments, fix it quickly. Your responsiveness to service quality concerns demonstrates that delegation doesn't mean reduced attention to client satisfaction.

Share client success stories that feature team members. "Last month Jessica worked with a client on a complex trust that required coordination with their accountant and financial advisor. The client specifically complimented how well Jessica managed all the moving pieces. She's excellent at this type of coordination."

These success stories build confidence that other clients will receive the same quality service through delegation.

Build team member expertise visibly over time. As team members develop specialized knowledge, let clients benefit from and recognize that expertise. "Jessica just completed advanced training in special needs trusts. If you ever have clients or family members who need that type of planning, she's now one of the most knowledgeable people in the state on that topic."

This visible expertise development shows clients that your team is continuously improving and that they benefit from those improvements.

Make team member contributions visible even when you're heavily involved. After handling a complex client matter personally, acknowledge team member contributions: "Jessica did excellent research that informed my strategy on this. Her thorough analysis of the case law made our approach much stronger."

This attribution builds team member credibility while also demonstrating your leadership in orchestrating team resources for client benefit.

Create premium service offerings that leverage delegation. Some clients might pay premium fees for even more responsive, thorough service that's only possible through effective team leverage. Position this as an advantage: "Our premium service includes a dedicated paralegal who manages every detail of your matter, with my oversight on all strategy and complex issues. You get white-glove service through this team approach."

The goal is clients who see your team as an asset that enhances their service rather than a substitute for your personal attention. When clients recognize that delegation makes their service better—faster, more thorough, more specialized, more cost-effective—resistance fades and appreciation grows.

The Virtual Assistant Dimension

The client relationship challenge becomes more complex when your team includes virtual assistants, particularly those based outside the United States. These remote team members can dramatically expand your capacity at a fraction of local hiring costs, but they also introduce considerations that don't exist with in-office staff.

Sarah discovered this when she hired her first VA—a talented professional based in the Philippines who could handle scheduling, document organization, and client intake coordination. The cost savings were compelling, and the VA's skills were strong. But Sarah hadn't thought through how to introduce this team member to clients, how to manage the ethical boundaries, or how to maintain security when someone halfway around the world was accessing client files.

Her first attempt nearly failed. A client expressed concern about "someone overseas" handling their confidential information. Another questioned whether it was even legal. A third simply refused to work with anyone they perceived as "not really part of the firm."

Sarah learned that VAs require the same thoughtful client relationship management as any team member, plus additional consideration for the unique concerns they raise.

Positioning VAs to Clients

The way you introduce and position VAs determines whether clients see them as a service enhancement or a cost-cutting measure that compromises quality.

Never hide VA usage or hope clients won't notice. Transparency builds trust; discovery of undisclosed offshore assistants destroys it. Instead, position VA usage proactively as part of your service model.

Sarah revised her approach. She now explains during initial consultations: "We've built a global team to serve you better. We have administrative specialists in different time zones, which means work continues on your matter even outside normal business hours. These team members handle scheduling, document preparation, and coordination under my direct supervision. They're bound by the same strict confidentiality requirements as our local staff, and they enable us to be more responsive than practices that rely only on local nine-to-five employees."

This framing accomplished several things. It positioned the global team as an advantage, not an apology. It emphasized the benefit to clients—extended working hours and faster service. It addressed confidentiality concerns proactively. And it maintained the supervision framework that clients expect.

Some clients will still express concern. When they do, acknowledge the concern and provide reassurance based on your actual safeguards.

"I understand your concern about having someone remote access your information. Let me explain our security protocols. All our virtual team members work through encrypted connections. They access only the specific information needed for their assigned tasks, never complete case files. Every piece of work they do is reviewed by me before it reaches you. And they sign comprehensive confidentiality agreements with severe penalties for any breach. In five years of using this model, we've never had a security incident."

This response validates the concern, demonstrates you've thought it through seriously, and provides concrete reassurance based on actual measures.

For particularly sensitive cases or clients who remain uncomfortable despite reassurances, offer flexibility. "If you prefer, I can handle your matter entirely with our U.S.-based team. The timeline may be slightly longer and the cost somewhat higher because we won't have the extended working hours, but we're happy to accommodate your preference."

Most clients, when they understand the actual safeguards and see the choice framed this way, become comfortable with VA involvement. Those who don't reveal that their concern is deeply held, and honoring that preference builds trust even if it reduces efficiency.

The Ethics and Security Framework

VAs create unique ethical considerations that require thoughtful management. The fundamental rule is simple: VAs cannot practice law. But the application can be nuanced.

Sarah learned to draw clear lines about what VAs could and couldn't do. Her VAs could schedule appointments, organize documents, prepare routine correspondence from templates, conduct factual research from public sources, and coordinate with courts on administrative matters. They could not give any legal advice, make strategy decisions, communicate legal opinions to clients, or exercise legal judgment of any kind.

The test she used: "If this task requires legal knowledge or judgment, only an attorney can do it. If it requires following clear instructions on administrative or factual matters, a VA can handle it."

Training VAs on these boundaries was critical. Sarah didn't just tell her VAs what they couldn't do; she explained why. "You cannot tell a client whether they should accept a settlement offer because that's legal advice. If a client asks, you say 'That's a legal strategy decision Attorney Sarah will discuss with you. Let me get her on the phone' or 'I'll have Attorney Sarah call you today to discuss that.'"

This training extended to recognizing situations that looked routine but actually required legal judgment. "If a client mentions something unusual—a new development in their case, a concerning conversation with opposing counsel, or anything that seems off— don't try to handle it yourself. Flag it for me immediately. It's better to escalate unnecessarily than to miss something important."

Security protocols had to be airtight. Sarah implemented several layers of protection. All VAs accessed firm systems through VPN connections. Multi-factor authentication was non-negotiable. VAs could view documents in the cloud-based practice management system but couldn't download files to personal devices unless absolutely necessary, and then only to encrypted drives that were wiped after task completion.

The principle of data minimization became standard practice. Before giving a VA access to any client information, Sarah asked herself: "Does this task truly require access to confidential details, or can I accomplish the goal with redacted or summarized information?" Often, she could provide only the specific information needed while keeping sensitive details restricted.

When a VA needed to organize documents chronologically, Sarah provided only the documents with dates visible—not entire case files. When a VA researched public records, Sarah gave them the factual information they needed to search without sharing case strategy or sensitive client details.

Regular security training reinforced these protocols. Monthly reminders about phishing threats, quarterly reviews of any security near-misses, and annual comprehensive refresher training kept security top of mind. Sarah learned that security awareness wasn't a one-time training topic; it required ongoing reinforcement.

Managing the Client Experience with Remote Team Members

The biggest client relationship challenge with VAs is maintaining the personal connection and responsiveness that clients expect when team members work different hours in different locations.

Sarah developed systems that made VA involvement invisible to clients in terms of service quality while being transparent about the team structure.

Communication handoffs were carefully managed. When a VA completed a task that required client notification, Sarah's process ensured the communication came from her or included clear context. A VA might draft a status update email, but it went through Sarah's review and was sent from her email address with appropriate personalization. Clients experienced seamless communication even though the underlying work was distributed across time zones.

For routine scheduling and administrative communication, VAs could interact with clients directly, but with clear protocols. The VA identified themselves: "This is Maria from Attorney Sarah's team" rather than ambiguously implying they were an attorney. They stayed within defined boundaries: scheduling, document requests, and administrative coordination were fine; anything touching case substance was immediately referred to Sarah.

Response time actually improved with VAs in different time zones. A client email sent at 8 PM Sarah's time might receive a response within an hour from a VA just starting their workday. What clients experienced was remarkable responsiveness; what enabled it was a thoughtfully managed global team.

The asynchronous nature of VA work required Sarah to be more intentional about task management. She couldn't just verbally explain what she needed; she had to document it clearly. This discipline, while initially time-consuming, actually improved her delegation to all team members. Clear written instructions with examples and decision criteria helped everyone work more independently.

Sarah used video recordings for complex instructions. When showing a VA how to prepare documents using a new template, she recorded herself doing it once with explanation. The VA could watch multiple times, pause to take notes, and reference it whenever needed. This was more efficient than repeated live explanations and worked despite timezone differences.

Building Trust Across Distance

The VAs Sarah never met in person could still become trusted, valued team members. But it required deliberate effort to build connection across distance and cultural differences.

She scheduled regular video calls during the few hours of timezone overlap. These weren't just about task management; they included personal connection. Sarah learned about her VAs' lives, their professional goals, their families and interests. She acknowledged their cultural holidays and celebrations. She showed genuine interest in them as people, not just as hired help.

Recognition and appreciation mattered even more with remote team members who didn't experience the daily affirmation of office interaction. Sarah publicly acknowledged excellent work in team messages. She provided specific, detailed positive feedback when VAs exceeded expectations. She gave bonuses for exceptional performance and provided references when VAs pursued other opportunities.

As her VA team grew, Sarah promoted her most experienced VA to a lead role. This Lead VA coordinated other VAs, conducted quality review before work reached Sarah, and provided first-line support for questions. This created a career path that showed VAs they weren't stuck in dead-end roles; excellence led to advancement.

The client relationship implications were significant. When Sarah's Lead VA had been with the practice for three years and deeply understood how everything worked, clients developed trust in her just as they did with long-term local staff. The geographic distance became irrelevant; the relationship and demonstrated competence mattered.

When to Use VAs vs. Local Team Members

Not every delegation opportunity is right for VAs, and understanding the distinction helps with both team building and client relationships.

Sarah learned that VAs excelled at clearly defined, repeatable tasks that didn't require real-time collaboration or legal judgment. Document organization, calendar management, basic research from public sources, social media management, routine client communication following templates, and administrative coordination were perfect VA tasks.

Work requiring nuanced legal judgment, extensive real-time collaboration, immediate access during business hours, or particularly sensitive client interaction was better suited to local team members or attorney handling.

The question wasn't "VA or local hire?" It was "What type of work needs what type of team member?" Both had their place in a well-designed team structure.

Clients understood this when it was explained in terms of optimal deployment of resources. "We have administrative specialists in different time zones who handle scheduling and coordination, which gives you 24-hour responsiveness. We have local paralegals who work directly with me on legal strategy and complex case tasks. And I personally handle all major decisions and client-facing legal work. Everyone works on what they do best, and you get the benefit of the entire team's expertise."

This explanation positioned different team members as complementary strengths rather than hierarchical quality levels. Clients saw the logic and experienced the benefits.

Sarah's VA Integration Success

Two years after her first struggled attempt with VA delegation, Sarah had built a seamlessly integrated global team. Three VAs in the Philippines handled administrative work, scheduling, document preparation, and research. Two local paralegals managed substantive case work and complex legal tasks. Sarah focused on strategy, major decisions, and key client interactions.

Clients no longer questioned the model; they praised the responsiveness and efficiency. Several specifically mentioned in reviews how impressed they were that someone from the firm always responded quickly, regardless of when they reached out.

The security framework had proven robust. Regular audits showed protocols were being followed. The one minor incident—a VA accidentally using unsecured WiFi—was caught immediately through monitoring, remediated quickly, and turned into a training opportunity for the entire team.

The cost structure allowed Sarah to build a larger, more capable team than she could have afforded with only local hires. The saved overhead went into higher-quality local team members for roles that truly required in-person collaboration, better technology, and increased profit that validated the business model.

Most importantly, client relationships remained strong. Clients who initially resisted working with VAs became advocates after experiencing the service quality. They understood that Sarah had built something better than a traditional solo practice—a coordinated team delivering superior service regardless of where individual team members were located.

Sarah had learned that VAs weren't a compromise or a cost-cutting measure. They were a strategic choice that, when implemented with proper protocols and client relationship management, enhanced her practice and improved client service.

The key was transparency, security, clear boundaries, and the same thoughtful client relationship management that any delegation requires. Get those elements right, and geographic distance becomes irrelevant to client satisfaction.

Practice Area-Specific Delegation Approaches

Different practice areas have different client relationship dynamics that affect delegation strategies. Here's how to tailor your approach:

Criminal Defense (Flat Fee)

Clients are often scared, stigmatized, and intensely focused on outcomes. They want reassurance from the person they believe controls their fate.

Delegation approach: You handle all court appearances, plea discussions, and substantive legal strategy conversations. Team handles routine scheduling, discovery updates, procedural explanations, and coordination with court and prosecution.

Key to success: Frame team involvement as "making sure nothing is missed while I focus on your defense." Emphasize that team coordination allows you to be better prepared for the moments that matter.

Client communication: "I'll be in court with you every time. I'll make all the decisions about how we defend your case. Jason handles the coordination and logistics so I can focus entirely on your defense strategy and court advocacy."

Personal Injury (Contingency)

Clients are often injured, in pain, financially stressed, and focused on compensation. They want to know their case is being worked and their settlement will be maximized.

Delegation approach: You handle case evaluation, major settlement negotiations, depositions, and trial work. Team handles medical record collection, lien resolution, demand letter drafting, routine settlement communications, and client updates.

Key to success: Emphasize that team efficiency speeds up their recovery and increases settlement value. Show how team handling of administrative work allows you to focus on maximizing their outcome.

Client communication: "My personal focus is on getting you the maximum settlement. Maria handles all the medical record collection, billing issues, and coordination so nothing slows down your case. When it's time to negotiate your settlement, I'll personally handle every dollar of it."

Estate Planning (Hourly)

Clients are often uncomfortable discussing mortality and family issues. They want thoughtful guidance on complex, personal matters. They're often fee-conscious and want value.

Delegation approach: You handle sophisticated planning strategy, complex family dynamics, tax planning, and major client discussions. Team handles document preparation, routine drafting, administrative coordination, and procedural explanations.

Key to success: Emphasize that team handling of document preparation keeps costs down while ensuring you spend your time (and their money) on the planning strategy that matters.

Client communication: "I'll personally design your estate plan based on your goals and family situation. Sarah will prepare all the documents following my design. This approach keeps your costs down because Sarah's time is less expensive than mine, while ensuring you get my expertise where it counts—on the strategy and planning."

Family Law

Clients are often emotional, dealing with major life transitions, and need both legal and emotional support. They're focused on outcomes that affect their children, finances, and future.

Delegation approach: You handle court appearances, negotiations, substantive legal strategy, and sensitive client counseling. Team handles discovery coordination, financial affidavit preparation, routine procedural work, and logistical coordination.

Key to success: Acknowledge the emotional difficulty while providing stable, responsive support through team members. Position team as providing the immediate responsiveness clients need during a difficult time.

Client communication: "I'll handle all court appearances and negotiations regarding your children and finances. My team will coordinate the day-to-day details and be available whenever you need immediate support. You'll get both my expertise on what matters most and responsive daily support from our team."

Corporate/Transactional

Clients are often business-savvy, focused on deals moving forward, and expecting sophisticated service. They value responsiveness and expertise.

Delegation approach: You handle deal structure, negotiations, complex drafting, and strategic advice. Team handles due diligence coordination, document management, routine contract review, and transaction logistics.

Key to success: Emphasize how team efficiency speeds deals and reduces costs. Business clients understand teams and often expect them—your job is ensuring quality and coordination.

Client communication: "I'll personally handle the deal structure and negotiation strategy. Our transaction team will coordinate all due diligence and documentation to keep things moving quickly. This approach gets your deal done faster and more cost-effectively."

Communication Protocols for Client-Facing Delegation

Clear protocols prevent confusion about who handles what and ensure nothing falls through the cracks.

Define clear ownership of client relationships. For every case, someone should be the primary contact. Usually this is a team member, with you as the strategic lead.

Make this explicit to the client: "Sarah is your primary contact. She'll handle all your day-to-day needs and questions. I'll be directly involved in [specific activities]. If you reach out to me directly on routine matters, I'll connect you with Sarah because she can help you faster."

Create communication workflows that route issues appropriately. When clients contact you directly, have a system for ensuring the right person responds.

Simple workflow:

- Client emails or calls you
- You assess if it requires your personal response or can be handled by team
- If team-appropriate, you forward to team member with context: "Maria, please handle. Client wants settlement timeline update"
- Team member responds to client and copies you
- You're informed but not doing the work

This takes you 30 seconds instead of 15 minutes, and the client gets a faster, more complete response.

Use technology to enable team access and responsiveness. Team members can't handle client communication if they don't have access to information.

Ensure team members can:

- Access complete case files and communications
- See your calendar to know when you're available for escalations
- View case management systems to track deadlines and developments

- Send communications from firm email addresses that clients recognize

Establish documentation standards for team-client interactions. When team members interact with clients, those interactions should be documented so you stay informed without being involved.

Simple documentation:

- Brief note in the case file after each client interaction
- Email summary to you on significant conversations
- Flag system for issues that need your attention
- Regular (weekly or biweekly) summary of all client communications on each case

This keeps you informed and allows you to spot issues without being the one handling every interaction.

Create escalation protocols that work smoothly. When something does need to be escalated to you, the process should be seamless for the client.

Protocol:

1. Team member identifies issue needing escalation
2. Team member tells client "I'll discuss this with the attorney and one of us will get back to you by [specific time]"
3. Team member brings issue to you with their assessment and recommendation
4. You decide how to handle
5. Either you respond to client or you brief team member to respond with your guidance

From the client's perspective, they got a commitment for a response and it was delivered. They don't feel bounced around—they feel well-served by a coordinated team.

Karen's Client Relationship Breakthrough

Six months after Margaret's email requesting to speak with Karen directly, the relationship dynamics had completely transformed. Margaret now contacted Jessica for most issues and specifically complimented the team-based approach when referring a friend to the practice.

The transformation didn't happen instantly. It required deliberate effort, strategic changes, and commitment to making delegation enhance rather than compromise client relationships.

Karen's first change was revising how she set expectations with new clients. Every initial consultation now included explicit discussion of the team approach, who handled what types of work, and how the collaborative approach benefited clients. New clients understood and accepted the team model from the beginning, eliminating surprise later.

Her second change was improving how she introduced Jessica and positioned her expertise. Instead of "my paralegal will help," Karen emphasized Jessica's specialized knowledge, extensive experience, and client service excellence. These confident introductions built client trust in Jessica from the first interaction.

Her third change was identifying the high-impact moments where her personal involvement mattered most and ensuring she showed up for those moments. The initial strategy session, mid-point review, and final planning conversation always involved Karen personally. Clients felt appropriately attended to even though routine work was delegated.

Her fourth change was creating feedback loops with clients about their experience working with Jessica. These conversations surfaced any concerns early and also often revealed positive experiences that reinforced the value of delegation.

Her fifth change was responding to "I want the attorney" requests with respect and curiosity. Instead of resistance, she honored requests while understanding what drove them. Often she could address underlying concerns while also strengthening Jessica's relationship with the client.

Her sixth change was making delegation advantages explicit rather than assumed. She actively educated clients about how team-based service delivered better responsiveness, more specialized expertise, and greater thoroughness than solo attorney service.

The results were compelling. Client satisfaction scores increased. Referrals grew. And perhaps most telling, clients who initially resisted working with Jessica specifically requested her involvement on subsequent matters. They'd experienced the advantages of the team approach and valued it.

Margaret became one of Karen's best advocates for the team approach. When referring her friend to the practice, she specifically mentioned: "Karen is excellent, but honestly, the whole team is fantastic. Jessica, her paralegal, knows everything about estate planning and responds immediately to any question. You get Karen's expertise on strategy and complex issues, plus Jessica's meticulous attention to detail on everything else. It's the best of both worlds."

That referral conversation captured exactly what Karen had been trying to build—clients who valued the team approach as a service enhancement rather than tolerating it as an accommodation.

Karen's practice transformed as a result. She served more clients without working longer hours. Her team members developed expertise and took on greater responsibility. Client satisfaction improved because responsiveness increased and thoroughness improved. And Karen focused her energy on the strategic work where her expertise created the most value.

The financial impact was significant too. By delegating routine work to Jessica at paralegal rates while focusing her own time on complex matters and client development, Karen's effective rate increased substantially. She billed fewer hours personally but generated more revenue because she deployed her time more strategically.

But the most meaningful change was the reduction in stress and the increase in professional satisfaction. Karen no longer felt torn between client service and business growth. The team approach allowed her to excel at both. She maintained strong client relationships while building a scalable practice.

She learned that client relationship challenges in delegation aren't obstacles to overcome through force; they're opportunities to build something better. When you set clear expectations, introduce team members effectively, maintain strategic personal involvement, respond respectfully to client preferences, and make delegation advantages visible, clients embrace the team approach.

The key insight was that clients don't inherently resist delegation. They resist unclear expectations, diminished service quality, lost personal connection, and feeling less important. Address those legitimate concerns and delegation becomes a relationship strength, not a weakness.

Karen reflected on how far she'd come from that initial email from Margaret. At the time, she'd felt defensive and uncertain. Should she accommodate Margaret's request for personal attention? Should she insist that Jessica was capable? Should she question whether delegation was worth the relationship risk?

Now she knew the answer was none of those. The right response was to honor client preferences while building confidence in team members, to provide strategic personal involvement while delegating effectively, and to make the team approach so valuable that clients appreciated rather than resisted it.

The client relationship challenge in delegation is real. But it's solvable. With the right approach, delegation doesn't damage client relationships—it enhances them by delivering better service than any solo attorney can provide.

Action Items for This Chapter

1. Revise Your Client Expectation-Setting Process

Update your intake conversation and engagement letter to clearly explain your team approach, specify what work you handle personally versus what team members handle, and frame delegation as a service advantage. Implement this with your next three new clients.

Updates made to: ☐ Intake script ☐ Engagement letter ☐ Team introduction process

Implementation deadline: _____

2. Create Strategic Personal Touchpoints

Identify the 3-5 high-impact moments in your typical client matter where your personal involvement matters most. Commit to personal involvement at those moments while confidently delegating surrounding work. Map this out for your most common matter type.

Matter type: _____

Personal touchpoint moments:

1. _____
2. _____
3. _____
4. _____
5. _____

3. Strengthen One Team Member Introduction

Select one team member who handles client-facing work. Revise how you introduce them to emphasize expertise, experience, and client service excellence. Practice the introduction and use it with the next five client interactions.

Team member: _____

New introduction language: _____

First use date: _____

4. Document Your Client Service Standards

Define the 5-7 most important standards for how your team should interact with clients. Make this a written reference for your team.

Our client service standards:

1. _____
2. _____
3. _____
4. _____
5. _____

5. Create Your Escalation Decision Tree

Build a simple green light/yellow light/red light framework showing your team when to handle issues independently vs. when to involve you. Share this with your team this week.

Green Light (handle independently):

- _____
- _____

Yellow Light (consult before responding):

- _____
- _____

Red Light (immediate escalation):

- _____
- _____

6. Practice the Warm Handoff Technique

This week, when a client contacts you with something a team member can handle, practice the warm handoff technique. Make the introduction personal and stay on briefly to build confidence.

Scheduled for: _____

7. Ask Three Current Clients for Feedback

Reach out to three clients and ask: "How has your experience been working with [team member name]?" Use their responses to identify what's working and what needs adjustment.

Client feedback summary:

_____

_____

_____

Before Moving to Chapter 7

You now understand how to manage the client relationship challenges that come with delegation. You know how to set expectations, train your team to maintain your standards, handle client resistance, create systems where clients prefer your team, adapt your approach to different practice areas, and leverage virtual assistants effectively while managing the unique considerations they present.

The next chapter focuses on creating the infrastructure and environment that makes delegation successful. Chapter 7 will show you how to build systems, processes, and tools that enable your team to work independently and effectively—from SOPs to communication protocols to the right technology stack.

Without the right environment, even the best people and clearest expectations will struggle. The next chapter ensures your delegation has the structural support it needs to succeed.

One Action Before Chapter 7

Schedule a 30-minute team meeting to introduce your team-based service approach and get their input on how to implement it effectively. Their buy-in is essential to success.

Team meeting scheduled for: _____

CHAPTER 7:

Mastering Deadlines and Tracking Systems

Marcus felt the familiar knot in his stomach as he walked into the office Monday morning. Something was wrong. He could feel it.

His paralegal, Amanda, was already at her desk, which was unusual. She typically arrived thirty minutes after he did. Her face was pale.

"We have a problem," she said quietly. "The Hendricks discovery responses were due Friday. I thought you were handling them. You thought I was handling them. They didn't get filed."

Marcus felt his blood pressure spike. The Hendricks case. Six-figure personal injury claim. Aggressive opposing counsel who would absolutely file a motion for sanctions over a missed discovery deadline. A client who was already anxious about every aspect of the case.

This wasn't Amanda's fault. It wasn't even really his fault. They simply didn't have a system. He'd mentioned the discovery deadline in a hallway conversation three weeks ago. She'd said "I'll take care of it," and he'd assumed she had it under control. She'd assumed he would review it before filing and had been waiting for him to ask for it.

No calendar entry. No task assignment. No deadline tracking. No accountability. Just two people with good intentions and a critical missed deadline that could cost their client the case.

The worst part? This wasn't the first time. Last month, they'd nearly missed a statute of limitations deadline because it was "on someone's list" but not in any shared system. Two months before that, they'd scrambled at the last minute to prepare for a hearing because no one had confirmed who was responsible for the prep work.

Marcus had built a successful practice, hired good people, and worked to delegate effectively. But without proper deadline management and tracking systems, his delegation efforts were built on quicksand.

Every delegated task carries a deadline. Some are court-imposed and catastrophic if missed. Others are client expectations or business operations deadlines. All of them matter.

This chapter shows you how to ensure that when you delegate work, deadlines get met and nothing falls through the cracks. You'll learn how to set clear deadlines, communicate them effectively, track delegated work without micromanaging, and build systems that catch problems before they become disasters.

Why Deadlines Matter in Delegation

Delegation without deadline management isn't delegation at all. It's hope masquerading as leadership.

When you keep all the work yourself, you might manage deadlines poorly, but at least you know what's on your plate. When you delegate work to others, deadline management becomes exponentially more complex. Now you need to know what's on everyone's plate, ensure they know their deadlines, confirm they have the resources to meet those deadlines, and verify that work is progressing appropriately.

In law firms, missed deadlines aren't just embarrassing. They're potentially career-ending. Courts don't accept "my paralegal didn't tell me" as an excuse for missing a filing deadline. Clients don't forgive "it fell through the cracks" when you miss a statute of limitations. The bar doesn't overlook deadline failures just because you delegated the work to someone else.

The attorney remains responsible even when the work is delegated. Model Rule 5.1 requires lawyers to make reasonable efforts to ensure that subordinate lawyers and nonlawyer assistants comply with professional obligations. That includes deadline obligations. You can delegate the work, but you cannot delegate the responsibility for meeting deadlines.

But there's a deeper issue beyond liability. Deadline management reveals whether your delegation is actually working. If team members consistently miss deadlines on delegated work, one of three things is happening. First, your deadlines might be unrealistic. Second, you might be delegating to people who lack the capacity or competence. Third, your systems might be inadequate.

Any of these problems will torpedo your delegation efforts. Clear deadline systems expose these issues early, when they can be fixed, rather than letting them fester until they cause disasters.

The Components of Effective Deadline Management

Setting a deadline is simple. Managing a deadline is complex. Effective deadline management in a delegation context requires several integrated components working together.

Clear deadline setting. The deadline must be specific, realistic, and understood by everyone involved. "Get this done soon" isn't a deadline. "Draft the motion to suppress and have it on my desk for review by 3 PM Thursday" is a deadline. Specificity eliminates ambiguity and creates accountability.

Shared visibility. Everyone who needs to know about a deadline should be able to see it. This typically means deadline information lives in a shared system, not just in one person's head or individual calendar. When Amanda thought Marcus was handling the Hendricks discovery and Marcus thought Amanda was handling it, the failure point was lack of shared visibility into who owned what deadline.

Buffer time and dependencies. Deadlines should account for the realities of how work flows. If a motion needs your review before filing, the paralegal's deadline should be at least a day before the court deadline. If a task depends on someone else completing prior work, the deadline needs to reflect that dependency. Deadlines set without considering buffer time and dependencies are really just optimistic fantasies.

Escalation triggers. Systems should flag when deadlines are at risk. If work isn't started within a reasonable time before the deadline, someone should notice. If a deadline passes without confirmation of completion, alarms should sound. Automatic escalation prevents small delays from becoming major problems.

Accountability mechanisms. Someone must own each deadline. When work is delegated, the person receiving the delegation owns the deadline. But the delegator retains responsibility for ensuring the system works. Clear ownership combined with systematic tracking creates accountability without micromanagement.

Completion confirmation. Just because a deadline passes doesn't mean the work is done. Systems should require explicit confirmation that work is complete and meets standards. This confirmation becomes part of the record and creates a clear handoff point.

How to Set Realistic Deadlines When Delegating

The most common deadline failure in delegation isn't missing deadlines; it's setting unrealistic ones in the first place. Attorneys who personally handle work often develop an instinctive sense of timing. They know roughly how long a motion takes to research and draft, how much time client communication requires, or how long case preparation takes for a hearing.

When you delegate that work to someone else, your instinctive timing often proves wrong. Your paralegal needs more time than you would because they have different skills and experience. Your associate might need less time than you expect because they're more current on certain areas of law. Setting realistic deadlines requires understanding the capabilities of the person receiving the delegation.

Start by involving the person receiving the delegation in setting the deadline. Instead of saying "I need this motion by Thursday," try "This motion needs to be filed by Friday. How much time do you need to draft it and get it to me for review?" This approach accomplishes several things simultaneously.

First, it gives you information about their capacity and workload. If they say they need a week when you expected two days, you've learned something important about either their capacity or your expectations. Second, it creates buy-in. People are more committed to deadlines they help set. Third, it surfaces conflicts or dependencies you might not know about. They might mention other deadlines or projects that affect their ability to meet your requested timeline.

But don't simply accept whatever timeline they propose. Engage in a conversation. Ask what's driving their time estimate. Discuss whether any steps can be shortened or whether any resources would help them work faster. Explore whether the deadline is truly necessary or whether you have some flexibility.

Consider the complexity and novelty of the work. Routine tasks that follow established procedures can have tighter deadlines. Novel work or complex matters require more buffer time. A standard discovery motion that follows a template might take three hours. A complex suppression motion on a novel legal issue might take twenty hours spread over several days. Set deadlines that match the work's complexity.

Account for interruptions and other demands. Your team member won't spend eight uninterrupted hours on your project. They'll field phone calls, respond to emails, handle client questions, and deal with unexpected issues. A project that requires eight hours of focused work might need three days on the calendar when interruptions and other demands are factored in.

Build in review and revision time. If you're delegating a client-facing deliverable or a court filing, you'll review it before it goes out. Budget time for that review and for any revisions that might be necessary. A motion that takes your paralegal two days to draft might need another day for your review and their revisions. The deadline to the paralegal should be two days before the court deadline, not the day before.

Consider external dependencies. Does the task require information from the client? Input from an expert? Documents from opposing counsel? Each dependency adds time and uncertainty. Build buffer time for each dependency, and make those dependencies explicit when setting the deadline.

Some deadlines aren't negotiable. Court deadlines, statutes of limitations, and contractual deadlines are fixed points. In these cases, work backward from the deadline to determine when internal deadlines must fall. If a brief is due to the court on the 15th, and you need a day for review, the draft must be ready by the 13th. If the draft requires a week to write, work must start by the 6th. Make these calculations explicit and share them with your team.

Document your deadline reasoning. When you set a deadline, explain why. "This needs to be done by Tuesday because the court deadline is Thursday and I need a day for review" is more powerful than just "Get this done by Tuesday." Understanding the why helps team members prioritize and helps them make good decisions if circumstances change.

Finally, track your deadline accuracy over time. If you consistently set deadlines that people struggle to meet, your estimation skills need recalibration. If deadlines are consistently met with days to spare, you're probably being too conservative. Find the right balance through observation and adjustment.

Communicating Deadlines Clearly

Setting a realistic deadline is only half the battle. The other half is ensuring that deadline is clearly understood by everyone involved. Miscommunication about deadlines is one of the most common delegation failures, and it's entirely preventable.

When you delegate work with a deadline, communicate in writing. Even if you discuss the deadline verbally, follow up with written confirmation. Email, task management systems, or project management platforms all work. The specific medium matters less than having a written record that both parties can reference.

Your written deadline communication should include several key elements. State the task clearly and specifically. Include what the final deliverable should look like. Specify the deadline with date and time. Explain any dependencies or prerequisites. Note who should review the work and when. Identify what happens next after the deadline is met.

For example: "Please draft the motion to suppress evidence for the Johnson case. The draft should include the statement of facts, legal argument with case citations, and proposed order. I need this on my desk by 3 PM Thursday, October 12th so I can review it Friday morning. The motion must be filed by Monday, October 16th. After I review your draft, we'll discuss any revisions needed and you'll prepare the final version for filing."

This communication is specific about the task, clear about the deadline, transparent about dependencies (your review), explicit about timing (you review Friday, they revise based on feedback, file Monday), and informative about the ultimate deadline (Monday filing).

Confirm understanding. After communicating a deadline, ask the recipient to confirm they understand the task and deadline. This doesn't mean you doubt their competence. It's a quality control measure that catches misunderstandings early. A simple "Please confirm you can meet this deadline and let me know if you have any questions" works well.

Pay attention to their confirmation. If they confirm but seem hesitant or uncertain, probe deeper. "You seem concerned about the timeline. What's your worry?" often reveals potential problems before they become actual failures. If they raise legitimate concerns about the deadline, take them seriously and adjust if possible.

Make deadline status visible. Use shared calendars, task management systems, or project boards where team members can see all pending deadlines at a glance. This visibility helps them prioritize, helps you monitor progress, and helps everyone avoid scheduling conflicts or capacity problems.

Distinguish between different types of deadlines. Some deadlines are hard and immovable (court filing dates, statutes of limitations). Others have more flexibility (internal review deadlines, client deliverables). Make these distinctions clear. You might code deadlines by color: red for court deadlines, yellow for client deadlines, green for internal goals. Whatever system you use, make sure your team understands what each deadline type means.

Update deadlines when circumstances change. If a court continues a hearing and pushes back a deadline, communicate that change immediately to everyone affected. If new information comes in that accelerates a deadline, don't assume people will figure it out. Proactive communication about deadline changes prevents people from working toward outdated targets.

Create a deadline culture where questions are encouraged. Team members should feel comfortable asking "Can you clarify exactly when this is due?" or "What takes priority if I can't meet both deadlines?" The goal is not blind deadline compliance; it's shared understanding and effective execution.

For complex projects with multiple deadlines and dependencies, consider a kickoff meeting where everyone involved reviews the timeline together. Walk through each major milestone, discuss dependencies, identify potential bottlenecks, and ensure everyone understands their piece of the puzzle. Fifteen minutes spent in collective planning can prevent weeks of deadline confusion.

Milestone and Interim Deadlines

Long-term projects or complex delegated work requires more than a final deadline. Without intermediate checkpoints, problems hide until they're too late to fix. Milestone and interim deadlines create visibility and accountability throughout the project lifecycle.

Think of interim deadlines as navigation checkpoints on a long journey. You don't just say "arrive in San Francisco by Saturday." You say "reach Sacramento by Thursday, then we'll assess and plan the final leg." If you're not in Sacramento by Thursday, you know you're behind and can adjust before the final deadline arrives.

The same principle applies to delegated legal work. If you delegate a complex brief that's due in three weeks, set interim deadlines for key milestones. Research complete by end of week one. Rough draft by end of week two. Final draft for review three days before filing.

Each milestone gives you visibility into progress and creates opportunities to course-correct if needed.

Interim deadlines should align with natural breakpoints in the work. For a motion, natural milestones might include research completion, first draft of facts section, first draft of legal argument, complete first draft, revised draft after review, and final version. Each represents a discrete deliverable that can be reviewed and assessed.

Make interim deadlines meaningful, not just arbitrary check-ins. Each milestone should produce something reviewable. "Made progress on research" is too vague. "Completed research and produced memo summarizing key cases with relevance to our facts" is a concrete milestone with a tangible deliverable.

The frequency of interim deadlines should match the project's complexity and risk. A routine motion might need just one interim deadline (draft ready for review). A complex appellate brief might need weekly milestones. A major transaction might need daily check-ins for certain phases. Higher stakes and greater complexity warrant tighter milestone intervals.

Interim deadlines serve several purposes beyond progress tracking. They create momentum by breaking large projects into manageable chunks. They provide feedback opportunities while there's still time to adjust. They reveal capacity and competency issues early. They reduce end-loading where all work happens in a panic at the final deadline.

When someone misses an interim deadline, treat it seriously but proportionately. Missing an early research deadline on a three-week project is a yellow flag, not a red alert. It signals the need for a conversation about priorities, obstacles, or capacity. Missing the final pre-review deadline on that same project is a different matter entirely and might require immediate intervention or reassignment.

Build buffer time between interim deadlines and the final deadline. If your paralegal's final draft is due to you on Wednesday and the filing deadline is Friday, you have buffer time for review and any necessary revisions. If their final draft is due Thursday afternoon and filing is Friday morning, there's no buffer. Missing that interim deadline almost guarantees missing the final deadline.

Use interim deadlines to provide coaching and feedback. When your associate submits research findings at the week-one milestone, review them and provide feedback. This improves the final product and develops the associate's skills. Interim deadlines are learning opportunities disguised as project management tools.

Don't create so many interim deadlines that they become burdensome. Each milestone requires time and attention from both the delegator and the person doing the work. Too many checkpoints transform helpful accountability into micromanagement. Find the right balance between oversight and autonomy.

Document milestone completion. When an interim deadline is met, note it. This creates a record of progress, provides positive reinforcement, and protects you if issues arise later. If someone claims they were on track with a project, you can point to documented milestone completion (or failure to complete).

Adjust milestones when circumstances change. If a client provides crucial information that changes the research direction, it might be reasonable to extend the research milestone and adjust subsequent deadlines. Milestones should serve the work, not become rigid obstacles to effectiveness.

Tracking Systems That Work Without Micromanaging

The challenge in tracking delegated work is maintaining visibility without hovering. You need to know whether work is progressing appropriately and deadlines are on track, but you don't want to undermine autonomy or waste time on excessive status updates.

Effective tracking systems provide the right information at the right time to the right people without creating bureaucratic overhead. The best systems are largely invisible when things are going well and immediately apparent when problems arise.

The foundation of good tracking is a shared system of record. Whether it's a practice management platform, project management tool, or customized database, there must be one authoritative source that shows who owns what work, when it's due, and what its status is. Every task or matter in your practice should exist in this system with clear ownership and deadline information.

This shared system eliminates the "I thought you were handling it" problem that plagued Marcus and Amanda. When task ownership and deadlines live in a shared system that everyone can access, there's no ambiguity. The system shows who owns the Hendricks discovery responses and when they're due. Both Marcus and Amanda can see it. Neither can assume the other is handling it without checking.

Task status updates should be part of normal workflow, not additional overhead. The best tracking happens as a byproduct of work completion, not as a separate reporting requirement. When your paralegal completes the research phase of a motion, they should mark that milestone complete in the system as part of finishing that work, not as a separate administrative task later.

Modern practice management systems can automate much of the tracking. Set up automatic alerts for approaching deadlines. Create dashboards that show all upcoming deadlines sorted by urgency. Configure notifications when tasks are at risk of missing deadlines. Use the technology to surface information that needs attention without requiring manual status requests.

Status-based tracking is more efficient than time-based tracking. Instead of asking for updates every Friday regardless of what's happening, use status triggers. When a task moves from "in progress" to "ready for review," you get notified. When a deadline is three days away and the status is still "not started," you get alerted. Information flows based on what's happening, not on arbitrary calendar intervals.

For longer projects or complex matters, create review schedules based on milestones rather than calendar dates. "Review after research is complete" is more useful than "review every Monday." The milestone approach focuses attention when there's actually something to review, not on random days that might not align with work progress.

Make status information easily accessible. Dashboards, visual project boards, or shared calendars should show at a glance what's on track, what's at risk, and what needs immediate attention. Color coding helps: green for on track, yellow for needs attention, red for overdue or at serious risk. You should be able to assess your team's deadline status in sixty seconds, not sixty minutes.

Build accountability for updating status into your culture and systems. Team members should understand that keeping task status current isn't administrative busywork; it's professional responsibility. When someone fails to update status and creates confusion, address it directly. Status discipline prevents problems.

Create exception-based reporting. Instead of requiring everyone to report on all their work, ask them to report only on items that are behind schedule, blocked, or need help. "Here's what's not on track and what I need" is more valuable than lengthy status reports covering things that are progressing fine.

Use standing meetings efficiently for status review. In a weekly team meeting, don't have everyone recite their task list. Instead, review items that are at risk or need coordination. Focus discussion on problems and decisions, not on routine updates that could be handled asynchronously in the tracking system.

For critical deadlines, implement staged alerts. First alert when 25% of the time has passed and work hasn't started. Second alert at 50% if insufficient progress. Third alert at 75% if still not on track. Final alert when deadline is imminent. These staged alerts catch problems early but don't create noise with constant notifications.

Document why deadlines are missed, not just that they were missed. When something falls behind, the system should capture the reason. Was it lack of information from the client? Unexpected complexity? Competing priorities? This information helps you improve future deadline setting and identifies systemic issues.

Review your tracking metrics periodically. Are you tracking the right things? Is the information you're collecting actually useful? Are there better ways to get the visibility you need? Tracking systems should evolve based on what you learn about your practice's needs.

The goal is a tracking system that provides confidence without constant checking. You should be able to focus on your own work knowing that if something is off track, you'll find out in time to fix it. That's the sweet spot between abdication and micromanagement.

When Deadlines Are Missed: Response Protocols

Despite your best planning, deadlines will occasionally be missed. How you respond to missed deadlines determines whether they become isolated incidents or recurring failures. Your response protocol should be swift, systematic, and focused on both immediate mitigation and long-term prevention.

The immediate priority when a deadline is missed is damage control. If it's a court deadline, what are the consequences and what can be done to minimize harm? Can you file a motion for an extension? Is there an opportunity to cure the default? Should you notify the client immediately or wait until you have a solution? Time is critical when deadlines are missed in legal matters.

Determine the scope and impact quickly. Was it just one missed deadline or are there multiple problems? Is this an isolated incident or part of a pattern? A paralegal who misses one internal deadline

240

after three years of reliability is very different from someone who chronically misses deadlines. Your response should match the severity and pattern.

Get the full story before drawing conclusions. Why was the deadline missed? Was it insufficient time? Unclear instructions? Competing priorities? Personal issues affecting capacity? Technical problems with systems? The reason matters for determining the appropriate response and preventing recurrence.

If the miss was due to system failure rather than individual failure, fix the system. If two people thought the other was handling a task, that's a visibility problem, not a performance problem. Add checks to your system to prevent that specific failure mode. Every missed deadline is an opportunity to strengthen your processes.

If the miss was due to individual performance issues, address them directly and promptly. Don't ignore deadline misses or make excuses for chronic under-performers. Have a direct conversation: "You missed this deadline. That's serious. What happened, and what will you do differently next time?"

Create accountability without punishment for honest mistakes. A good team member who makes a rare error should be supported, not berated. But accountability still matters. They should own the mistake, understand its impact, and commit to preventing recurrence. "I apologize for missing the deadline. I underestimated the complexity. Going forward, I'll build in more buffer time for similar projects" demonstrates accountability and learning.

For serious misses or patterns of missed deadlines, implement performance improvement plans with specific, measurable expectations. "Meet all deadlines for the next thirty days" is measurable. "Try harder" is not. Tie specific consequences to continued failures. Without consequences, accountability is just aspiration.

Document missed deadlines and your response. If the miss was serious (court deadline, statute of limitations risk, client harm), create a written record of what happened, why, and what corrective action was taken. This documentation protects you if issues escalate and provides evidence of reasonable supervision efforts.

After addressing the immediate situation, conduct a post-mortem on significant deadline misses. Gather everyone involved and walk through what happened chronologically. Identify the failure point. Determine what warning signs were missed. Decide what systemic changes would prevent this specific failure. Implement those changes.

Use deadline misses as teaching moments. If an associate missed a deadline because they were working on too many matters simultaneously, that's an opportunity to teach prioritization and capacity management. If a paralegal missed a deadline because they didn't understand its importance, that's a chance to explain the why behind deadlines.

Track patterns across your practice. If one person misses multiple deadlines, that's an individual performance issue. If multiple people miss deadlines on a particular type of matter, that might indicate unrealistic expectations or inadequate resources. Pattern analysis reveals whether you have personnel problems or systems problems.

Adjust your delegation approach based on deadline performance. Someone who consistently meets deadlines might earn more autonomy and looser oversight. Someone with a pattern of missed deadlines needs tighter supervision until they demonstrate improvement. Let performance inform how you delegate and track.

Distinguish between misses that harm clients and those that don't. Missing an internal review deadline but still meeting the court deadline is different from missing the court deadline itself. Both matter, but they require different levels of response. Save your most serious interventions for the most serious failures.

Create a graduated response protocol. First miss of a minor internal deadline might warrant just a conversation. Second miss gets documented and discussed more formally. Third miss triggers a performance plan. This graduated approach is fair to team members while maintaining clear standards.

Finally, recognize that some deadline misses reveal that you, not your team, need to change. If you consistently set unrealistic deadlines, provide inadequate resources, or fail to communicate priorities clearly, the missed deadlines are on you. Be honest about your contribution to the problem and adjust your delegation practices accordingly.

Technology Tools for Deadline Management

The right technology can transform deadline management from a constant source of stress into a reliable, automated system that works in the background. But technology is only valuable if it's properly implemented and consistently used. The best deadline management tool poorly used is worse than a simple shared calendar used religiously.

Practice management platforms are the foundation of deadline management for most law firms. Platforms like Clio, MyCase, PracticePanther, or Smokeball integrate deadline tracking with matter management, document storage, billing, and client communication. When deadlines are part of your core practice management system, they're more likely to be entered accurately and monitored consistently.

These platforms typically offer deadline calculation tools that automatically compute response deadlines, appeal deadlines, and other court-driven dates based on the triggering event. If you enter that you received a complaint on a certain date, the system calculates the answer deadline based on your jurisdiction's rules. This automation eliminates calculation errors and ensures deadlines are tracked from the moment a triggering event occurs.

Task management systems like Asana, Monday.com, or Trello work well for managing complex projects with multiple interim deadlines and dependencies. These platforms let you create project templates for recurring work types. A "motion practice" template might include tasks for research, draft preparation, attorney review, revision, finalization, and filing, each with appropriate due dates calculated from the project start date.

Visual project boards help teams see work flow and deadline status at a glance. A board might have columns for "Not Started," "In Progress," "Ready for Review," "Revisions Needed," and "Complete." Cards representing tasks move across the board as work progresses. Deadlines display prominently on each card. Color coding indicates deadline urgency. This visual approach makes status obvious to everyone.

Calendar integration is crucial. Deadlines that live only in a task management system might not get the attention they deserve. Integration with Google Calendar, Outlook, or Apple Calendar puts deadlines where people already look. When your paralegal checks their calendar each morning, they see their deadlines alongside their meetings and appointments.

Automated alerts and notifications prevent deadlines from being forgotten. Configure your systems to send alerts at multiple intervals: when a task is created, when 25% of time has elapsed, at the halfway point, when 75% of time has passed, and as the deadline approaches. Customize alert frequency based on deadline importance and typical task duration.

Mobile access is increasingly important. Your team needs to check deadline status, update task progress, and receive alerts when they're out of the office. Cloud-based systems with strong mobile apps enable deadline management regardless of location. Your associate can update a task status from court. Your paralegal can check deadline priorities from home.

Shared calendars dedicated to deadline tracking provide simplicity and visibility. A firm-wide "Deadlines Calendar" shows every upcoming deadline in one place. Color code by matter type, responsible person, or deadline category. Anyone in the firm can see what deadlines are approaching and who owns them. This transparency creates collective awareness and accountability.

Document management systems that integrate with deadline tracking ensure the right documents are available when deadlines approach. When a motion filing deadline nears, the system might automatically surface the draft motion, the supporting documents, and the relevant research. This integration reduces the time spent hunting for materials and increases the likelihood of timely completion.

Workflow automation can eliminate manual deadline tracking steps. When a new matter is opened in your practice management system, automated workflows can create all standard deadlines, assign tasks to appropriate team members, set up notification schedules, and even generate template documents with deadline-driven instructions. What used to take thirty minutes of manual setup now happens automatically in seconds.

Communication tools like Slack or Microsoft Teams can integrate with deadline systems to send notifications where your team already communicates. A Slack channel dedicated to upcoming deadlines might post daily or weekly summaries of what's due. Team members can acknowledge deadlines, ask questions, or flag issues without leaving their primary communication platform.

Reporting and analytics tools help you understand deadline performance over time. How many deadlines are being met? Which types of deadlines are most often missed? Which team members have the best deadline track record? Is deadline performance improving or declining? Data-driven insights inform process improvements and resource allocation.

Time tracking integration reveals whether deadline misses correlate with workload issues. If someone consistently misses deadlines during periods when they're billing excessive hours, the problem might be capacity, not capability. Connecting deadline data with time data provides a more complete picture of performance and capacity.

Client portals that show case deadlines and milestones increase client confidence and reduce status inquiries. When clients can log into a portal and see exactly when key deadlines are approaching and what progress has been made, they feel more informed and involved. This transparency builds trust and reduces the time you spend providing routine updates.

The key to technology success is integration and simplicity. The more systems you require your team to check for deadline information, the more likely something will be missed. Strive for a unified view where deadlines from all sources flow into a single, authoritative system that everyone uses. Technology should reduce complexity, not add to it.

Training is essential. Even the best deadline management system fails if your team doesn't know how to use it properly. Invest time in training when you implement new tools. Create written procedures for how deadlines should be entered, updated, and monitored. Designate a system champion who can answer questions and troubleshoot issues.

Review your technology stack regularly. Are you using all the features you're paying for? Are there gaps in functionality that new tools could fill? Have your needs evolved beyond your current systems' capabilities? Technology should evolve with your practice, not remain static while your practice grows.

Remember that technology supports human processes; it doesn't replace them. The best deadline management system in the world won't save you if your team doesn't have the discipline to use it consistently. Combine good technology with good habits, clear expectations, and consistent accountability.

Creating a Culture of Deadline Accountability

Systems and technology provide the infrastructure for deadline management, but culture determines whether that infrastructure actually works. A culture of deadline accountability means everyone understands that meeting deadlines is non-negotiable, that excuses are rarely acceptable, and that deadline performance is a core measure of professional competence.

Culture starts with leadership modeling. If you consistently meet your own deadlines, communicate when you can't, and take deadline commitments seriously, your team will follow. If you blow past deadlines without acknowledgment, make excuses for your own failures, or treat deadlines as suggestions, your team will mirror that behavior. Your deadline discipline sets the standard for everyone else.

Make deadline expectations explicit, not assumed. During onboarding, explain that deadline reliability is a fundamental expectation of the role. Describe the consequences of missed deadlines for clients, for the firm, and for individual careers. Don't assume people understand the seriousness of deadlines; teach it explicitly.

Connect deadline performance to consequences both positive and negative. Meeting deadlines consistently should factor into raises, bonuses, and advancement opportunities. Missing deadlines should factor into performance reviews and improvement plans. When deadline performance has real consequences, people take it seriously.

Create psychological safety for deadline concerns. Team members should feel comfortable saying "I'm not going to make this deadline" without fear of punishment. The earlier you know about a potential deadline miss, the more options you have to address it. If people hide deadline problems until they become disasters, your culture punishes honesty.

Respond differently to deadline misses based on how they're handled. Someone who proactively communicates three days before a deadline that they're behind and proposes a solution demonstrates responsibility even though they're missing the deadline. Someone who lets a deadline pass without communication and makes excuses afterward demonstrates neither responsibility nor accountability. Your response should reflect that difference.

Celebrate deadline successes, especially challenging ones. When your team successfully juggles multiple urgent deadlines, pulls together to meet a sudden court-imposed timeline, or consistently delivers quality work on time despite difficult circumstances, acknowledge it. Recognition reinforces the behaviors and standards you want to see.

Make deadline reliability a hiring criterion. In interviews, ask candidates about their approach to deadlines. Describe a scenario where multiple deadlines conflict and ask how they would handle it. Check references specifically about deadline reliability. Hire people who already have strong deadline discipline rather than hoping to instill it after the fact.

Address deadline failures directly and promptly. Don't let a missed deadline slide without comment. Don't accept poor excuses. Don't rationalize away patterns of deadline failures. Direct feedback delivered quickly helps people understand that deadline reliability matters and that their performance fell short of expectations.

Build in redundancy for critical deadlines. High-stakes deadlines shouldn't depend on a single person's memory or reliability. Set up automatic reminders. Have a second person verify that critical deadlines are being tracked. Create backup plans. Redundancy isn't a sign of distrust; it's recognition that critical deadlines are too important to risk on any single point of failure.

Distinguish between deadline discipline and deadline flexibility. Good deadline culture doesn't mean rigidity. When legitimate reasons justify deadline adjustments, make them. When priorities shift and deadlines need to change, communicate those changes clearly. The goal is reliability and transparency, not inflexibility.

Teach time estimation skills. Many deadline failures stem from poor time estimation. Help your team learn to estimate realistically by tracking actual time against estimated time, discussing where estimates went wrong, and building buffer time into estimates. Time estimation is a learnable skill that improves deadline reliability.

Create deadline rituals that reinforce accountability. A Monday morning review of the week's deadlines helps everyone start the week aligned. A Friday afternoon confirmation that all week's deadlines were met or appropriately handled provides closure. These rituals make deadline awareness a consistent part of your practice rhythm.

Use past deadline failures as teaching tools. When a deadline is missed, after addressing the immediate situation, use it as a case study. What went wrong? What were the warning signs? What could have prevented it? How will we ensure this specific failure doesn't happen again? Transform failures into learning opportunities that strengthen future performance.

Encourage ownership, not blame-shifting. When deadlines are missed, team members should own their role rather than pointing fingers at others. "I missed the deadline because the client was slow getting me information" might be factually accurate, but it's also deflecting responsibility. Better: "I missed the deadline. I should have followed up with the client sooner or alerted you when I saw the information wasn't coming in time."

Normalize deadline conversations. Deadlines shouldn't be taboo topics discussed only when problems arise. Regular discussions about upcoming deadlines, capacity to meet them, potential conflicts, and resource needs should be routine. When deadline talk is normal, problems surface early and solutions are easier to find.

Build a reputation for deadline reliability. Your firm's external reputation should include reliability. Clients should know that when you commit to a deadline, you meet it. Opposing counsel should expect your filings on time. Courts should view your firm as responsible and professional. This external reputation reinforces internal culture because everyone takes pride in reliability.

Address systemic deadline issues with systemic solutions. If your firm chronically struggles with a particular category of deadline (discovery responses, client deliverables, court filings), don't just blame individuals. Examine whether your processes, resources, or expectations are the real problem. Fix systems, not just people.

Create escalation paths for deadline help. When someone realizes they can't meet a deadline alone, they should know exactly who to ask for help and how. Clear escalation paths turn potential failures into collaborative solutions. "I'm stuck on this research and the deadline is Thursday; who can help me?" should have an obvious answer in your culture.

Measure and communicate deadline performance metrics. Track firm-wide deadline compliance rates. Share those metrics with your team monthly or quarterly. Celebrate improvements. Discuss declines. Transparency about performance creates collective ownership of deadline culture.

Remember that deadline culture serves client interests, not just firm efficiency. Every deadline met is a commitment kept to a client. Every deadline missed potentially harms someone who trusted you with their legal matter. Connect deadline accountability to the deeper purpose of serving clients well.

A culture of deadline accountability isn't built overnight. It requires consistent reinforcement, clear expectations, fair consequences, and leadership modeling. But once established, it becomes self-sustaining. New team members absorb deadline standards from existing team culture. Deadline reliability becomes "just how we do things here." That's when deadline management transforms from a constant challenge into a reliable strength.

Marcus's Transformation: From Crisis to Confidence

Six months after the Hendricks discovery disaster, Marcus walked into the office Monday morning with coffee in hand and no knot in his stomach. He checked his dashboard, saw the week's deadlines clearly displayed, and felt confident rather than anxious.

The transformation hadn't happened overnight. It had required hard work, honest conversations, and systematic changes to how his practice managed delegated work and deadlines.

The first change was implementing a shared task management system. Every matter now had an authoritative record of deadlines, task ownership, and status. Marcus and Amanda could both see who owned what and when it was due. The "I thought you were handling it" problem was impossible because the system showed explicit ownership.

The second change was establishing clear communication protocols for deadline delegation. When Marcus delegated work, he sent a written confirmation with specific details: the task, the final deliverable, the deadline with date and time, review timelines, and ultimate filing dates. Amanda confirmed receipt and flagged any capacity concerns immediately.

The third change was implementing milestone tracking for complex matters. Instead of just tracking the final deadline, they identified interim checkpoints. Research complete by X date. Draft ready for review by Y date. Final version prepared by Z date. These milestones gave visibility into progress and created opportunities to course-correct before final deadlines arrived.

The fourth change was automated alerting. Their system now sent alerts when deadlines approached, when tasks sat too long without progress, and when interim milestones were missed. These alerts caught problems early when fixes were still easy.

The fifth change was weekly deadline review meetings. Every Monday morning, Marcus and Amanda spent fifteen minutes reviewing the week's deadlines, discussing capacity, identifying potential conflicts, and ensuring alignment. These meetings prevented surprises and created shared awareness.

The sixth change was a response protocol for deadline risks. When Amanda identified that she couldn't meet a deadline, she immediately notified Marcus with an explanation and proposed solution. They addressed the issue together rather than letting it silently become a disaster. This proactive communication turned potential failures into manageable challenges.

Most importantly, the culture changed. Deadline reliability became a core value, not just an aspiration. Both Marcus and Amanda treated deadlines as sacred commitments. They built their days around deadline priorities. They communicated early and often about deadline status. They took personal responsibility for deadline performance.

The results were dramatic. In six months, they hadn't missed a single deadline. Client satisfaction increased because deliverables arrived on time and clients felt well-informed. Marcus's stress level plummeted because he had confidence in the system. Amanda felt more trusted and empowered because she had clear ownership and the tools to succeed.

The financial impact was significant too. Marcus reclaimed hours previously spent in crisis management when deadlines were missed or nearly missed. He focused that time on higher-value work: complex case strategy, client development, and practice growth. His effective rate increased, his revenue grew, and his profitability improved.

But the most meaningful change was personal. Marcus took his first real vacation in five years. He flew to Hawaii with his wife for their anniversary. He left his laptop at home. He checked his phone once per day for true emergencies. The practice ran smoothly without him because the deadline management systems worked, Amanda had the tools and authority to handle anything that arose, and the culture of accountability ensured nothing fell through the cracks.

On the beach in Maui, watching the sunset with his wife, Marcus reflected on the journey. The Hendricks discovery disaster had been painful, embarrassing, and expensive. But it had been the catalyst for transformation. It had forced him to confront the reality that delegation without deadline systems was just organized chaos.

He'd learned that effective delegation required more than just assigning work to capable people. It required clear deadline setting, explicit communication, systematic tracking, appropriate technology, and a culture that valued accountability. It required viewing deadline management not as administrative overhead but as core infrastructure for a successful practice.

He'd learned that deadlines delegated without clear systems were deadlines waiting to fail. But deadlines managed with good systems and good culture became reliable, sustainable, and stress-free.

Most of all, he'd learned that the investment in deadline management systems paid dividends far beyond just meeting deadlines. It enabled true delegation. It created team confidence. It improved client service. It reduced stress. It made growth possible. It transformed a practice from chaos to calm.

As the sun dipped below the Hawaiian horizon, Marcus smiled. His phone stayed in his pocket. His mind stayed present with his wife. His practice ran smoothly thousands of miles away. The systems were working. The deadlines were being met. The delegation was successful.

For the first time in years, Marcus was truly on vacation. And it felt extraordinary.

Action Items for This Chapter

1. Implement Your Deadline Tracking Foundation

Choose one action that will have the biggest immediate impact on your deadline management: implement a shared task management system, create deadline communication templates, or set up automated deadline alerts. Focus on getting one thing working well before adding complexity.

Action selected: _____

Completion deadline: _____

2. Conduct a Deadline Failure Analysis

Select one deadline that was missed or nearly missed recently. Identify the root cause: Was it unrealistic timing? Poor communication? Lack of tracking? Missing milestones? Fix that specific failure point with a concrete systemic change.

Deadline reviewed: _____

Root cause: _____

Fix implemented: _____

3. Protect Your Highest-Risk Deadline

Identify the one deadline in the next 30 days that would cause the most damage if missed. Apply everything from this chapter to protect it: clear communication, interim milestones, automated tracking, and escalation protocols.

Highest-risk deadline: _____

Due date: _____

Protection measures: _____

Before Moving to Chapter 10:

Deadline management is the most visible and consequential aspect of delegation. When deadlines are met consistently, delegation works. When they're missed, everything falls apart. The systems and practices in this chapter transform deadline management from a source of stress into a reliable strength.

You now understand how to set realistic deadlines, communicate them clearly, create interim milestones, track progress without micromanaging, respond to deadline failures, leverage technology effectively, and build a culture of accountability.

The next chapter addresses what happens when delegation goes wrong—how to identify failures, diagnose root causes, course-correct effectively, and know when to pull work back versus push through problems.

Even the best delegation systems experience failures. Chapter 10 ensures you're prepared to handle them skillfully when they occur.

One final commitment before moving forward:

Identify the one highest-risk deadline in your practice right now—the one that would cause the most damage if missed. Apply everything from this chapter to that specific deadline: clear communication, interim milestones, automated tracking, escalation protocols, and accountability mechanisms.

Protect that deadline as if your practice depends on it. Because it might.

Highest-risk deadline: _____

Due date: _____

Systems applied: _____

Confidence level (1-10): _____

CHAPTER 8:

When Delegation Fails

Nicole discovered the problem at 4:47 PM on a Friday.

Her associate, Brian, had been handling a suppression motion for one of their DUI clients. It was a critical motion—if successful, the breathalyzer results would be excluded and the case would likely be dismissed. If unsuccessful, their client faced significant consequences including jail time and license suspension.

Brian had assured Nicole the motion was solid. He'd been working on it for two weeks. She'd checked in twice and both times he'd reported good progress. The motion was due to be filed Monday morning, and Brian had told her it would be ready for her final review Friday afternoon.

At 4:47 PM, Brian walked into her office with a draft motion. Nicole began reading. By the second page, her stomach dropped. The legal research was superficial. The argument was weak. The case citations were barely relevant to their specific facts. The writing was mediocre at best.

This wasn't a motion that needed minor revisions. This was a motion that needed to be completely rewritten from scratch. And they had one weekend to do it.

Nicole felt the familiar surge of frustration and regret that comes with delegation failure. Why had she trusted Brian with this? Why hadn't she reviewed it sooner? Should she have known this would happen? Was this her fault or his?

She had two immediate problems. First, she needed a viable motion filed by Monday morning. Second, she needed to understand why this delegation had failed so spectacularly and ensure it never happened again.

The weekend Nicole spent rewriting that motion was exhausting. But the conversation she had with Brian the following Monday morning was even harder. Because she had to confront an uncomfortable truth: this delegation failure wasn't just about Brian's performance. It was also about her delegation approach, her supervision, and her systems.

Every attorney who delegates work will experience delegation failures. The question isn't whether it will happen, but how you'll respond when it does. This chapter shows you how to identify delegation failures early, diagnose their root causes, decide whether to course-correct or pull work back, learn from failures, and build resilience into your delegation systems.

Recognizing the Warning Signs

Delegation failures rarely happen without warning. Most disasters signal their arrival through subtle warning signs that, if recognized early, allow intervention before catastrophe strikes. The key is knowing what to look for and taking those signals seriously rather than explaining them away.

The first warning sign is communication breakdown. When someone who normally provides regular updates suddenly goes quiet, that's a red flag. When responses to your check-in questions become vague or evasive, alarm bells should ring. When someone stops asking questions on a complex matter they should have questions about, something's wrong.

Nicole had this warning sign with Brian. His check-in responses were brief and positive but lacked specifics. When she asked "How's the motion coming?" he responded "Good progress, right on track." That should have prompted a follow-up: "Great, walk me through your argument structure." But she accepted the vague reassurance and moved on.

The second warning sign is missed interim deadlines or milestones. If you've set up checkpoint deliverables and someone misses the first one, that's predictive of missing the final deadline too. The research memo that was due Wednesday but arrives Friday afternoon signals trouble. The first draft that keeps getting pushed back indicates problems ahead.

The third warning sign is scope creep or confusion. When someone asks questions that suggest they misunderstand the scope of work, or when they start pursuing tangents that aren't relevant to the core task, delegation is off track. If your paralegal starts asking about issues well beyond the assigned motion, they might be confused about what they're actually supposed to deliver.

The fourth warning sign is lack of initiative or problem-solving. When someone brings you every small obstacle without attempting to solve it themselves, or when they wait for your direction on routine decisions they should handle independently, the delegation isn't working. Delegation requires the recipient to take ownership. If that's not happening, the delegation has failed even if the work eventually gets completed.

The fifth warning sign is quality inconsistency. If someone's work quality suddenly drops on a particular project compared to their normal standard, investigate immediately. It might signal that they're overwhelmed, confused about expectations, dealing with personal issues, or working beyond their competence level.

Whatever the cause, the quality drop is a warning that delegation is at risk.

The sixth warning sign is defensive behavior when you ask about progress. If simple status questions trigger defensive responses, justifications, or excuses, you're likely heading toward a failure. Someone confident in their progress answers straightforwardly. Someone who knows they're behind but doesn't want to admit it becomes defensive.

The seventh warning sign is isolation. When someone stops collaborating with others on the team, stops participating in meetings normally, or seems to be working in a silo on the delegated project, warning lights should flash. Isolation often means they're struggling but unwilling to ask for help.

The eighth warning sign is last-minute intensity. If someone shows no visible stress or urgency about a project until the final hours before deadline, then suddenly works frantically, they've likely procrastinated. This pattern suggests poor time management, avoidance behavior, or lack of understanding about the project's complexity.

Nicole had several of these warnings with Brian. His communication became vague. He missed the informal milestone of having research complete by the end of week one. He worked in isolation rather than discussing his approach with the team. And he showed no urgency about the project until the very last day.

The critical skill is recognizing these warning signs and taking action rather than hoping they resolve themselves. When you see these signals, investigate immediately. Don't wait for the scheduled check-in. Don't assume things will improve. Probe deeper, ask specific questions, request work samples, and assess whether the delegation is on track or headed for failure.

Many delegation failures could be prevented if the warning signs were heeded early. A conversation on Tuesday when communication becomes vague can prevent a disaster on Friday when the work is due. An intervention when the first milestone is missed can salvage a project that would otherwise fail completely.

Trust your instincts. If something feels off about a delegated project, it probably is. Experienced attorneys develop a sixth sense for trouble. When that sense tingles, investigate. Better to discover that your concern was unwarranted than to discover too late that it was justified.

Diagnosing the Root Cause

When delegation fails, the immediate instinct is often to blame the person who failed to deliver. But that's frequently wrong or at least incomplete. Delegation failures usually have multiple contributing causes, and fixing the problem requires understanding all of them.

Nicole's initial reaction to Brian's terrible motion was anger at Brian. He'd let her down. He'd failed to deliver competent work. He'd put their client at risk. All of that was true. But as she reflected more deeply, she recognized her own contributions to the failure.

Root cause analysis for delegation failures typically reveals issues in one or more of these categories: competence, capacity, clarity, support, or systems.

Competence issues mean the person lacked the skills or knowledge to do the work. Brian had handled motions before, but never a suppression motion with this level of complexity. Nicole had assumed his general motion practice skills would transfer. They didn't. The specialized knowledge required for Fourth Amendment suppression arguments was beyond his current capability. This was a competence gap.

When competence is the issue, you've delegated work to someone who wasn't ready for it. This might be because you overestimated their abilities, because you didn't properly assess the work's difficulty, or because you were desperate and delegated to whoever was available. Whatever the reason, the solution is different than if other factors caused the failure.

Capacity issues mean the person had the skills but not the time or bandwidth. Someone capable of excellent work will produce mediocre work when they're overwhelmed with too many competing demands. You might delegate a task that would take someone eight focused hours to complete well, but if they can only spare three rushed hours because of other obligations, the work will suffer.

Nicole learned that Brian had been juggling five other active matters during the two weeks he worked on the suppression motion. Each of those matters had their own deadlines and demands. He simply didn't have the capacity to give the motion the time it required. That wasn't entirely his fault—it was a resource allocation problem.

Clarity issues mean the person didn't understand what was expected. Vague instructions, unclear standards, or ambiguous deliverable descriptions lead to delegation failures. If you ask someone to "handle the discovery" without specifying exactly what that means, you'll likely be disappointed with the result. They might think you meant draft initial interrogatories. You might have meant comprehensive discovery plan with document requests, interrogatories, and deposition strategy.

Brian had some clarity issues too. Nicole had told him to "draft a motion to suppress the breath test." She hadn't specified the standard she expected, the depth of research required, or the argument structure she had in mind. Brian drafted what he thought was adequate. Nicole expected something much more thorough. The gap between expectation and delivery stemmed partly from lack of clarity.

Support issues mean the person needed resources, guidance, or collaboration they didn't receive. Maybe they needed access to a particular database for research. Maybe they needed input from an expert. Maybe they needed someone to brainstorm with about strategy. If necessary support is absent, delegation fails even when competence, capacity, and clarity align.

Nicole never asked Brian if he needed help. She assumed he would ask if he did. Brian assumed he should figure it out independently to demonstrate competence. Neither checked their assumptions. If Nicole had offered to spend an hour discussing the legal strategy with Brian, or if she'd connected him with another attorney who had handled similar motions, the outcome might have been different.

System issues mean the processes, tools, or infrastructure weren't adequate for successful delegation. Maybe there's no good way to track project status. Maybe deadline alerts don't work properly. Maybe there's no clear escalation path when problems arise. Maybe the practice doesn't have templates or precedents for the type of work delegated.

Nicole's practice had no template or model for suppression motions. Brian was essentially starting from scratch. If a strong precedent motion had been available, Brian could have followed that structure and focused his energy on applying the law to the specific facts. Without that infrastructure, he had to invent everything.

The diagnostic process requires honest assessment of all these potential causes. Resist the urge to attribute failure solely to individual performance when systemic or leadership issues contributed. Ask yourself:

- Did this person have the competence required for this work at this level?
- Did they have adequate time and capacity given their other obligations?
- Were my instructions and expectations clear and specific?
- Did they have the support, resources, and guidance they needed?
- Are our systems and infrastructure adequate for this type of delegation?

Often you'll find multiple contributing factors. Brian had a competence gap on this specific type of motion. He also had capacity constraints from too many competing matters. Nicole's instructions lacked the specificity needed. Support wasn't offered or requested. And the practice lacked the infrastructure of templates and precedents.

Diagnosing all these contributing causes is essential because each requires a different solution. If you attribute a competence problem to laziness, you might respond with discipline when training is what's needed. If you attribute a capacity problem to inability when it's actually workload, you might pull work from a capable person who just needs bandwidth.

The diagnosis should be collaborative when possible. Talk to the person who failed to deliver. Ask them what happened from their perspective. Ask what obstacles they encountered. Ask what would have helped. Their input might reveal causes you didn't recognize.

Nicole's conversation with Brian revealed his anxiety about asking for help on a complex matter. He didn't want to appear incompetent, so he struggled alone rather than seeking guidance. That's a cultural issue Nicole needed to address—her practice didn't feel safe enough for people to acknowledge when they were in over their heads.

Proper diagnosis transforms delegation failures from simple performance problems into learning opportunities that strengthen your entire delegation approach. Each failure reveals something about your systems, your leadership, your team's capabilities, or your practice's infrastructure. Learn those lessons and you'll prevent similar failures in the future.

The Pull-Back Decision: When to Reclaim Work

When delegation is clearly failing, you face a critical decision: pull the work back and handle it yourself, or push through the challenges and course-correct while keeping the work delegated. This decision has immediate and long-term implications that extend far beyond the specific task.

Nicole made the pull-back decision immediately when she saw Brian's motion. She took it back, worked through the weekend, and rewrote it herself. The motion got filed on time and was ultimately successful. But pulling the work back had costs beyond her weekend.

The case for pulling work back is straightforward. When quality or deadlines are at serious risk, when client interests are threatened, or when the person delegated to is clearly incapable of completing the work adequately, pulling it back is the responsible choice. Your professional obligations to clients supersede your delegation goals.

Certain situations demand pulling work back. When a critical deadline is imminent and the work is nowhere near acceptable, you don't have time to coach someone through completion. When the work quality could lead to malpractice exposure, client harm, or bar discipline, the risk is too high to continue delegating. When someone is so far out of their depth that success is impossible regardless of support, pulling back is necessary.

The cost of not pulling back in these situations is potentially catastrophic. A missed statute of limitations because you kept work delegated to someone who couldn't complete it is indefensible. A terrible brief filed in a client's case because you were committed to delegation at all costs is malpractice. When client interests are at stake, pull the work back.

But pulling work back also has costs. It signals to the person you pulled it from that you don't trust them. It reinforces their own doubts about their abilities. It creates a pattern where difficult work always flows back to you, preventing your team from developing capability on challenging matters. It burns your time on work that should have been delegated. And it reinforces the very bottleneck problems you're trying to solve through delegation.

The case for pushing through and course-correcting is about long-term capability building. Sometimes keeping work delegated, providing intensive support to get it across the finish line, develops skills and confidence that benefit the practice for years to come. The short-term pain of heavy involvement produces long-term gain of team capability.

When the deadline allows time for coaching and revision, when the person has foundational competence and just needs guidance, when the quality issues are fixable with direction, and when the learning value is high, pushing through often makes sense. You invest more time in the immediate situation but build capability that makes future delegation easier.

The decision framework requires assessing several factors:

Time availability. How much time remains before the absolute deadline? If you have a week, course-correction might work. If you have a day, pulling back is probably necessary.

Gap size. How far is the current work from acceptable? If it needs minor revisions and polishing, push through. If it needs complete reconceptualization, pull back.

Learning value. How much capability will be built if you push through? If this is a one-time unusual task, the learning value is low. If this is a task type you'll need to delegate repeatedly, the learning value is high.

Person's capacity to improve. Can this person actually get the work to acceptable quality with guidance, or are they fundamentally incapable? Honest assessment of their ability to improve with support is crucial.

Risk tolerance. What are the consequences if pushing through fails? If the consequences are serious (client harm, malpractice risk, major financial loss), err toward pulling back. If the consequences are manageable, you can take more risk by pushing through.

Pattern recognition. Is this a one-time delegation failure or part of a pattern? A single failure from a normally reliable person might warrant pushing through. A pattern of failures suggests pulling back and addressing larger performance issues.

Nicole faced this decision framework with Brian. Time availability was minimal—she had a weekend. The gap was enormous—the motion needed complete rewriting. The learning value was moderate—they had suppression motions occasionally but not frequently. Brian's capacity to improve in the available time was low—learning to write excellent suppression motions takes longer than a weekend. The risk was high—client freedom was at stake. And while this was Brian's first major failure, there had been smaller quality concerns previously.

Given those factors, pulling back was the right call. But Nicole made a plan for the future. Next time they had a suppression motion with adequate lead time, she would assign it to Brian with intensive scaffolding: a detailed outline of argument structure, regular check-ins, provision of model motions, and early draft review. She'd build his capability deliberately rather than through sink-or-swim delegation.

Sometimes the best decision is a hybrid approach. Pull back the parts of work that are most critical or most problematic, but leave other components delegated. Nicole might have pulled back the legal argument section that required sophisticated analysis, but left Brian to complete the statement of facts and procedural history. This limits immediate risk while preserving some learning opportunity.

Whatever you decide, communicate it clearly. If you pull work back, explain why: "This motion is too critical to our client and the deadline is too tight for me to feel comfortable with the current draft. I'm going to rewrite it myself. This isn't a reflection of your overall capabilities, but this specific situation requires my direct involvement."

If you decide to push through with intensive support, explain that too: "This motion isn't where it needs to be, but we have time and I believe you can get it there with guidance. We're going to work together closely this week to improve it. This is a learning opportunity for you on complex suppression motions."

The pull-back decision is never easy. It requires balancing immediate client interests against long-term team development, weighing risks against learning opportunities, and assessing time constraints against capability gaps. But making that decision consciously and strategically, rather than reactively, leads to better outcomes both immediately and over time.

Course-Correcting Failed Delegation

When you decide to push through rather than pull back, course-correction must be swift, specific, and systematic. The goal is to salvage the current project while building capability for future work.

Course-correction starts with honest feedback. The person needs to understand clearly that the current work is inadequate and why. Vague criticism like "this isn't quite there yet" doesn't help. Specific feedback does: "This motion lacks the depth of Fourth Amendment analysis the court will expect. The cases you cite are relevant but not the strongest authority available. Your fact-to-law connection needs to be more explicit."

After delivering feedback, shift immediately to problem-solving mode. Don't dwell on the failure. Focus on the path forward. "Here's what we need to do to get this motion where it needs to be" is more productive than extended discussion of why it's currently inadequate.

Create a detailed remediation plan with specific steps. For Brian's motion, that might look like: "Today you'll complete additional research focusing specifically on the checkpoint stop cases I'm sending you. Tomorrow morning we'll meet to discuss how those cases apply to our facts. Tomorrow afternoon you'll rewrite the legal analysis section incorporating that research. Wednesday morning I'll review the revised section and provide feedback. Wednesday afternoon you'll finalize it."

This level of detailed planning removes ambiguity and creates clear accountability. Each step has a concrete deliverable and deadline. Progress is visible. The path to completion is mapped.

Provide resources and support generously during course-correction. Share model documents. Direct them to specific resources. Spend time discussing strategy. Course-correction requires more of your time than successful initial delegation would have, but it's still less than doing all the work yourself.

Increase check-in frequency dramatically. Daily or even multiple times daily check-ins might be appropriate during intensive course-correction. These aren't about micromanaging; they're about ensuring the course-correction is working and catching new problems immediately.

Consider reducing the scope if necessary. If you realize the original delegated task was too ambitious given time and capability constraints, narrow it. Perhaps Brian writes the facts section and procedural history while you handle the complex legal analysis. Partial delegation that succeeds is better than complete delegation that fails.

Involve others if helpful. Maybe another attorney can provide a different perspective. Maybe a paralegal can help with research. Maybe you can find an external resource like a motion bank or consultation with a specialist. Solving the immediate problem matters more than maintaining the original delegation structure.

Document what's being learned through the course-correction process. "Here's how to structure Fourth Amendment suppression arguments" becomes a resource for future similar work. The intensive work required to salvage one failed delegation can create infrastructure that prevents future failures.

Set explicit quality standards. Don't assume the person knows what "excellent" looks like. Show them. "Here's an example of the depth of analysis I expect" or "This case citation is strong because it's factually similar, recent, and from our jurisdiction" teaches standards while addressing the immediate problem.

Build confidence where possible. Course-correction is inherently deflating. Where you can, acknowledge what's working: "Your factual summary is actually quite strong. The problem is only in the legal analysis section. Let's focus our energy there."

Monitor your own frustration. Course-correcting failed delegation is time-consuming and stressful. But taking that frustration out on the person you're trying to help is counterproductive. They already know they failed. What they need now is supportive guidance to succeed.

Create accountability for improvement. "We're investing significant time in getting this motion right. I expect that next time you handle a similar motion, you'll apply what you're learning here and produce higher quality initial work." This frames the course-correction as a learning investment with future payoff expectations.

Be realistic about outcome probability. Sometimes despite best course-correction efforts, the work doesn't get to acceptable quality in the available time. Have a backup plan. Be prepared to pull the work back even after attempting course-correction if it's not working. Knowing when to cut your losses is part of effective delegation management.

After successful course-correction, debrief thoroughly. What went wrong initially? What would have prevented the problem? What systems or support would help avoid similar issues? This debriefing transforms a near-failure into a practice improvement opportunity.

Nicole's course-correction approach with Brian evolved over subsequent months. The next suppression motion had a three-week timeline. She gave Brian extensive scaffolding: a detailed outline, weekly meetings to discuss progress, early review of the research memo, mid-point review of a rough draft, and time for substantive revision before final review.

Brian's motion still needed revisions, but it was fundamentally sound. The course-correction investment from the first failure paid off. By the third suppression motion, Brian needed only moderate oversight. By the fifth, he was producing work that required minimal revision.

That's the power of effective course-correction. Short-term pain yields long-term capability. The key is committing to the process, providing the support needed, and maintaining standards while building skills.

Learning from Delegation Failures

Every delegation failure contains lessons. The question is whether you'll learn them or repeat the same mistakes indefinitely. Systematic learning from failures transforms delegation disasters into practice improvements.

Start by creating a written record of significant delegation failures. Document what was delegated, to whom, what went wrong, what contributed to the failure, how it was addressed, and what you learned. This written record serves multiple purposes. It creates accountability for actually learning and changing. It provides data over time about patterns. And it creates institutional memory so lessons aren't lost.

Nicole created a simple delegation failure log. Each entry included: Date, Project Description, Person Involved, What Went Wrong, Contributing Factors, Immediate Response, Changes Made, and

Future Prevention Strategy. After a year, she had eight entries. Reviewing them revealed patterns she hadn't noticed in the moment.

Three of the eight failures involved unclear expectations. Nicole learned she needed to be more specific in her initial delegation conversations, confirm understanding more thoroughly, and document expectations in writing. That pattern recognition led to creating delegation templates with built-in expectation clarification.

Two of the eight failures involved capacity issues—people had too many competing demands to complete delegated work well. This led Nicole to implement a workload tracking system so she could see total commitments before delegating additional work. It also led to conversations about saying no when truly at capacity.

Pattern recognition across multiple failures reveals systemic issues one failure alone might not show. If every failure involves a particular type of work, maybe you need better systems or training for that work type. If every failure involves a particular person, maybe you have a performance or fit issue to address. If failures cluster around certain times (end of quarter, trial season), maybe you have seasonal capacity problems to solve.

Distinguish between unique failures and recurring ones. A truly unusual situation that creates a one-time delegation failure might not warrant systemic changes. But if you see the same failure mode repeatedly, systemic change is essential. Nicole's clarity issue appeared in three different failures—that's a clear pattern requiring systematic solution, not just individual course-correction.

Share lessons learned with your team when appropriate. If a delegation failure revealed a gap in your processes, tell your team what you learned and what you're changing. This transparency builds trust and creates collective learning. "We've struggled with delegation on complex research projects. I've realized I need to be more specific about the depth and scope I expect. Going forward, I'll provide more detailed guidance upfront" models accountability and continuous improvement.

Create preventive systems based on failure lessons. Each lesson learned should lead to a concrete change that prevents similar failures. If unclear expectations caused problems, create expectation clarification checklists. If capacity issues recurred, implement workload tracking. If certain skill gaps appeared repeatedly, develop training. Transform lessons into systems.

Some lessons are about your own delegation practices. Nicole learned she had a tendency to delegate and then go hands-off too quickly on complex matters. She now builds in structured check-ins early in delegation timelines, especially on challenging work. That's a personal practice change driven by failure lessons.

Other lessons are about team capabilities and development needs. Nicole learned that none of her associates had strong suppression motion skills because the practice hadn't deliberately taught them. She created a motion practice training series and started having associates observe her in suppression hearings. That's a capability development response to identified gaps.

Still other lessons are about systems and infrastructure. Nicole's failure log showed that delegated work without clear interim milestones failed more often than work with defined checkpoints. She implemented milestone planning for all significant delegated projects. That's a systematic infrastructure change.

Celebrate when failure lessons lead to improvements. When Nicole's new expectation clarification process prevented a delegation failure that would have happened under the old approach, she acknowledged it with the team. "Six months ago, this project would have gone off track. But because we learned from past problems and created better upfront clarity, it's going well. That's progress."

Review your failure lessons periodically. Every quarter, Nicole reviewed her delegation failure log looking for new patterns, assessing whether implemented changes were working, and identifying any emerging issues. This regular review kept lessons fresh and ensured changes were actually preventing problems.

Don't just learn from your own failures. Learn from near-misses too. When something almost went wrong but was caught just in time, treat that as a learning opportunity. Ask what made it a near-miss instead of an actual failure, and whether you can systematize whatever saved it.

Learn from others' delegation failures when possible. Conversations with other law firm owners about their delegation challenges can reveal problems you haven't encountered yet and solutions you can implement proactively. Professional networks, mastermind groups, or peer learning communities offer vicarious learning opportunities.

The ultimate test of whether you're learning from delegation failures is whether they decrease over time. If you experience the same types of failures year after year, you're not learning effectively. If failures become less frequent and less severe as your systems improve and you apply lessons learned, you're doing it right.

Nicole's delegation failure rate dropped dramatically over two years. Year one, she had eight significant failures. Year two, she had three. Year three, just one. And that one failure was a novel situation—a type of work she'd never delegated before, not a repeat of past mistakes. That progression demonstrated real learning and systemic improvement.

Delegation failures are inevitable. Stagnation after failures is optional. Choose learning over repetition, systemization over blame, and improvement over defensiveness. Every failure is tuition paid in the school of delegation mastery. Make sure you're getting the education you're paying for.

Building Resilience Into Your Delegation Approach

The goal isn't to eliminate delegation failures entirely—that's impossible. The goal is to build resilience so failures are caught early, addressed effectively, and cause minimal harm. Resilient delegation systems can absorb failures without catastrophic consequences.

Resilience starts with redundancy on critical matters. For work that's truly high-stakes, don't rely on a single person. Have a second set of eyes review it. Build in multiple check-points. Create backup coverage. Yes, this reduces efficiency. But for work where failure could be devastating, resilience matters more than efficiency.

Nicole implemented a rule: any motion or filing with major consequences for a client must be reviewed by a second attorney before filing. This catches errors before they become problems. It's redundant by design, but that redundancy is resilience.

Build buffer time into critical deadlines. If a court filing is due Friday, set your internal deadline for Wednesday. This buffer creates time to catch problems, make corrections, or even redo work completely if necessary. Tight deadlines maximize efficiency but minimize resilience. Buffer time is insurance against failure.

Create escalation paths that encourage early problem surfacing. When team members know they can raise concerns without punishment, problems get flagged while they're still fixable. When people hide struggles to avoid looking bad, problems fester until they're disasters. Psychological safety is a resilience mechanism.

Nicole explicitly told her team: "If you're struggling with delegated work, I want to know immediately. There's no shame in saying 'this is harder than I expected' or 'I need help.' What's not okay is hiding struggles until deadlines are missed. Early warning gives us options. Late discovery gives us only damage control."

Implement staged review for complex work. Instead of one final review right before deadline, build in early rough draft review, mid-point substantial review, and final polishing review. Each stage catches different types of problems at different points when they're easier to fix.

Develop bench strength so you have alternatives when primary delegation fails. If the person you delegated to can't complete the work, who else could step in? Cross-training, skill development across your team, and maintaining awareness of everyone's capabilities gives you options when failures occur.

Create forcing functions that reveal problems early. Required status updates, interim deliverable deadlines, and scheduled check-ins force visibility into delegation progress. Problems that might otherwise hide until the last minute get exposed early when intervention is still possible.

Build quality criteria into the delegation itself. When you delegate work, specify not just what needs to be done but what "good" looks like. Provide examples of excellent work. Define quality standards explicitly. This helps the person receiving delegation recognize when they're off track, ideally before you need to tell them.

Maintain some hands-on involvement even when delegating. The best delegators don't disappear entirely. They stay engaged enough to notice warning signs, ask useful questions, and provide guidance when needed. Total abdication isn't effective delegation; it's just abandonment.

Document key knowledge so delegation doesn't depend entirely on tribal knowledge in people's heads. Written procedures, templates, precedents, and decision frameworks make delegation more resilient because the knowledge is accessible even when specific people aren't available.

Create a learning culture where failures are analyzed, not hidden. When delegation failures are treated as learning opportunities rather than shameful secrets, you build organizational knowledge about what works and what doesn't. That collective learning makes the entire practice more resilient.

Build relationships with outside resources you can tap in emergencies. Know which specialists you can consult on short notice. Maintain relationships with contract attorneys who could step in if needed. Have expert databases and research services readily available. These external resources add resilience when internal delegation fails.

Maintain your own skills even as you delegate more work. If you delegate all motion practice but never write motions yourself anymore, you lose the ability to step in when delegation fails. Strategic personal involvement in work you're delegating maintains the skills needed for rescue operations.

Track leading indicators of delegation failure, not just the failures themselves. Monitor stress levels in your team, workload distribution, quality trends, and deadline near-misses. These indicators predict failures before they happen, allowing preventive action.

Plan for absence. If the person handling delegated work becomes unavailable unexpectedly, what happens? Build systems that allow work to be picked up by others. Document where things stand. Create visibility into work status. Resilience means the practice can function even when key people are unavailable.

Accept that some failures will happen despite all precautions. Resilience isn't about preventing every failure. It's about responding well when failures occur, learning from them, and maintaining practice viability even when things go wrong. Perfect delegation is a myth. Resilient delegation is achievable.

Nicole's practice became measurably more resilient over time. Early in her delegation journey, a single failure could create a crisis. Later, with resilience built in, failures were handled smoothly. Problems were caught early. Backup plans existed. Buffer time allowed course-correction. The practice absorbed delegation failures without client harm or attorney panic.

That's the goal: delegation systems robust enough that when failures happen—and they will—they're manageable bumps rather than catastrophic disasters. Build that resilience deliberately and your delegation confidence will grow alongside your practice capabilities.

Nicole's Hard-Won Wisdom

Three years after the Friday afternoon disaster with Brian's motion, Nicole sat in her office reflecting on how much had changed. She'd just reviewed an excellent appellate brief written by Brian. It needed only minor edits. She'd approved it and sent it for filing with complete confidence.

The transformation hadn't been easy. That first delegation failure had been painful, expensive, and embarrassing. Nicole had worked through the weekend to rewrite the motion. She'd lost sleep worrying about whether her client would suffer from her poor delegation judgment. She'd questioned whether she was cut out for leading a practice with other attorneys.

But she'd also learned invaluable lessons that transformed her delegation approach and ultimately her practice.

She learned that delegation failures are feedback, not verdicts. That first failure with Brian taught her about gaps in her delegation process, not Brian's fundamental incompetence. She learned to diagnose contributing causes instead of just blaming individuals. She discovered that most failures had multiple causes, many of which were within her control to fix.

She learned the importance of scaffolding, especially when delegating complex or unfamiliar work. Instead of throwing people into the deep end, she now built careful progressions. Brian's next suppression motion came with extensive support. The one after that needed less. Eventually he could handle them independently. But that independence was earned through supported practice, not demanded immediately.

She learned that clear expectations prevent most quality failures. Her delegation conversations became much more specific. She confirmed understanding explicitly. She documented expectations in writing. She provided examples of what excellent work looked like. These practices virtually eliminated the "I thought you wanted something different" failures.

She learned that capacity management is as important as capability development. Even highly skilled people produce poor work when they're overwhelmed. Nicole became much more thoughtful about workload distribution. She implemented systems to track total commitments before delegating additional work. She gave people permission to say when they truly couldn't take on more.

She learned that psychological safety enables early problem detection. When Brian felt he couldn't admit he was struggling, the motion failure was inevitable. Nicole worked hard to create a culture where asking for help was valued, not penalized. Problems surfaced earlier. Course-corrections happened while there was still time. Disasters became rare.

She learned that redundancy and buffer time are investments, not waste. The second-attorney review on critical matters caught errors before they harmed clients. The buffer time between internal deadlines and court deadlines allowed for fixes when delegation didn't go perfectly. These "inefficiencies" actually protected the practice and its clients.

She learned to distinguish between one-time failures and patterns. A single delegation failure from a good team member warranted course-correction and learning. A pattern of failures warranted different intervention—performance management, role reassessment, or potentially separation. She learned to respond appropriately to each.

She learned that her own growth as a delegator mattered as much as her team's growth in receiving delegation. She had to become better at setting expectations, providing support, tracking progress, giving feedback, and building systems. Effective delegation required as much skill development from her as it did from her team.

She learned that failure documentation creates institutional memory. Her delegation failure log became one of her most valuable practice management tools. Reviewing it quarterly revealed patterns she would have missed otherwise. It informed training priorities, system improvements, and hiring decisions.

She learned that resilience matters more than perfection. Her goal shifted from preventing all delegation failures to building systems that could absorb failures without catastrophe. Buffer time, redundancy, escalation paths, and backup plans made her practice resilient even when individual delegations failed.

Most importantly, she learned that persistence through failures leads to mastery. Her early delegation attempts were rough. She made mistakes. Work fell through cracks. Quality sometimes suffered. But she kept learning, kept adjusting, and kept delegating. Each failure taught lessons that improved future delegation.

Three years in, Nicole's practice was unrecognizable from where it started. Brian was now handling complex appellate work independently. Her other associates had developed specialized expertise through progressive delegation. Her paralegals operated with high autonomy on matters within their competence. Her firm administrator managed operations without constant oversight.

Nicole's own practice had transformed too. She focused almost exclusively on the work only she could do: complex case strategy, key client relationships, major negotiations, and practice development. The routine work, the administrative tasks, the standard motions—all were handled capably by others.

Her revenue had increased substantially, but more importantly, her stress had decreased dramatically. She took real vacations without her laptop. She left the office at reasonable hours. She had time for strategic thinking instead of constant firefighting. She built a practice that served her instead of consuming her.

The transformation started with failures. Each delegation disaster forced learning. Each problem revealed gaps to fill. Each crisis created motivation for systematic improvement. The failures weren't obstacles to success; they were the path to it.

Nicole's advice to other attorneys struggling with delegation was simple: expect failures, learn from them systematically, and build resilience. Delegation isn't a skill you acquire and then execute perfectly. It's a journey of continuous learning where failures are the best teachers.

The Friday afternoon motion disaster with Brian had felt like her worst professional moment. In retrospect, it was one of her best learning opportunities. It forced her to confront her delegation weaknesses and build the systems that ultimately transformed her practice.

She kept the original terrible draft of Brian's motion in a file. Occasionally she'd pull it out and compare it to his recent work. The contrast reminded her how far they'd both come. It reminded her that failure is temporary but learning is permanent.

Delegation mastery isn't about avoiding failures. It's about responding to them skillfully, learning from them systematically, and building practices resilient enough to thrive despite them.

Nicole had learned that lesson through hard experience. And her practice was stronger because of it.

Action Items for This Chapter

1. Create Your Delegation Failure Learning System

Establish a simple log or journal where you'll document significant delegation failures. Include what was delegated, to whom, what went wrong, contributing factors, your response, and lessons learned. Commit to reviewing this quarterly to identify patterns.

Log created: Yes / No

Location: _____

First quarterly review scheduled for: _____

2. Diagnose One Past Delegation Failure Thoroughly

Select a recent delegation failure and analyze it using the five-category framework: competence, capacity, clarity, support, or systems. Identify all contributing causes, not just the obvious one. Implement one concrete change based on your diagnosis.

Failure selected: _____

Contributing causes identified: _____

Change implemented: _____

3. Build One Resilience Mechanism

Choose one way to add resilience to your delegation approach: build buffer time into critical deadlines, implement second-attorney review for high-stakes work, create clearer escalation paths, or develop bench strength through cross-training. Implement it this week.

Resilience mechanism selected: _____

Implementation complete: Yes / No

First test/use: _____

Before Moving to Chapter 11:

Delegation failures are inevitable, but stagnation after failures is optional. The practices in this chapter transform failures from disasters into learning opportunities that strengthen your delegation approach.

You now know how to recognize warning signs early, diagnose root causes accurately, make smart pull-back decisions, course-correct effectively, extract lessons systematically, and build resilience into your systems.

The next chapter shifts focus to one of the most challenging aspects of delegation: the client relationship. How do you maintain the personal touch clients expect while delegating client-facing work to your team? How do you build client confidence in your team? How do you prevent the "I want to speak to the attorney" problem from undermining delegation?

Chapter 11 provides the strategies and language you need to delegate client work successfully while maintaining the relationships that drive your practice.

One reflection before moving forward:

Think about your most painful delegation failure. What would have been different if you'd had the frameworks from this chapter? What will you do differently when the next failure occurs?

Reflection: _____

CHAPTER 9:

The Client Relationship Challenge

The email arrived at 9:23 AM on a Tuesday. Karen, a successful estate planning attorney, read it with a sinking feeling.

"Dear Karen, I've been working with your paralegal Jessica on updating my estate plan, and while she seems nice, I really need to speak with you directly about some decisions. I hired you, not your assistant. When can we schedule a call? Best, Margaret."

Margaret was a good client. Sophisticated, reasonable, willing to pay appropriate fees. But she'd just articulated the fundamental challenge of delegating client-facing work: clients hire you, not your team. They want your expertise, your judgment, your personal attention. Delegation feels to them like bait and switch.

Karen had carefully delegated much of Margaret's estate plan update to Jessica. Jessica was highly competent, detail-oriented, and excellent with clients. The work was well within her capabilities. But Margaret wanted Karen, and no amount of competent paralegal work would satisfy that expectation.

This wasn't unique to Margaret. Over the past month, three other clients had made similar requests. "I appreciate your team, but I really need to talk to you." "Can we schedule time with you directly?" "I'm sure your associate is capable, but I'd prefer you handle this."

Karen faced a dilemma that every attorney confronts when delegating client work. She needed to leverage her team to grow the practice and serve more clients effectively. But clients expected personal attorney attention and felt disappointed when they got team member attention instead.

If she gave in to every client request for personal attention, delegation failed and she remained the bottleneck. If she insisted on team member handling without client buy-in, client satisfaction suffered and retention decreased. She needed a middle path that preserved client relationships while enabling effective delegation.

This chapter shows you how to navigate the client relationship challenges inherent in delegation. You'll learn how to set expectations that make delegation acceptable to clients, introduce team members in ways that build client confidence, maintain the personal touch while delegating substantial work, handle the "I want to speak to the attorney" objection, and ensure client-facing delegation enhances rather than damages relationships.

Why Clients Resist Delegation

Understanding why clients resist delegation is the first step to overcoming that resistance. Client objections to delegation aren't irrational; they're based on legitimate concerns that deserve acknowledgment and thoughtful response.

The first reason clients resist delegation is the personal relationship they've built with you. They trust you because they know you, have worked with you, and feel confident in your judgment. Your paralegal or associate might be equally competent, but the client doesn't know that yet. The relationship is with you, not with your practice. Delegation asks them to extend trust to someone they don't know based only on your assurance that it's appropriate.

Margaret's resistance to working with Jessica stemmed partly from this relationship factor. Margaret had worked with Karen for five years. They'd developed rapport. Margaret knew Karen's communication style, understood how she thought about estate planning issues, and trusted her judgment completely. Jessica might be equally skilled, but Margaret would need time to develop similar trust.

The second reason is perceived value. Clients pay attorney rates for attorney expertise. When a paralegal handles their work, even if that's appropriate and efficient, clients sometimes feel they're not getting what they paid for. The billing rate logic doesn't matter—emotionally, they want the person they're paying premium rates for to do the work, not delegate it to someone with lower credentials.

This perception is especially strong in legal services because credentials matter so much. A J.D. and bar admission signal expertise in ways a paralegal certificate doesn't, even when the paralegal's skills for a specific task might be superior. Clients conflate credentials with competence and want the most credentialed person handling their matters.

The third reason is control and importance. Clients want to feel their matter is important enough to merit the attorney's personal attention. When work is delegated, some clients interpret it as "my matter isn't important enough for the attorney to handle personally." This isn't about actual quality of service; it's about feeling valued and prioritized.

The fourth reason is concern about quality and accountability. Clients worry that delegated work might not meet the same standards as attorney work. They wonder if the team member has adequate knowledge, whether mistakes might be made, and whether there's proper oversight. These are legitimate concerns about quality control in the delegation process.

The fifth reason is communication preferences. Some clients simply communicate better with attorneys than with other team members. They speak the same professional language. They understand attorney communication style. They worry that working with support staff will involve translation inefficiencies or communication breakdowns.

The sixth reason is past bad experiences. Many clients have had experiences with delegation gone wrong—work delegated to incompetent team members, matters handled by people without adequate knowledge, poor communication from non-attorney staff, or errors made because work was delegated inappropriately. These experiences create understandable skepticism about delegation.

Karen realized that Margaret's resistance likely stemmed from several of these factors. Margaret valued her relationship with Karen specifically. She equated Karen's personal involvement with quality and importance. And she'd mentioned once that a prior attorney had delegated work to an incompetent paralegal who made costly errors.

Understanding these root causes shaped Karen's response. She couldn't just insist that Jessica was competent and expect Margaret to accept it. She needed to address the underlying concerns: relationship building with Jessica, demonstrating value despite delegation, ensuring Margaret felt important, providing quality assurance, facilitating good communication, and acknowledging past bad experiences while distinguishing this situation.

The key insight is that client resistance to delegation is rarely about stubborn unreasonableness. It's about legitimate concerns that deserve respectful attention. When you understand what's driving resistance, you can respond in ways that address root concerns rather than just pushing back against surface objections.

Setting Client Expectations From the Start

The easiest client relationship challenges to solve are the ones you prevent. Setting appropriate expectations from the beginning of the client relationship makes delegation feel normal rather than unexpected.

The intake conversation is your first opportunity to establish delegation expectations. Before the client signs on, explain how your practice works. Describe your team structure. Explain what work you handle personally and what work team members handle. Make delegation part of the value proposition, not a secret to be revealed later.

Karen revised her intake approach based on lessons learned. She now explained: "I lead an experienced team that includes two senior paralegals and an associate attorney. For your estate planning work, I'll personally handle all strategic decisions about your plan structure, meet with you for key planning conversations, and review all final documents. My senior paralegal Jessica will handle document preparation, routine updates, and day-to-day communication. This team approach allows us to be more responsive and thorough than if I tried to do everything myself."

This framing accomplished several things. It described the team as an asset, not a liability. It specified exactly what work Karen would handle personally, giving the client certainty about her involvement. It explained the benefits of the team approach in terms the client cared about—responsiveness and thoroughness. And it set expectations before the client formed assumptions about how the engagement would work.

The engagement letter should reinforce these expectations in writing. Include language about team-based service delivery. Specify which team members may work on the matter and their roles. Explain billing rates for different team members and why the team approach creates value.

Karen's engagement letters now included: "Your matter will be handled by our estate planning team, led by Attorney Karen Mitchell and including Senior Paralegal Jessica Thompson. Karen will personally handle all strategic planning, complex legal issues, and final document review. Jessica will prepare documents, coordinate execution, and serve as your primary point of contact for routine questions and updates. This collaborative approach ensures you receive expert attention at each stage while maintaining efficiency and responsiveness."

The language in engagement letters matters because it creates the framework for the entire relationship. If the letter says "Attorney Karen Mitchell will handle your matter" with no mention of a team, clients reasonably expect that Karen will personally do all the work. If it explains a team approach upfront, delegation aligns with stated expectations.

Introduce team members early and personally. Don't just mention that others will be involved; make personal introductions that build confidence. In the first client meeting, introduce the paralegal or associate who will work on the matter. Explain their background, expertise, and role. Create a personal connection, not just an announcement that others exist.

Karen started bringing Jessica into initial client meetings for ten minutes. She'd introduce Jessica, have Jessica explain her background and experience, and then Jessica would ask a few questions about the client's goals. This personal introduction made Jessica real to the client rather than just a name on an email.

Set specific communication expectations. Explain who the client should contact for different types of issues. Make it clear that the team member is the appropriate first contact for routine matters, with you available for complex issues or upon request. This guidance helps clients know when to expect your personal involvement and when team member involvement is normal.

Karen told clients: "For routine questions about document preparation, timeline updates, or scheduling, reach out to Jessica directly. She's fully equipped to help you and will respond more quickly than I can. For complex planning questions, strategy discussions, or if you ever just want to connect with me directly, contact me anytime. Jessica and I communicate constantly, so we're always aligned on your matter."

Explain the quality control process. Clients worry about quality when work is delegated. Address that concern proactively by explaining how you ensure quality. Describe your review process. Explain how team member work is supervised. Make quality assurance visible.

Karen explained: "All documents Jessica prepares go through my review before you see them. I personally check every detail to ensure accuracy and alignment with your goals. Jessica's work is excellent, and my review adds an additional quality check. You get the benefit of Jessica's meticulous preparation and my oversight."

Build in personal touchpoints throughout the engagement. Even when substantial work is delegated, create moments of personal attorney contact. These touchpoints reassure clients that you're engaged and aware, even if you're not doing all the work yourself.

Karen scheduled three personal touchpoints for estate planning clients: initial strategy session, mid-point check-in after documents are drafted, and final review before execution. These touchpoints were Karen's personal involvement, while Jessica handled the work in between. Clients felt appropriately attended to without requiring Karen's involvement in every detail.

Use language that emphasizes "we" rather than delegation. Instead of "I'm delegating this to Jessica," say "We'll be working on this together, with Jessica handling preparation and me providing oversight and strategic direction." The "we" framing emphasizes collaboration rather than handoff.

The goal of expectation setting is to make the team approach feel like a feature, not a bug. Clients should understand from the beginning that they're getting a team's collective expertise, not just one attorney's time. They should know what work you'll handle personally and what work team members will handle. And they should feel confident that the team approach benefits them through better responsiveness, more attention to detail, and appropriate deployment of expensive attorney time on the work that truly requires it.

When expectations are set well from the start, delegation doesn't feel like a disappointment. It feels like exactly what the client signed up for.

Introducing Team Members to Build Confidence

Even when expectations are set appropriately, clients need to develop confidence in team members. The way you introduce and position team members determines whether clients embrace them or resist working with them.

The introduction should highlight expertise, not apologize for non-attorney status. Don't say "My paralegal will help with this." Say "Jessica, our senior estate planning paralegal with twelve years of experience, will prepare your documents." Lead with competence, credentials, and experience that build confidence.

Karen learned to introduce Jessica with specific expertise signals: "Jessica is our senior paralegal and she's been with the practice for eight years. She's prepared over a thousand estate planning documents and has deep knowledge of both simple and complex planning strategies. Frankly, she knows the technical details of document preparation better than I do. She's also fantastic with clients—patient, detail-oriented, and great at explaining complex issues in clear terms."

This introduction accomplished several things. It established Jessica's extensive experience. It specified her expertise area. It positioned her knowledge as potentially superior to Karen's in certain respects, which is credible and builds confidence. And it highlighted client service skills that matter to clients.

Introduce team members in person when possible, not just via email. Personal introduction creates connection that email cannot. The client sees the team member, hears their voice, observes their professionalism, and begins forming a relationship. Email introductions are functional but don't build the same rapport.

When in-person isn't possible, use video introduction. A brief video call where you introduce the team member, they explain their role and background, and the client can ask questions creates much stronger connection than email alone.

Have team members explain their own experience and approach, not just you vouching for them. When Jessica speaks about her background, experience, and how she works with clients, it's more powerful than Karen describing the same things. Let team members showcase their own competence.

In introduction meetings, Karen would ask Jessica questions that allowed her to demonstrate expertise: "Jessica, could you explain to Margaret how we'll handle the trust funding process?" Jessica's knowledgeable response built confidence more effectively than Karen's assurance that Jessica was competent.

Address the "what work will each of us do" question explicitly. Clients want to understand the division of labor. Walk them through a typical matter and explain who does what at each stage. This transparency removes uncertainty about roles.

Karen would explain: "Here's how we'll work together on your estate plan. First, you and I will meet to discuss your goals, family situation, and planning priorities—that's the strategic foundation. Then Jessica will prepare initial draft documents based on our discussion. I'll review those drafts to ensure they perfectly match your goals. You'll review them with Jessica, who will explain each provision and answer your questions. Any complex legal questions that come up, Jessica will bring me in. We'll make any needed revisions together. Then I'll do a final review before you sign. At the signing, Jessica will walk you through execution, and I'll be available if needed."

This detailed walkthrough showed exactly when the client would interact with each team member and what each person's role was at each stage. It removed mystery and created appropriate expectations.

Use collaborative language that emphasizes the team working together. Instead of positioning team members as substitutes for you, position them as specialists working alongside you. "Jessica and I" rather than "Jessica instead of me."

Share stories of past client successes involving the team member. "Jessica recently worked with a client whose estate plan was similar to yours in complexity. The client specifically mentioned how helpful Jessica's explanations were and how much they appreciated her attention to detail." Third-party validation builds confidence.

Create opportunities for the client to experience the team member's competence directly. After introduction, delegate a small, low-stakes task to the team member where the client will directly experience their capability. Success on that small task builds confidence for larger delegation.

Karen would have Jessica handle a simple initial task after introduction—perhaps gathering information about assets or explaining how certain documents work. Margaret's positive experience with Jessica on this small task built trust for more significant involvement later.

Demonstrate your confidence in team members through your own behavior. If you constantly second-guess their work in front of clients, you undermine their credibility. If you show confidence in their abilities and judgment, clients mirror that confidence.

Karen was careful never to undercut Jessica in client interactions. If a client asked a question Jessica could answer, Karen would let her answer or defer to her: "Jessica, you've handled this exact situation before. Can you explain how we typically approach it?" This deference signaled Karen's trust in Jessica's knowledge.

Acknowledge that developing comfort with team members takes time. Some clients will immediately embrace working with your team. Others need time to develop trust. Acknowledge that reality and give permission for the relationship to develop gradually.

Karen would sometimes say: "I know you hired me specifically and want to work with me. As you get to know Jessica, I think you'll find she's excellent to work with. But I'm always available if you need me. Over time, many clients find they're very comfortable working directly with Jessica for most matters, but there's no pressure. We'll work together in whatever way feels right to you."

This acknowledgment of the client's preference, combined with patience about relationship development and assurance of your continued availability, often helps clients relax and give team members a genuine chance.

Finally, create feedback loops where clients can express any concerns about working with team members. "How has your experience working with Jessica been so far?" asked genuinely and with openness to honest feedback, helps surface and address issues before they become serious problems.

The goal is clients who see your team members as trusted advisors in their own right, not just as intermediaries to you. That level of confidence doesn't come from a single introduction. It comes from thoughtful positioning, demonstrated competence, successful experiences, and time to develop trust.

Training Teams to Maintain Your Client Service Standards

Delegating to capable people isn't enough. They need to represent your practice in a way that maintains your standards and reflects your approach to client service.

Start by defining what "your standard" actually means. Many attorneys have an intuitive sense of good client service but have never articulated what that looks like. Your team can't replicate what you haven't defined.

Document your client service standards:

- Response time expectations (same-day for urgent, 24 hours for routine)
- Tone and manner of communication (professional but warm, empathetic but not overly familiar)
- Information clients should always receive (proactive updates on key developments, explanation of next steps)
- How to handle different emotional states (anxious clients need reassurance, frustrated clients need action plans, grieving clients need patience)

A criminal defense practice might define standards as: "Clients are often scared and sometimes feel judged. We never judge. We explain clearly without legal jargon. We respond to calls within 4 hours. We proactively update clients before court dates."

A personal injury practice might establish: "Clients are often in pain and financially stressed. We acknowledge their hardship. We explain the timeline early so they know what to expect. We return calls same-day. We never promise outcomes we can't guarantee."

An estate planning practice might set: "Clients are trusting us with deeply personal family and financial information. We maintain strict confidentiality. We explain complex concepts in plain English. We're patient with questions. We respect family dynamics without taking sides."

Create frameworks, not rigid scripts. You don't want team members to sound robotic, but you do want consistency in how common situations are handled.

For common client questions, provide language frameworks. Not word-for-word scripts (which sound fake), but approaches and key phrases to include.

For "When will my case settle?" in a personal injury practice:

- Framework: Acknowledge the question, explain the variables, give a realistic range if possible, commit to updates
- Key phrases: "That's the question every client asks, and I understand why..." "Several factors affect timing..." "Based on similar cases..." "I'll keep you updated as we learn more..."

For "What are my chances?" in a criminal defense practice:

- Framework: Explain why we can't guarantee outcomes, discuss strengths and challenges, focus on process and preparation
- Key phrases: "I can't make promises about outcomes..." "Here's what we know in your favor..." "Here are the challenges we'll address..." "I can promise we'll prepare thoroughly and fight hard..."

For "Is this normal?" in an estate planning practice:

- Framework: Validate their concern, explain what's typical, address any legitimate issues, reassure where appropriate
- Key phrases: "That's a common question..." "In estate planning, it's typical to..." "Let me explain why we do it this way..." "I'll make sure the attorney reviews this with you..."

Role-play difficult scenarios in team training. Talking about how to handle upset clients is different from actually doing it. Practice builds confidence and competence.

Create realistic scenarios based on actual situations:

- The client who calls angry that their case isn't moving faster
- The client who's scared after reading something online about their situation
- The client who wants guarantees you can't provide
- The client who's difficult to reach but complains about not being updated

Have team members practice responses. Provide feedback on what worked and what didn't. This builds muscle memory for handling tough conversations.

The Escalation Decision Tree

Teach the escalation decision tree explicitly. Team members need crystal-clear criteria for when to handle something themselves versus when to involve you.

Create a simple framework:

Green light (handle independently):

- Routine questions with established answers
- Scheduling and administrative matters
- Status updates on cases proceeding normally
- Client concerns that can be addressed with information

Yellow light (consult before responding):

- Questions about case strategy or legal advice
- Client concerns about outcomes or timelines
- New developments that might affect the case
- Situations where the client seems particularly upset or the issue is sensitive

Red light (immediate escalation):

- Ethical issues or conflicts

- Potential malpractice situations
- Client threatening to fire you or file a complaint
- Emergency situations affecting the client or case
- Anything involving media or public attention

Monitor and provide feedback on actual client interactions. Training doesn't end after onboarding. Regular feedback on real interactions helps team members improve.

Listen to recorded calls (with appropriate consent). Review email exchanges. Ask clients about their experience with team members. Provide specific, actionable feedback:

"When that client was upset about the delay, you did a great job acknowledging their frustration. Next time, also give them a specific timeline for next steps so they know what to expect."

Celebrate excellent client service. When a team member handles a difficult situation well, acknowledge it publicly. This reinforces your standards and shows others what excellent looks like.

Maintaining Personal Touch While Delegating

The biggest fear in delegating client-facing work is losing the personal connection that drives client relationships. But delegation and personal touch aren't mutually exclusive. You can delegate substantial work while maintaining the relationship equity that matters to clients.

The key is strategic personal involvement—identifying the moments that matter most to clients and preserving your personal involvement in those moments while delegating surrounding work.

Certain interactions carry disproportionate relationship weight. Initial consultations, strategy sessions, difficult conversations, major decisions, and problem resolution are high-impact client interactions. Your personal involvement in these moments preserves the relationship even when routine work is delegated.

Karen identified four high-impact moments in estate planning: initial goal-setting conversation, reviewing the first draft to confirm it matches expectations, addressing any family complexity or difficult decisions, and the final pre-signing review. She personally handled these four touchpoints even when Jessica handled all the work in between.

Clients who experienced Karen's personal involvement at these critical moments felt well-served even though Jessica handled 70% of the total work. The strategic touchpoints created perception of high personal engagement despite extensive delegation.

Routine communications can be delegated; personalized communications should come from you. Status updates, scheduling coordination, and information requests can come from team members. But acknowledgment of milestones, responses to client concerns, or celebration of successes should include your personal touch.

When Margaret's estate plan was completed, the routine "your documents are ready for signing" email came from Jessica. But Karen sent a separate personal note: "Margaret, I've reviewed your completed estate plan and it beautifully accomplishes your goals for your family. I'm confident you'll have peace of mind knowing your affairs are properly arranged. Looking forward to seeing you at the signing."

That personal note took Karen two minutes to write but created relationship value far exceeding the time invested. It showed personal attention and care that delegation alone might not convey.

Create personal contact even when delegating the work. After delegating a matter to an associate, call the client yourself to confirm the associate has everything they need and ask if there are any questions or concerns they want to discuss with you. This call takes five minutes but reinforces your engagement.

Use personal outreach when team members report concerns. If Jessica mentioned that Margaret seemed uncertain about a trust provision, Karen would personally call Margaret to discuss it. This converts a potential weakness of delegation into a relationship strength—the client gets team member attention for routine matters and attorney attention immediately when questions or concerns arise.

Share team member successes with clients in a way that reflects well on you. "Jessica caught an important detail in your asset list that we need to address" positions you as the leader of a sharp team, not as someone who's checked out. You get credit for building and leading a team that serves clients well.

Maintain visibility through check-ins even when delegating execution. "I know Jessica is handling the day-to-day work on your matter, but I wanted to check in personally to make sure everything is going smoothly and you're getting what you need." This check-in reassures the client while respecting the delegation to Jessica.

Personalize your involvement based on client preferences. Some clients are happy with efficient team-based service. Others want more personal attorney contact. Flexibility in adapting your involvement level to individual client preferences maintains satisfaction across different client types.

Karen learned that some clients thrived with heavy delegation to Jessica and minimal attorney contact. Others needed more of Karen's personal involvement to feel comfortable. She adjusted her approach based on individual client preferences rather than applying a rigid formula to everyone.

Use technology to scale personal touch. Personalized video messages, voice memos, or short personal emails don't require much time but create strong perception of personal attention. A 90-second video message from you explaining a complex issue feels highly personal even though it's more efficient than a phone call.

Create exclusive value in your personal interactions. When you do engage with clients personally, bring insights, expertise, or perspective that team members can't provide. Make it clear why your personal involvement adds value beyond what capable team members deliver.

When Karen met with Margaret for strategy sessions, she brought sophisticated planning insights, creative solutions to complex family situations, and nuanced judgment about trade-offs between different approaches. Margaret left those meetings appreciating why Karen's personal involvement mattered, even though Jessica could handle the technical execution.

Remember that relationship maintenance happens in small moments, not just big ones. A personal response to a client email, a quick call to check on them during a difficult time, or remembering and asking about something important in their life builds relationship equity that makes delegation more acceptable.

The goal isn't constant personal attention, which isn't scalable. The goal is strategic personal attention at moments that matter, combined with excellent team-based service for everything else. When clients feel personally cared for even while much of the work is delegated, you've achieved the right balance.

Handling "I Want to Speak to the Attorney"

Despite your best efforts at expectation-setting and team building, you'll still hear "I want to speak to the attorney." How you respond to this request determines whether it derails delegation or becomes an opportunity to strengthen both the client relationship and team dynamics.

The first principle is never dismissing or minimizing the request. "My paralegal can handle this" or "This doesn't require an attorney" might be factually accurate but feels dismissive to clients. They've expressed a preference. Honor it, even if you ultimately provide context that shapes how it's fulfilled.

When Margaret emailed requesting to speak with Karen directly, Karen didn't respond "Jessica is fully capable of helping you with this" even though that was true. Instead she responded "Absolutely, I'm happy to talk with you. I'll call you this afternoon. In the meantime, I want to make sure we're addressing your specific concerns. What questions or issues would you like to discuss?"

This response did several things. It immediately honored the request, showing respect for Margaret's preference. It created a specific plan rather than a vague promise. And it gathered information about what was driving the request, which helped Karen prepare and potentially address some concerns before the call.

Understanding what's driving the "I want the attorney" request is crucial. Sometimes it's about a specific complex issue that genuinely requires attorney involvement. Sometimes it's about relationship preferences—the client simply communicates better with you. Sometimes it's about control or importance. Each driver requires a different response.

On the call with Margaret, Karen discovered the issue was actually complex—Margaret had questions about tax implications that were beyond Jessica's scope. This was a legitimate need for attorney involvement. Karen addressed the tax questions, then explained: "These tax issues are exactly the kind of thing I should handle personally. Jessica knows to flag these for me, and I'm glad you raised them. For questions like this, I'm always your right contact. For document details, timeline, or execution logistics, Jessica is actually more knowledgeable than I am because she focuses on that daily."

This response validated Margaret's instinct to reach out to Karen while also reinforcing that Jessica was the right contact for other issues. It educated about appropriate division of labor without making Margaret feel wrong for wanting attorney contact.

Sometimes the request is driven by lack of confidence in the team member. The client might have had a communication breakdown, received a confusing answer, or simply not connected well with the team member. In these cases, address the underlying issue rather than just providing your attention.

If Margaret had said "Jessica's answers just confused me more," Karen's response would be different: "I'm sorry Jessica's explanation wasn't clear. Let's make sure you get answers that make sense. I'll walk through this with you now. And let's also figure out how Jessica can communicate with you more effectively going forward. She's excellent at what she does, but everyone has different communication styles."

This addresses the immediate need while also working to improve the team member relationship rather than bypassing it.

The Warm Handoff Technique

Use "I want the attorney" requests as opportunities to strengthen team member credibility. After addressing the client's concern personally, you can often create opportunities for team members to demonstrate capability on related issues.

After discussing tax implications with Margaret, Karen might say: "Now that we've resolved the tax questions, Jessica will prepare revised documents reflecting our discussion. She'll walk you through exactly how the changes address the tax issues we discussed. If any new tax questions come up, bring me back in. But Jessica is excellent at explaining how the documents implement planning decisions."

This gives Jessica an opportunity to demonstrate her competence in explaining documents, potentially building Margaret's confidence for future delegation.

The warm handoff technique is particularly powerful for building trust:

Instead of: "My paralegal can help you with that" (which feels like a brush-off).

Try: "Let me connect you with Maria right now. She's our case manager and knows your file inside and out. She'll have the information you need and can help you immediately. I'll stay on the line to introduce you."

Then: "Maria, this is John Smith calling about his settlement timeline. I know you've been working on his case and can give him a complete update. John, Maria has all the details and can answer your questions. I'll let you two talk. John, if you need me for anything after talking with Maria, just let her know and I'll call you back."

This shows the client you're not abandoning them—you're connecting them with someone competent who can help them faster.

Sometimes clients need permission to work with team members. The "I want the attorney" request might really mean "I'm not sure if the paralegal is adequate for this." Giving explicit permission helps: "This is exactly the kind of thing Jessica handles regularly, and she's genuinely better at it than I am because she does it every day. You're in great hands with her. But I'm always here if you need me or prefer to work with me directly."

Create a path back to the team member after addressing the client's request. "I'm glad we had this conversation. Going forward, Jessica can handle updates on this issue—she and I will be aligned. But anytime something comes up that you want to discuss with me, just let me know."

This satisfies the immediate request while creating expectations that routine future contact on the issue can go through the team member.

Be honest about efficiency and responsiveness trade-offs when appropriate. Some clients are highly responsive to understanding the practical implications of their preferences: "I'm always happy to speak with you personally. I do want you to know that Jessica typically responds within an hour or two, while I might take a day to respond because of court schedule and other demands. For time-sensitive questions, Jessica will actually get you answers faster. But it's completely up to you—whatever works better for you is fine with me."

This gives clients information to make informed choices without pressuring them. Many clients, when they understand the responsiveness difference, become comfortable with team member contact.

Train your team on how to respond when clients request attorney involvement. Team members should never be defensive or take it personally. They should facilitate the connection: "Absolutely, I'll have Karen call you today. In the meantime, can you tell me what specific questions you have so I can give her context?"

Jessica learned to handle Margaret's attorney requests smoothly, providing Karen with background on the client's questions so Karen could prepare. This made attorney responses more effective and also sometimes revealed that Jessica could actually address the issue if she understood it better.

Track patterns in "I want the attorney" requests. If many clients ask for you specifically, that might indicate team members need additional training, your expectation-setting needs improvement, or your client base has legitimately higher needs for attorney involvement. If only certain clients make this request, you can adjust your approach with those specific clients.

Karen noticed that sophisticated business owner clients tended to request her involvement more frequently than individual clients with straightforward estates. This pattern led her to adjust her approach with business owners, providing more direct attorney involvement upfront because that's what the client segment valued.

Remember that some delegation isn't worth the relationship cost. If a particular client really wants your personal involvement and resists delegation despite your best efforts, it might be more valuable to provide that involvement than to insist on delegation. High-value clients or complex relationships might warrant less delegation than your standard approach.

Karen had one ultra-high-net-worth client who simply wouldn't work with anyone but her. Rather than fight it, she accepted it and billed accordingly. That one client's fees justified the personal attention even though it was inefficient by her normal delegation standards.

The goal isn't to eliminate "I want the attorney" requests. The goal is to respond to them in ways that address client needs, maintain relationships, strengthen team member credibility where possible, and educate clients about when attorney involvement is most valuable. Handle these requests skillfully and they become opportunities rather than obstacles.

Making Delegation Enhance Client Service

The ultimate goal is making delegation a client service enhancement rather than a necessary evil. When done well, team-based service delivers better outcomes than solo attorney service. Making that reality visible to clients transforms delegation from something they tolerate to something they value.

The first way delegation enhances service is through responsiveness. A well-trained paralegal or associate who responds within hours is more valuable to clients than an attorney who takes days to respond. Make this advantage explicit to clients.

Karen started framing it this way: "Jessica checks email constantly throughout the day and typically responds within an hour or two.

My court schedule and client meetings mean my responses often take longer. By working with Jessica on routine matters, you'll get faster answers and quicker turnaround. That's better service for you."

Framed as a service advantage rather than an accommodation to attorney workload, delegation becomes attractive. Clients prefer quick responses to credentialed responses when the quality is equivalent.

The second way delegation enhances service is through specialized expertise. Team members who focus on specific tasks often develop deeper knowledge in those areas than attorneys who split attention across many different tasks. Highlight this specialization.

"Jessica prepares trust documents every day. She knows every technical requirement, every potential issue, and every detail that matters. My practice is broader—estate planning, probate, business succession. In the specific area of trust document preparation, Jessica's focused expertise means fewer errors and more attention to detail than if I prepared everything myself."

This honest acknowledgment of specialized expertise builds team member credibility while also explaining why delegation serves clients better.

The third way delegation enhances service is through thoroughness. Team members with more bandwidth can spend more time on matters than overwhelmed attorneys can. That additional time often produces better work product.

"If I personally handled every aspect of your estate plan, I'd be rushing because I have twenty other clients competing for attention. With Jessica handling document preparation, she can give your documents the meticulous attention they deserve. She'll catch details I might miss when I'm juggling too much. That thoroughness protects you."

The fourth way delegation enhances service is through continuity. Team members who aren't in court, at trials, or juggling emergencies provide more consistent availability and follow-through. Emphasize this reliability.

"Jessica is always available to answer questions or address concerns. I'm sometimes in court all day or handling urgent matters. By working with Jessica for routine issues, you have a reliable contact who's always accessible. For complex issues or major decisions, you get me. You're getting the best of both—consistent daily support from Jessica and specialized attorney attention when it matters most."

The fifth way delegation enhances service is through multiple perspectives. When both an attorney and team member work on a matter, different perspectives catch different issues. Position this as quality enhancement.

"Jessica prepares the documents and I review them. This two-person approach means four eyes on everything, with different types of expertise. Jessica catches technical details and execution issues. I catch strategic and legal concerns. You benefit from both perspectives, which produces better results than either of us working alone."

The sixth way delegation enhances service is through appropriate cost management. Clients appreciate getting value for fees paid. Delegation allows attorney time to focus on high-value work while team members handle routine work at lower rates.

"By having Jessica handle document preparation at her rate and me focusing on strategy and complex legal issues at my rate, we're managing your costs effectively. You're paying for attorney expertise where it matters and paralegal support where that's sufficient. This approach keeps your total fees lower than if I personally handled everything."

This transparent discussion of cost efficiency positions delegation as client-focused rather than practice-focused.

Create feedback loops that demonstrate service quality from delegation. Ask clients specifically about their experience working with team members. When feedback is positive, it reinforces that delegation is working.

Karen would ask: "How has your experience working with Jessica been? Is she giving you the service and support you need?" When Margaret responded positively, as she usually did, it reinforced that delegation was serving her well.

When feedback identifies issues, address them immediately. If a client reports that a team member was slow to respond, unresponsive to concerns, or failed to meet commitments, fix it quickly. Your responsiveness to service quality concerns demonstrates that delegation doesn't mean reduced attention to client satisfaction.

Share client success stories that feature team members. "Last month Jessica worked with a client on a complex trust that required coordination with their accountant and financial advisor. The client specifically complimented how well Jessica managed all the moving pieces. She's excellent at this type of coordination."

These success stories build confidence that other clients will receive the same quality service through delegation.

Build team member expertise visibly over time. As team members develop specialized knowledge, let clients benefit from and recognize that expertise. "Jessica just completed advanced training in special needs trusts. If you ever have clients or family members who need that type of planning, she's now one of the most knowledgeable people in the state on that topic."

This visible expertise development shows clients that your team is continuously improving and that they benefit from those improvements.

Make team member contributions visible even when you're heavily involved. After handling a complex client matter personally, acknowledge team member contributions: "Jessica did excellent research that informed my strategy on this. Her thorough analysis of the case law made our approach much stronger."

This attribution builds team member credibility while also demonstrating your leadership in orchestrating team resources for client benefit.

Create premium service offerings that leverage delegation. Some clients might pay premium fees for even more responsive, thorough service that's only possible through effective team leverage. Position this as an advantage: "Our premium service includes a dedicated paralegal who manages every detail of your matter, with my oversight on all strategy and complex issues. You get white-glove service through this team approach."

The goal is clients who see your team as an asset that enhances their service rather than a substitute for your personal attention. When clients recognize that delegation makes their service better—faster, more thorough, more specialized, more cost-effective—resistance fades and appreciation grows.

Practice Area-Specific Delegation Approaches

Different practice areas have different client relationship dynamics that affect delegation strategies. Here's how to tailor your approach:

Criminal Defense (Flat Fee)

Clients are often scared, stigmatized, and intensely focused on outcomes. They want reassurance from the person they believe controls their fate.

Delegation approach: You handle all court appearances, plea discussions, and substantive legal strategy conversations. Team handles routine scheduling, discovery updates, procedural explanations, and coordination with court and prosecution.

Key to success: Frame team involvement as "making sure nothing is missed while I focus on your defense." Emphasize that team coordination allows you to be better prepared for the moments that matter.

Client communication: "I'll be in court with you every time. I'll make all the decisions about how we defend your case. Jason handles the coordination and logistics so I can focus entirely on your defense strategy and court advocacy."

Personal Injury (Contingency)

Clients are often injured, in pain, financially stressed, and focused on compensation. They want to know their case is being worked and their settlement will be maximized.

Delegation approach: You handle case evaluation, major settlement negotiations, depositions, and trial work. Team handles medical record collection, lien resolution, demand letter drafting, routine settlement communications, and client updates.

Key to success: Emphasize that team efficiency speeds up their recovery and increases settlement value. Show how team handling of administrative work allows you to focus on maximizing their outcome.

Client communication: "My personal focus is on getting you the maximum settlement. Maria handles all the medical record collection, billing issues, and coordination so nothing slows down your case. When it's time to negotiate your settlement, I'll personally handle every dollar of it."

Estate Planning (Hourly)

Clients are often uncomfortable discussing mortality and family issues. They want thoughtful guidance on complex, personal matters. They're often fee-conscious and want value.

Delegation approach: You handle sophisticated planning strategy, complex family dynamics, tax planning, and major client discussions. Team handles document preparation, routine drafting, administrative coordination, and procedural explanations.

Key to success: Emphasize that team handling of document preparation keeps costs down while ensuring you spend your time (and their money) on the planning strategy that matters.

Client communication: "I'll personally design your estate plan based on your goals and family situation. Sarah will prepare all the documents following my design. This approach keeps your costs down because Sarah's time is less expensive than mine, while ensuring you get my expertise where it counts—on the strategy and planning."

Family Law

Clients are often emotional, dealing with major life transitions, and need both legal and emotional support. They're focused on outcomes that affect their children, finances, and future.

Delegation approach: You handle court appearances, negotiations, substantive legal strategy, and sensitive client counseling. Team handles discovery coordination, financial affidavit preparation, routine procedural work, and logistical coordination.

Key to success: Acknowledge the emotional difficulty while providing stable, responsive support through team members. Position team as providing the immediate responsiveness clients need during a difficult time.

Client communication: "I'll handle all court appearances and negotiations regarding your children and finances. My team will coordinate the day-to-day details and be available whenever you need immediate support. You'll get both my expertise on what matters most and responsive daily support from our team."

Corporate/Transactional

Clients are often business-savvy, focused on deals moving forward, and expecting sophisticated service. They value responsiveness and expertise.

Delegation approach: You handle deal structure, negotiations, complex drafting, and strategic advice. Team handles due diligence coordination, document management, routine contract review, and transaction logistics.

Key to success: Emphasize how team efficiency speeds deals and reduces costs. Business clients understand teams and often expect them—your job is ensuring quality and coordination.

Client communication: "I'll personally handle the deal structure and negotiation strategy. Our transaction team will coordinate all due diligence and documentation to keep things moving quickly. This approach gets your deal done faster and more cost-effectively."

Communication Protocols for Client-Facing Delegation

Clear protocols prevent confusion about who handles what and ensure nothing falls through the cracks.

Define clear ownership of client relationships. For every case, someone should be the primary contact. Usually this is a team member, with you as the strategic lead.

Make this explicit to the client: "Sarah is your primary contact. She'll handle all your day-to-day needs and questions. I'll be directly involved in [specific activities]. If you reach out to me directly on routine matters, I'll connect you with Sarah because she can help you faster."

Create communication workflows that route issues appropriately. When clients contact you directly, have a system for ensuring the right person responds.

Simple workflow:

- Client emails or calls you
- You assess if it requires your personal response or can be handled by team
- If team-appropriate, you forward to team member with context: "Maria, please handle. Client wants settlement timeline update"
- Team member responds to client and copies you
- You're informed but not doing the work

This takes you 30 seconds instead of 15 minutes, and the client gets a faster, more complete response.

Use technology to enable team access and responsiveness. Team members can't handle client communication if they don't have access to information.

Ensure team members can:

- Access complete case files and communications
- See your calendar to know when you're available for escalations
- View case management systems to track deadlines and developments

- Send communications from firm email addresses that clients recognize

Establish documentation standards for team-client interactions. When team members interact with clients, those interactions should be documented so you stay informed without being involved.

Simple documentation:

- Brief note in the case file after each client interaction
- Email summary to you on significant conversations
- Flag system for issues that need your attention
- Regular (weekly or biweekly) summary of all client communications on each case

This keeps you informed and allows you to spot issues without being the one handling every interaction.

Create escalation protocols that work smoothly. When something does need to be escalated to you, the process should be seamless for the client.

Protocol:

1. Team member identifies issue needing escalation
2. Team member tells client "I'll discuss this with the attorney and one of us will get back to you by [specific time]"
3. Team member brings issue to you with their assessment and recommendation
4. You decide how to handle
5. Either you respond to client or you brief team member to respond with your guidance

From the client's perspective, they got a commitment for a response and it was delivered. They don't feel bounced around—they feel well-served by a coordinated team.

Karen's Client Relationship Breakthrough

Six months after Margaret's email requesting to speak with Karen directly, the relationship dynamics had completely transformed. Margaret now contacted Jessica for most issues and specifically complimented the team-based approach when referring a friend to the practice.

The transformation didn't happen instantly. It required deliberate effort, strategic changes, and commitment to making delegation enhance rather than compromise client relationships.

Karen's first change was revising how she set expectations with new clients. Every initial consultation now included explicit discussion of the team approach, who handled what types of work, and how the collaborative approach benefited clients. New clients understood and accepted the team model from the beginning, eliminating surprise later.

Her second change was improving how she introduced Jessica and positioned her expertise. Instead of "my paralegal will help," Karen emphasized Jessica's specialized knowledge, extensive experience, and client service excellence. These confident introductions built client trust in Jessica from the first interaction.

Her third change was identifying the high-impact moments where her personal involvement mattered most and ensuring she showed up for those moments. The initial strategy session, mid-point review, and final planning conversation always involved Karen personally. Clients felt appropriately attended to even though routine work was delegated.

Her fourth change was creating feedback loops with clients about their experience working with Jessica. These conversations surfaced any concerns early and also often revealed positive experiences that reinforced the value of delegation.

Her fifth change was responding to "I want the attorney" requests with respect and curiosity. Instead of resistance, she honored requests while understanding what drove them. Often she could address underlying concerns while also strengthening Jessica's relationship with the client.

Her sixth change was making delegation advantages explicit rather than assumed. She actively educated clients about how team-based service delivered better responsiveness, more specialized expertise, and greater thoroughness than solo attorney service.

The results were compelling. Client satisfaction scores increased. Referrals grew. And perhaps most telling, clients who initially resisted working with Jessica specifically requested her involvement on subsequent matters. They'd experienced the advantages of the team approach and valued it.

Margaret became one of Karen's best advocates for the team approach. When referring her friend to the practice, she specifically mentioned: "Karen is excellent, but honestly, the whole team is fantastic. Jessica, her paralegal, knows everything about estate planning and responds immediately to any question. You get Karen's expertise on strategy and complex issues, plus Jessica's meticulous attention to detail on everything else. It's the best of both worlds."

That referral conversation captured exactly what Karen had been trying to build—clients who valued the team approach as a service enhancement rather than tolerating it as an accommodation.

Karen's practice transformed as a result. She served more clients without working longer hours. Her team members developed expertise and took on greater responsibility. Client satisfaction improved because responsiveness increased and thoroughness improved. And Karen focused her energy on the strategic work where her expertise created the most value.

The financial impact was significant too. By delegating routine work to Jessica at paralegal rates while focusing her own time on complex matters and client development, Karen's effective rate increased substantially. She billed fewer hours personally but generated more revenue because she deployed her time more strategically.

But the most meaningful change was the reduction in stress and the increase in professional satisfaction. Karen no longer felt torn between client service and business growth. The team approach allowed her to excel at both. She maintained strong client relationships while building a scalable practice.

She learned that client relationship challenges in delegation aren't obstacles to overcome through force; they're opportunities to build something better. When you set clear expectations, introduce team members effectively, maintain strategic personal involvement, respond respectfully to client preferences, and make delegation advantages visible, clients embrace the team approach.

The key insight was that clients don't inherently resist delegation. They resist unclear expectations, diminished service quality, lost personal connection, and feeling less important. Address those legitimate concerns and delegation becomes a relationship strength, not a weakness.

Karen reflected on how far she'd come from that initial email from Margaret. At the time, she'd felt defensive and uncertain. Should she accommodate Margaret's request for personal attention? Should she insist that Jessica was capable? Should she question whether delegation was worth the relationship risk?

Now she knew the answer was none of those. The right response was to honor client preferences while building confidence in team members, to provide strategic personal involvement while delegating effectively, and to make the team approach so valuable that clients appreciated rather than resisted it.

The client relationship challenge in delegation is real. But it's solvable. With the right approach, delegation doesn't damage client relationships—it enhances them by delivering better service than any solo attorney can provide.

Action Items for This Chapter

1. Revise Your Client Expectation-Setting Process

Update your intake conversation and engagement letter to clearly explain your team approach, specify what work you handle personally versus what team members handle, and frame delegation as a service advantage. Implement this with your next three new clients.

Updates made to: ☐ Intake script ☐ Engagement letter ☐ Team introduction process

Implementation deadline: _____

2. Create Strategic Personal Touchpoints

Identify the 3-5 high-impact moments in your typical client matter where your personal involvement matters most. Commit to personal involvement at those moments while confidently delegating surrounding work. Map this out for your most common matter type.

Matter type: _____

Personal touchpoint moments:

1. _____
2. _____
3. _____
4. _____
5. _____

3. Strengthen One Team Member Introduction

Select one team member who handles client-facing work. Revise how you introduce them to emphasize expertise, experience, and client service excellence. Practice the introduction and use it with the next five client interactions.

Team member: _____

New introduction language: _____

First use date: _____

4. Document Your Client Service Standards

Define the 5-7 most important standards for how your team should interact with clients. Make this a written reference for your team.

Our client service standards:

1. _____
2. _____
3. _____
4. _____
5. _____

5. Create Your Escalation Decision Tree

Build a simple green light/yellow light/red light framework showing your team when to handle issues independently vs. when to involve you. Share this with your team this week.

Green Light (handle independently):

- _____
- _____

Yellow Light (consult before responding):

- _____
- _____

Red Light (immediate escalation):

- _____
- _____

6. Practice the Warm Handoff Technique

This week, when a client contacts you with something a team member can handle, practice the warm handoff technique. Make the introduction personal and stay on briefly to build confidence.

Scheduled for: _____

7. Ask Three Current Clients for Feedback

Reach out to three clients and ask: "How has your experience been working with [team member name]?" Use their responses to identify what's working and what needs adjustment.

Client feedback summary:

_____

_____

_____

Before Moving to Chapter 11

You now understand how to manage the client relationship challenges that come with delegation. You know how to set expectations, train your team to maintain your standards, handle client resistance, create systems where clients prefer your team, and adapt your approach to different practice areas.

The next chapter focuses on creating the infrastructure and environment that makes delegation successful. Chapter 11 will show you how to build systems, processes, and tools that enable your team to work independently and effectively—from SOPs to communication protocols to the right technology stack.

Without the right environment, even the best people and clearest expectations will struggle. The next chapter ensures your delegation has the structural support it needs to succeed.

One Action Before Chapter 11

Schedule a 30-minute team meeting to introduce your team-based service approach and get their input on how to implement it effectively. Their buy-in is essential to success.

Team meeting scheduled for: _____

CHAPTER 10:

Decision-Making Frameworks That Empower

Daniel counted the interruptions. By 3:00 PM on Tuesday, his team had asked him to make seventeen decisions. Should they file this motion or wait? Which expert should they hire? How should they respond to opposing counsel's discovery requests? What settlement range should they communicate to the client? Should they schedule the deposition now or after more discovery?

Seventeen decisions. None of them particularly complex. Most within his team's capability to make if they had a framework for decision-making. But they didn't, so every decision flowed to Daniel.

He'd successfully delegated tasks. His associate handled motion practice. His paralegals managed discovery. His office manager oversaw administration. But he hadn't delegated decision-making authority, so the task delegation created a constant stream of "What should I do?" questions that consumed his day.

Daniel had become a decision bottleneck. He'd offloaded the execution of work but retained all the decision-making. His team could do things, but they couldn't decide things. That made delegation only marginally effective.

The breakthrough came when Daniel's business coach asked a simple question: "When your team asks what to do, what percentage of the time do you already know they're going to make the same decision you would if they just thought it through?"

Daniel estimated 80%. His team usually had the information and capability to make good decisions. They just lacked confidence in their judgment and a structured way to think through decisions. So they asked him, and he became the bottleneck.

That conversation led Daniel to implement decision-making frameworks—structured approaches his team could use to make decisions independently while maintaining quality and alignment with practice standards. The impact was immediate and dramatic.

This chapter introduces decision-making frameworks that transform your team from task-executors who need constant direction into empowered decision-makers who solve problems independently. You'll learn when to use each framework, how to implement them effectively, and how to build decision-making confidence across your team.

Why Decision Delegation Matters

Task delegation without decision delegation is incomplete delegation. You can assign someone to handle discovery, but if they have to ask your approval for every decision within that discovery process, you haven't truly delegated the work. You've just created a decision queue that consumes your time and slows everything down.

The cost of decision bottlenecks is substantial. Every decision that flows to you takes time—not just the seconds to make the decision, but the interruption cost, the context-switching, and the delay while the requester waits for your response. Multiply that across dozens of daily decisions and you've spent hours on decisions others could have made.

Decision bottlenecks also slow work velocity. When team members can't proceed without your decision, work stalls. Discovery that should take three days takes a week because multiple points required your decision and you were in trial. Motions that should be filed promptly get delayed because someone was waiting for your go-ahead.

Perhaps most significantly, decision bottlenecks prevent team development. People don't develop decision-making judgment by always asking someone else. They develop it by making decisions, seeing consequences, learning from outcomes, and gradually building confidence. When you retain all decisions, you prevent that development.

Daniel realized his team hadn't developed decision-making capability because he'd never required it. They'd learned to execute tasks competently but always with his direction. They were skilled technicians, not empowered professionals.

The solution isn't telling people "just decide yourself." That creates anxiety, inconsistency, and errors. People need structure for decision-making—frameworks that guide their thinking, align their decisions with practice standards, and build confidence in their judgment.

Decision-making frameworks provide that structure. They're systematic approaches to thinking through decisions that help people reach good conclusions independently. With the right frameworks, your team can make 80% of decisions without involving you while maintaining quality and consistency.

The 1-3-1 Framework: Structured Problem-Solving

The 1-3-1 framework is perhaps the most versatile decision tool for law practices. It requires the person facing a decision to: define one problem clearly, develop three possible solutions, and recommend one course of action with reasoning.

The beauty of 1-3-1 is that it shifts the mental work from you to the person requesting the decision. Instead of "What should I do about X?" they must think through the problem and solutions before involving you. Often in the process of developing three options and selecting one, they realize they don't need your input at all.

Here's how Daniel implemented 1-3-1. He told his team: "Going forward, when you face a decision you want my input on, don't just ask what to do. Instead, bring me the 1-3-1: one clear problem statement, three possible solutions with pros and cons of each, and one recommendation of which solution you think is best and why."

The first week was awkward. People had to learn the framework. Several times someone started with "What should I do about..." and Daniel gently redirected: "Use the 1-3-1 framework. Come back when you've thought through the problem, options, and your recommendation."

But within two weeks, the transformation was obvious. People were coming to Daniel with thoughtful analysis rather than raw problems. Many were making decisions independently after working through the framework and realizing their recommendation was solid. And when they did seek Daniel's input, the conversations were far more efficient because the thinking was already done.

The 1-3-1 framework works because it creates disciplined thinking. Defining one clear problem forces clarity about what actually needs to be decided. Many apparent decision requests are actually unclear thinking. "What should we do about this case?" isn't a decision request; it's fuzzy thinking. "Should we move to dismiss based on statute of limitations or proceed to discovery to gather more facts?" is a clear decision.

Developing three options forces creative problem-solving. It's easy to see two options—the obvious choice and the alternative. Finding a third option requires more creative thinking and often produces the best solution. Three options also demonstrate thoroughness— you've actually thought this through, not just presented the first idea that came to mind.

Recommending one option with reasoning forces commitment and accountability. You can't just lay out options and ask someone else to choose. You have to evaluate the options, weigh the factors, and take a position. This builds decision-making confidence and also gives the final decision-maker insight into your reasoning, which helps them teach you better judgment.

Daniel found that 1-3-1 revealed who had good judgment and who needed development. His associate consistently presented well-reasoned 1-3-1s where Daniel almost always agreed with the recommendation. His junior paralegal's 1-3-1s showed logical thinking but sometimes missed important factors. Those gaps became teaching opportunities.

The framework also created documentation. When decisions were made through 1-3-1 analysis, there was a written record of the problem, options considered, and reasoning. This protected against second-guessing and provided precedent for similar future decisions.

Implementing 1-3-1 requires commitment to the process. You'll be tempted to just answer when someone asks what to do, especially if you know the answer immediately. Resist. Redirect them to the framework. The short-term inefficiency of making them go through the process yields long-term efficiency as they internalize the framework and start using it automatically.

Create templates or forms for 1-3-1 if helpful. A simple structure like:

Problem: [One sentence clearly stating the decision to be made]

Option 1: [Description]

- Pros: [List advantages]
- Cons: [List disadvantages]

Option 2: [Description]

- Pros: [List advantages]
- Cons: [List disadvantages]

Option 3: [Description]

- Pros: [List advantages]
- Cons: [List disadvantages]

Recommendation: [Which option and why]

Reasoning: [Explanation of your recommendation]

This template makes the framework concrete and ensures people include all necessary components.

The 1-3-1 framework is appropriate for decisions with multiple viable options, decisions that benefit from creative problem-solving, decisions where you want to develop team judgment, and decisions where you're genuinely open to their recommendation. It's less appropriate for decisions with clear right/wrong answers, decisions you've already made and just need to communicate, or emergencies requiring immediate action.

The Eisenhower Matrix: Prioritization Decisions

Your team faces constant prioritization decisions. Multiple tasks compete for attention. Multiple deadlines loom. Multiple clients need service. How do they decide what to work on first? Without a framework, they'll either ask you constantly or make poor prioritization choices that create problems.

The Eisenhower Matrix provides a simple prioritization framework. It categorizes tasks based on two factors: urgency (time-sensitive or not) and importance (significant consequences or not). This creates four quadrants:

Quadrant 1: Urgent and Important - Do immediately. Court deadlines, client emergencies, critical problems requiring immediate attention.

Quadrant 2: Important but Not Urgent - Schedule deliberately. Strategic work, planning, relationship building, skill development, prevention activities.

Quadrant 3: Urgent but Not Important - Delegate or minimize. Interruptions, some emails, some meetings, other people's minor emergencies.

Quadrant 4: Not Urgent and Not Important - Eliminate. Busy work, time wasters, activities with no meaningful value.

Daniel taught his team the Eisenhower Matrix and gave them decision authority for their own prioritization using this framework. Instead of asking "What should I work on next?" they learned to categorize their tasks and prioritize accordingly.

The power of the matrix is its simplicity. Anyone can quickly assess whether a task is urgent and whether it's important. Those two assessments determine prioritization without requiring complex analysis.

Daniel's implementation included specific practice definitions for each category:

Urgent and Important in our practice:

- Court deadlines within 48 hours
- Client emergencies (arrest, imminent hearing, crisis situations)
- Critical errors discovered that could harm clients
- Serious practice issues requiring immediate attention

Important but Not Urgent in our practice:

- Case strategy development
- Thorough legal research
- Client relationship building
- Team training and development
- Practice improvement projects
- Prevention activities (conflicts checks, quality reviews, system improvements)

Urgent but Not Important in our practice:

- Most emails (respond within 24 hours, but rarely truly urgent)
- Many phone calls (return promptly but schedule for efficiency)
- Minor administrative tasks with arbitrary deadlines
- Other people's poor planning creating artificial urgency

Not Urgent and Not Important:

- Tangential research that doesn't advance cases
- Excessive meeting attendance
- Low-value administrative busy work
- Social media browsing disguised as marketing

These practice-specific definitions gave team members concrete guidance for categorization. What seemed urgent to someone inexperienced (every email, every call) could be properly categorized using these definitions.

The key decision authority Daniel gave his team was this: "You own your Quadrant 2 and 3 decisions. Schedule important non-urgent work deliberately to ensure it gets done. Minimize urgent but unimportant work—delegate it, batch it, or handle it efficiently. For Quadrant 1 urgent and important items, you have authority to prioritize them immediately and adjust other commitments accordingly. Just keep me informed of any major shifts."

This authority transformed team member confidence in prioritization. They knew they could make these decisions without asking. They understood the framework for making good choices. And Daniel's time was freed from constant "What should I do next?" questions.

The Eisenhower Matrix also helped address the common problem of urgent-but-unimportant work crowding out important-but-not-urgent work. Daniel's team had been spending most of their time in Quadrant 1 (urgent/important) and Quadrant 3 (urgent/not important), leaving no time for Quadrant 2 strategic work.

By making Quadrant 2 a priority and giving team members authority to protect time for important work, Daniel's practice became more proactive and less reactive. Strategic work got done. Prevention activities reduced crises. Planning improved outcomes.

One implementation key is teaching people to question urgency. Many "urgent" items aren't actually urgent—they just feel that way or someone else is treating them as urgent. Daniel taught his team to ask: "What are the actual consequences if this waits until tomorrow? If those consequences are minimal, it's not truly urgent."

Another key is recognizing that importance should trump urgency for most decisions. An important project due next week should often take priority over an unimportant task due tomorrow. The Eisenhower Matrix makes that clear and gives people permission to make that prioritization.

Track your team's prioritization patterns over time. If someone consistently categorizes everything as urgent and important, they either face truly exceptional workload or need help distinguishing urgency from anxiety. If someone's Quadrant 2 time is always zero, they're not making strategic work a priority and need course-correction.

The Eisenhower Matrix works best for ongoing prioritization decisions, workload management decisions, and helping people develop judgment about what matters. It's less useful for one-time decisions or choices between equally important options.

RAPID: Clarifying Decision Roles

Many decision paralysis problems stem from confusion about roles. Who should recommend? Who needs to agree? Who will perform? Who provides input? Who decides? When these roles are unclear, decisions stall or involve the wrong people.

RAPID is an acronym that clarifies decision roles:

Recommend - Who recommends a course of action? **Agree** - Who must agree before the decision proceeds? **Perform** - Who will implement the decision? **Input** - Who should provide input? **Decide** - Who makes the final decision?

Daniel applied RAPID to recurring decision types in his practice. For settlement decisions, he defined:

Recommend: Associate attorney handling the case reviews all factors and recommends settlement range **Agree:** Daniel must agree before any settlement offer is communicated **Perform:** Associate communicates settlement position to opposing counsel or client **Input:** Client provides input on acceptable outcomes; senior partner provides input on firm precedent for similar cases **Decide:** Daniel makes final decision on settlement authority and strategy

This clarity eliminated confusion. The associate knew their role was to develop a thorough recommendation, not just raise the question. Daniel knew his role was to review and approve, not generate the recommendation from scratch. The client knew they'd be consulted, not just informed afterward.

For hiring decisions, Daniel defined different RAPID roles:

Recommend: Office manager screens candidates and recommends finalists **Agree:** Daniel must agree on any offer before it's extended

Perform: Office manager conducts interviews, checks references, makes offer, handles onboarding **Input:** Team members who will work closely with the new hire provide input on fit **Decide:** Daniel makes final hiring decision

For routine administrative decisions like software purchases under $500:

Recommend: Team member who needs the software or identified the issue **Agree:** No agreement required (delegated authority) **Perform:** Office manager processes purchase **Input:** IT support consultant if technical decision **Decide:** Office manager decides based on recommendation

Notice how decision authority shifts based on decision type. Settlement decisions require Daniel's approval. Hiring requires his final decision. But routine software purchases are fully delegated to the office manager.

The power of RAPID is making implicit assumptions explicit. Before RAPID, Daniel's team often wasn't sure who should be involved in decisions. Should they recommend and wait for approval? Should they decide independently? Should they gather extensive input first? RAPID removes that uncertainty.

Implementing RAPID requires documenting decision roles for your most common decision types. Create a RAPID matrix showing different decisions and who fills each role. Share it with your team. Reference it when confusion arises.

RAPID also reveals over-involvement or under-involvement. If the "Agree" list for most decisions includes many people, you've created approval bottlenecks. If the "Input" list is empty for complex decisions, you're missing valuable perspectives.

Daniel discovered he was in the "Agree" role for too many decisions. Routine matters that his team should handle independently still required his approval. He deliberately removed himself from the "Agree" role for an entire category of decisions and moved to "Input" instead—available if consulted, but not required for approval.

The framework also helps with delegation conversations. When delegating a type of decision, walk through RAPID: "For these client communication decisions, I want you to recommend the approach, get agreement from me initially until you build confidence, perform the communication yourself, get input from the client relations manager on sensitive situations, and I'll ultimately decide until you've handled ten of these successfully. Then the 'Decide' role transfers to you."

This clarity about role progression helps people understand the path to greater decision authority. They know what competence they need to demonstrate and when authority will expand.

Use RAPID to diagnose decision dysfunction. When decisions are taking too long, map the RAPID roles. Often you'll find too many people in "Agree," unclear "Decide" authority, or failure to get necessary "Input." Clarifying roles accelerates decisions.

RAPID works best for recurring decision types, complex decisions involving multiple people, and situations where confusion about roles is causing problems. It's overkill for simple one-person decisions and less useful for novel situations where roles haven't been established.

The OODA Loop: Fast Decision-Making Under Uncertainty

Some decisions can't wait for deliberate frameworks like 1-3-1. Crisis situations, rapidly evolving circumstances, or competitive situations require faster decision-making. The OODA Loop provides structure for effective decisions under pressure.

OODA stands for Observe, Orient, Decide, Act—a cycle that repeats continuously as situations evolve.

Observe: Gather current information about the situation. What's happening? What's changed? What new data is available?

Orient: Analyze the information in context of your knowledge, experience, and goals. What does this mean? How does it relate to our objectives? What patterns do I recognize?

Decide: Choose a course of action based on your analysis. What will we do?

Act: Implement the decision quickly. Execute.

Then loop back to Observe—gather information about the results of your action and how the situation has evolved, continuing the cycle.

Daniel taught OODA to his trial team for in-trial decision-making. During trial, situations evolve rapidly. A witness says something unexpected. Opposing counsel makes a surprise motion. The judge signals a concern about your approach. You need to make quick decisions with imperfect information.

His associate learned to use OODA when the prosecution introduced surprise evidence:

Observe: Prosecution just introduced text messages we didn't know existed. Judge allowed them over our objection. Jury is paying close attention.

Orient: These messages are damaging but not devastating. They contradict our client's timeline but don't prove guilt. We have cross-examination opportunity. Our defense strategy needs adjustment but not abandonment.

Decide: I'll cross-examine the witness about message authenticity and context. I'll adjust closing argument to address the messages directly rather than ignore them.

Act: Conduct aggressive cross-examination now. Make notes for closing argument revision.

Then Observe: How did the cross go? How is the jury responding? What's the prosecution doing in response? The loop continues.

The power of OODA is its speed and adaptability. You're not trying to make perfect decisions with complete information. You're making good-enough decisions quickly, then adjusting as new information emerges. This works well in dynamic situations where waiting for certainty means missing opportunities or falling behind.

Daniel gave his team OODA authority for specific situations:

Crisis response: Client arrested unexpectedly, emergency hearing scheduled, immediate action needed. Team members should use OODA to respond quickly, keeping Daniel informed but not waiting for detailed approval.

Opposing counsel surprise moves: Discovery you weren't expecting, scheduling changes, procedural maneuvers. Team should Observe what happened, Orient to our case strategy, Decide on response, Act quickly, then update Daniel.

Trial or hearing adaptation: Unexpected testimony, judge rulings, new information emerging in real-time. Authorized to make tactical adjustments using OODA without breaking for consultation.

The key to successful OODA delegation is trust in team judgment and acceptance of imperfect decisions. OODA decisions won't always be optimal. But they'll be timely, and timeliness often matters more than perfection in fast-moving situations.

Training for OODA effectiveness includes practice scenarios. Daniel would describe a situation: "You're in motion hearing. Judge just indicated she's skeptical of our argument. What's your OODA response?" Team members would walk through: Observe (judge's skepticism, specific concerns she raised), Orient (our argument has merit but we're not connecting with her priorities), Decide (shift emphasis to the case law she seems to favor), Act (adjust oral argument accordingly).

These practice sessions built confidence in using the framework under pressure. Team members internalized the rapid decision cycle and could apply it when real situations arose.

OODA also works for business development decisions. Potential client calls. Do you quote a fee immediately or schedule a consultation? OODA: Observe (client's apparent sophistication, urgency, matter complexity), Orient (our capacity, our expertise in this area, fee expectations for similar work), Decide (either quote range for simple matter or schedule detailed consultation for complex matter), Act (execute the decision), Observe (client's response, whether approach is working).

The limitation of OODA is that it prioritizes speed over thoroughness. Don't use it for decisions that deserve deliberate analysis. Don't use it when stakes are high and you have time for better frameworks. But when circumstances demand quick decisions with imperfect information, OODA provides structure that improves decision quality while maintaining speed.

Building Decision-Making Confidence

Frameworks are tools, but confidence determines whether people will use them. Many team members have the capability for good decisions but lack confidence in their judgment. Building that confidence requires deliberate practice, positive reinforcement, and creating safety for imperfect decisions.

Start with small, low-stakes decisions and gradually increase complexity. Don't begin by delegating major case strategy decisions. Begin with scheduling decisions, routine client communication, vendor selection for minor purchases, or administrative processes. Build success and confidence on simple decisions before progressing to complex ones.

Daniel created a decision progression for his associate:

Month 1-2: Motion hearing scheduling, routine discovery responses, standard client status updates **Month 3-4:** Motion practice on routine issues, deposition scheduling and preparation, client meeting planning **Month 5-6:** Strategy recommendations for standard case types, settlement position development for minor cases, witness preparation plans **Month 7-12:** Complex motion practice, significant settlement negotiations, trial strategy input

This progression built confidence systematically. Each level of decision-making success prepared for the next level of complexity and responsibility.

Provide feedback on decision outcomes, not just decision correctness. Sometimes a reasonable decision produces poor outcomes due to factors beyond the decision-maker's control. Sometimes a questionable decision works out due to luck. Focus feedback on decision process and reasoning, not just results.

When Daniel's paralegal made a vendor selection that seemed reasonable but the vendor underperformed, Daniel's feedback focused on the decision process: "Your evaluation process was sound. You compared pricing, checked references, and assessed fit with our needs. The vendor's poor performance wasn't predictable from available information. The lesson isn't about the specific decision—it's about building in trial periods or guarantees for new vendors to manage risk."

This feedback validated the decision process while extracting learning for future decisions. It built confidence in the paralegal's approach rather than undermining it because of an outcome they couldn't control.

Celebrate good decisions explicitly. When someone makes a decision you would have made or handles something well independently, acknowledge it: "Excellent decision on how to handle that client communication. You read the situation perfectly and responded appropriately. That's exactly the kind of judgment I want you using."

This positive reinforcement accelerates confidence development. People internalize what good decisions look like and trust their ability to make them.

Create safety for wrong decisions. Not every decision will be optimal. Some will be wrong. How you respond to wrong decisions determines whether people will keep making decisions or retreat to constant approval-seeking.

When Daniel's associate made a motion filing decision that turned out poorly, Daniel's response was: "That motion strategy didn't work. Let's analyze why. What information did you have when you made the decision? What would have changed your thinking? What can we learn for similar situations?" This collaborative analysis extracted learning without punishment.

Contrast that with responses that destroy confidence: "Why did you do that? You should have asked me first. This is a mess." Such responses guarantee the person will never make an independent decision again without explicit approval.

Use the "what would you do?" technique even when you've already decided. When you know the answer to a decision, sometimes ask your team member what they would do before revealing your thinking. Their response shows their judgment and creates teaching opportunities.

Daniel would ask: "I've already decided how we're handling this discovery issue, but I want to hear your thinking. What would you do?" The associate would present their analysis. Often it matched Daniel's thinking, which built confidence. When it differed, Daniel could explain his reasoning and develop the associate's judgment.

Document decision outcomes to create organizational learning. When team members make decisions, track outcomes. Decisions that worked become precedent and build confidence: "You successfully handled a similar situation three months ago. Apply the same approach here."

Build decision-making confidence through group discussion of scenarios. "Here's a client situation. What would you each decide and why?" Different perspectives and reasoning reveal multiple valid approaches, showing team members that reasonable people can reach different conclusions and that there isn't always one perfect answer.

Daniel's team meetings included regular decision scenarios. The collaborative discussion built confidence because people saw others wrestling with similar uncertainties, heard various reasoning approaches, and recognized that good judgment involves weighing factors, not achieving perfection.

Create increasing decision authority as confidence grows. Daniel implemented a graduated authority system:

Level 1 - Recommend: Present decision for approval before acting
Level 2 - Inform: Make decision and inform Daniel before acting
Level 3 - Act and Report: Make decision, act, and report afterward **Level 4 - Full Authority:** Make decision, act, report only if requested

Team members progressed through levels based on demonstrated judgment. The progression gave them clarity about their current authority and motivation to demonstrate judgment that would advance them to the next level.

The goal is team members who make decisions confidently within their authority, seek input appropriately when needed, and continuously develop better judgment through practice and feedback. Frameworks provide structure, but confidence provides the courage to use that structure independently.

Maintaining Quality While Delegating Decisions

The biggest fear in delegating decision-making is loss of quality. How do you ensure team members make good decisions without reviewing every decision beforehand? The answer is thoughtful quality systems, not constant oversight.

Define clear decision boundaries. Specify what decisions team members can make independently and what requires consultation or approval. These boundaries should be based on impact, complexity, and team member experience, not arbitrary control.

Daniel's decision boundaries:

Independent authority (no approval needed):

- Scheduling within established case timelines
- Routine discovery responses following templates
- Standard client status communications
- Vendor selection under $500
- Administrative decisions affecting only the specific team member's work

Consultation recommended (seek input but decide):

- Non-routine discovery strategy
- Client communication on sensitive topics
- Deviations from standard case procedures
- Vendor selection $500-$2000
- Decisions affecting other team members' work

Approval required (recommend but don't decide):

- Settlement positions
- Motion practice strategy on complex issues
- Client communication with significant risk
- Expenditures over $2000

- Decisions affecting case outcomes or client relationships significantly

These clear boundaries eliminated confusion. Team members knew exactly what they could decide independently, where they should seek input, and what required approval.

Implement spot-checking rather than pre-approval. Instead of reviewing all decisions before they're made, review a sample after they're made. This maintains quality oversight while allowing decisions to proceed without delay.

Daniel spot-checked 20% of independent decisions. He'd randomly select decisions from the past week and review them. If quality was consistently good, he'd reduce spot-checking frequency. If issues emerged, he'd increase it and provide targeted training.

Create decision templates or checklists for complex decisions. "Before making X decision, consider these factors..." The template ensures consistent thought process without requiring your involvement in each decision.

For settlement decisions, Daniel created a template:

Settlement Decision Checklist: ☐ Client's stated priorities and acceptable outcomes ☐ Strength of liability evidence (scale 1-10) ☐ Strength of damages evidence (scale 1-10) ☐ Risks of trial (best/worst likely outcomes) ☐ Client's risk tolerance ☐ Costs of continued litigation ☐ Comparable settlements in similar cases ☐ Timing considerations (client needs, strategic timing) ☐ Opposing counsel's indicated flexibility ☐ Recommended settlement range with reasoning

Team members using this template made more thorough decisions because the template prompted consideration of all relevant factors.

Build in escalation triggers for concerning decisions. "If the decision involves X, Y, or Z factors, escalate to me even if it's normally within your authority." This creates safety valves without removing decision authority.

Daniel's escalation triggers included:

- Any decision where team member feels uncertain
- Decisions involving angry or upset clients
- Situations with potential malpractice implications
- Matters where opposing counsel is being unreasonable or aggressive
- Cases with unusual circumstances not covered by standard approaches

These triggers caught edge cases while allowing normal decisions to proceed independently.

Review decision patterns, not individual decisions. Look for trends across multiple decisions. Is someone consistently too aggressive? Too conservative? Missing certain factors? Pattern analysis reveals judgment issues that individual decision review might miss.

Daniel's quarterly decision reviews examined patterns: "Your settlement recommendations average 15% lower than what we ultimately achieve. Let's discuss whether you're consistently undervaluing cases or whether I'm pushing too hard." This pattern-based feedback improved future decision-making more effectively than critiquing individual decisions.

Create peer review for significant decisions. Before finalizing a major decision, have another team member review it using the relevant framework. Peer review catches errors while developing judgment in both the decision-maker and the reviewer.

Build decision quality metrics. Track decision outcomes over time. How often do independent decisions need to be reversed? How often do they lead to good outcomes? Metrics reveal whether decision delegation is working and where improvement is needed.

Daniel tracked:

- Percentage of independent decisions that needed revision
- Client satisfaction with team member decisions
- Time saved by decision delegation
- Decision quality ratings from spot checks

These metrics showed decision delegation was working (98% of independent decisions required no revision) and identified specific areas for improvement (client communication decisions needed more development).

The goal isn't perfection in delegated decisions. The goal is good-enough decisions made efficiently, with quality systems that catch and correct the inevitable errors. Perfect decisions that require constant attorney oversight are slower and more expensive than good delegated decisions with appropriate quality checks.

Daniel's Decision Delegation Transformation

Four months after implementing decision frameworks, Daniel's practice had fundamentally changed. The constant stream of "What should I do?" questions had slowed to a trickle. His team was making dozens of decisions daily without his involvement. And decision quality was excellent—maybe better than when Daniel made all decisions himself because team members closer to the details often had better information.

The transformation required systematic effort. Daniel hadn't just announced "Make more decisions yourselves." He'd implemented specific frameworks, defined clear authorities, built team confidence, and created quality systems. Each piece was necessary for the transformation to work.

The 1-3-1 framework became the default for any complex decision requiring input. Team members automatically structured their thinking: problem definition, three options, recommendation with reasoning. Daniel's role shifted from making decisions to reviewing well-developed recommendations and usually approving them.

The Eisenhower Matrix transformed prioritization. Team members managed their own work priorities using the urgent/important framework. Quadrant 2 strategic work got protected time. Quadrant 3 busywork was minimized. Daniel's constant reprioritization of team member work was no longer necessary.

RAPID role clarity eliminated confusion about who should be involved in decisions. Everyone knew whether they should recommend, agree, provide input, perform, or decide. Decisions that had stalled due to role confusion now moved forward smoothly.

OODA equipped the team for fast decisions under pressure. Trial situations, client crises, and time-sensitive opportunities were handled effectively without waiting for Daniel's direction. The team could adapt quickly while keeping him informed.

The impact on Daniel's practice was profound. He reclaimed hours daily that had been consumed by decision-making. Those hours were redeployed to strategic work—complex case strategy, business development, and practice improvement. His effective hourly rate increased dramatically because he focused on the highest-value work.

Team member engagement increased substantially. People who felt empowered to make decisions were more invested in their work. They took ownership of outcomes. They developed expertise more quickly because they were thinking strategically, not just executing tasks.

Client service improved because decisions were faster. Previously, work would stall while waiting for Daniel's decision. Now decisions were made promptly by the people closest to the details. Responsiveness increased, which clients noticed and appreciated.

The financial impact was significant. Daniel could handle a higher volume of cases with the same team size because decision-making was distributed rather than bottlenecked through him. Revenue increased without proportional increase in costs.

But perhaps the most valuable change was Daniel's own stress reduction. The constant cognitive load of making dozens of daily decisions had been exhausting even when individual decisions were easy. That load was now distributed across the team. Daniel felt lighter, more focused, and more energized.

He reflected on how much unnecessary control he'd been holding. Most decisions his team asked about, they were capable of making. They just needed frameworks for thinking through decisions and confidence that their judgment was trusted.

The decision frameworks provided structure without rigidity. They guided thinking without dictating outcomes. They built confidence without eliminating accountability. And they created a practice where decision-making happened at the right level—the people with the best information and closest connection to the work.

Daniel's advice to other attorneys struggling with decision bottlenecks was straightforward: "Implement frameworks, define authorities clearly, build confidence deliberately, and trust your team's judgment. You'll be amazed how many decisions they can make well without you. And the decisions they do need your help with will be better developed and more efficiently resolved because they've already done the thinking using good frameworks."

The transformation from decision bottleneck to empowered team decision-making was one of the most valuable changes Daniel made to his practice. And it all started with structured frameworks that gave his team the tools to think through decisions independently.

Action Items for This Chapter

1. Implement the 1-3-1 Framework This Week

Introduce the 1-3-1 framework (one problem, three options, one recommendation) to your team. For the next week, redirect all decision requests to use this framework. Track how many decisions are made independently after working through the framework.

Framework introduced: Yes / No

Team training date: _____

Decisions resolved independently: _____ out of _____

2. Define Decision Authority Boundaries

Create a three-tier list of decisions for your practice: (1) Team member decides independently, (2) Team member decides after consultation, (3) Requires your approval. Share this with your team so everyone knows their decision authority.

Authority boundaries documented: Yes / No

Shared with team: Yes / No

Implementation date: _____

3. Choose One Additional Framework to Implement

Select either the Eisenhower Matrix (for prioritization), RAPID (for role clarity), or OODA (for fast decisions) based on your practice's biggest decision-making challenge. Teach it to your team and implement it for relevant decisions over the next two weeks.

Framework selected: _____

Why this one: _____

Training completed: Yes / No

First successful use: _____

Before Moving to Chapter 13:

Decision delegation is one of the most powerful leverage points in your practice. When team members can make good decisions independently, your bottleneck effect disappears and your practice can scale without your constant involvement in every choice.

You now have four proven frameworks—1-3-1 for structured problem-solving, Eisenhower Matrix for prioritization, RAPID for role clarity, and OODA for fast decisions under pressure. You understand how to build decision-making confidence, maintain quality while delegating decisions, and create the systems that make empowered decision-making sustainable.

The next chapter addresses one of the most critical and often overlooked aspects of delegation: feedback and accountability. How do you provide feedback that improves performance without crushing confidence? How do you create accountability without micromanaging? How do you address performance issues while maintaining relationships?

Chapter 13 provides the communication skills and accountability systems that make delegation sustainable over the long term.

One commitment before moving forward:

Identify the decision type that creates the biggest bottleneck in your practice right now. Commit to implementing one framework from this chapter for that specific decision type within the next week.

Biggest decision bottleneck: _____

Framework to use: _____

Implementation deadline: _____

CHAPTER 11:

Feedback, Coaching, and Accountability

Rebecca had delegated extensively. Her estate planning practice ran largely through her team—two paralegals and an associate attorney who handled most client work. She'd implemented systems, clarified expectations, and given her team appropriate authority. By most measures, her delegation was working.

But she had a growing problem she didn't know how to address. Her senior paralegal, Maria, had developed a habit of cutting corners. Nothing egregious enough to harm clients, but enough to create inefficiencies and occasional cleanup work. Maria would skip steps in their document review process, assuming things were fine. She'd rush through client communications without the thoroughness Rebecca expected. She'd mark tasks complete before they were truly finished.

Rebecca noticed these issues but said nothing. She'd rationalize: "Maria's been here eight years. She knows what she's doing. Maybe I'm being too picky." Or she'd think: "I don't want to micromanage. Isn't delegation about trusting people?" Or she'd worry: "If I give negative feedback, will Maria get defensive? Will it damage our relationship?"

So Rebecca remained silent while the problems persisted. She'd quietly redo some of Maria's work. She'd work around the corner-cutting. She'd hope the issues would resolve themselves.

They didn't. They got worse. Maria interpreted Rebecca's silence as approval. The corner-cutting became more pronounced. Quality issues multiplied. And Rebecca's resentment grew alongside her reluctance to address it.

Finally, a client complaint forced the issue. The client had received documents with errors that should have been caught in the review process Maria had skipped. Rebecca could no longer avoid the conversation.

The feedback discussion went poorly. Maria was shocked that Rebecca was unhappy—after all, Rebecca had never mentioned concerns before. Maria felt blindsided and defensive. Rebecca was uncomfortable and unclear in her communication. The conversation resolved nothing and damaged their relationship.

Rebecca learned a hard lesson: delegation without feedback and accountability isn't actually delegation. It's abdication. Effective delegation requires ongoing communication about performance, clear expectations about quality, coaching to improve capability, and accountability when standards aren't met.

This chapter shows you how to provide feedback that improves performance, create accountability without micromanaging, coach team members to higher capability, and address performance issues constructively. These skills are essential for sustainable delegation.

The Feedback Avoidance Trap

Most attorneys are terrible at giving feedback. This isn't surprising—law school doesn't teach feedback skills, and attorney training emphasizes criticism and finding flaws rather than constructive development. But avoiding feedback destroys delegation effectiveness.

The reasons attorneys avoid feedback are predictable. Fear of conflict tops the list. Attorneys spend their professional lives in adversarial contexts, so they often view difficult conversations as confrontations to avoid. Giving critical feedback feels like picking a fight with someone you work with daily.

Rebecca's fear of conflict kept her silent for months. Each time she noticed an issue with Maria's work, she'd think: "Is this worth the awkwardness? Can I just fix it myself and move on?" The short-term conflict avoidance felt comfortable but created long-term dysfunction.

The second reason is uncertainty about how to give feedback effectively. What exactly should you say? How critical should you be? How do you balance honesty with kindness? Without a framework, feedback conversations feel risky and unpredictable.

The third reason is fear of damaging relationships. You work closely with your team. You might genuinely like them. The prospect of giving feedback that might hurt their feelings or damage the relationship is uncomfortable. Better to say nothing than risk the relationship, right?

Wrong. Avoiding feedback doesn't preserve relationships; it corrodes them. Resentment builds when you're silently frustrated by someone's performance. Trust erodes when people don't know where they stand. And team members miss opportunities to improve when you withhold information they need.

The fourth reason is the belief that feedback equals micromanagement. "If I'm always giving feedback on how they do things, aren't I just controlling everything? Isn't delegation about letting go?" This confusion between feedback and control prevents necessary communication.

The fifth reason is simple discomfort. Many attorneys are conflict-averse in personal relationships even if they're comfortable in professional adversarial contexts. The intimacy of workplace relationships makes feedback conversations more uncomfortable than courtroom confrontations.

Rebecca struggled with all of these. She feared conflict, didn't know how to structure feedback conversations, worried about damaging her relationship with Maria, believed that frequent feedback contradicted delegation, and was personally uncomfortable with difficult conversations.

But avoiding feedback had clear costs. Maria's performance didn't improve—it declined because silence was interpreted as approval. Quality issues multiplied and eventually reached clients. Rebecca's own workload increased as she compensated for Maria's shortcuts. Her resentment grew to the point where she considered firing Maria rather than having a direct conversation.

The feedback avoidance trap is thinking that silence is neutral. It's not. Silence about performance issues is actually negative feedback—it signals that you don't care about quality, don't notice problems, or don't have the courage to address them. None of those messages serves your practice or your team.

Breaking the feedback avoidance trap requires recognizing that feedback is a gift, not a punishment. When you give someone honest information about their performance, you're giving them the opportunity to improve, succeed, and advance. Withholding that information is actually unkind because it prevents growth.

It also requires understanding that feedback is essential to delegation. You can't delegate work and then ignore how it's being done. Delegation requires ongoing communication about quality, coaching to develop capability, and course-correction when performance drifts from expectations.

Rebecca's breakthrough came when she reframed feedback as a professional responsibility rather than a personal preference. Her job as a practice owner wasn't just delegating work; it was ensuring that delegated work met quality standards and helping team members develop capability. Feedback was how she fulfilled that responsibility.

The Elements of Effective Feedback

Effective feedback follows predictable patterns. Understanding and applying these patterns makes feedback conversations more comfortable and more productive.

Feedback should be timely. Don't wait weeks or months to address an issue. Provide feedback soon after observing the behavior that needs to change. Timely feedback connects clearly to specific situations. Delayed feedback feels abstract and is harder to act on.

Rebecca's mistake was waiting months before addressing Maria's corner-cutting. By the time they finally talked, Rebecca had examples spanning eight months and Maria had no idea there had been concerns. If Rebecca had addressed the first instance immediately— "Maria, I noticed you skipped the final review step on the Johnson documents. What happened?"—the pattern might never have developed.

Feedback should be specific. Vague feedback like "Your work quality needs improvement" provides no actionable guidance. Specific feedback like "The Smith trust had three numerical errors in the distribution provisions, which could have created problems at funding" gives clear information about what needs to change.

When Rebecca finally talked with Maria, she started with vague generalities: "I need you to be more thorough." Maria had no idea what that meant. Only when Rebecca provided specific examples— "Yesterday you marked the Williams file complete before the execution copies were prepared" and "Last week the Henderson documents went to the client without the final proofread"—did Maria understand the actual issues.

Feedback should be behavioral, not personal. Focus on what the person does, not who they are. "You've been rushing through the review process" is behavioral. "You're careless" is personal. Behavioral feedback can be changed. Personal feedback feels like character assassination.

Feedback should be balanced. Pure criticism without acknowledgment of strengths demoralizes people. Pure praise without addressing issues prevents improvement. Effective feedback recognizes what's working while clearly addressing what needs to change.

Rebecca learned to start feedback conversations with genuine acknowledgment: "Maria, you're excellent with clients and your technical knowledge is strong. That's why these quality issues surprised me—they're not consistent with your capability." This acknowledgment made the critical feedback more receivable.

Feedback should include impact explanation. Help people understand why the issue matters. Don't just say what's wrong; explain the consequences. "When documents aren't thoroughly reviewed, we risk sending clients materials with errors, which undermines their confidence in us and creates potential liability issues."

Understanding impact motivates change more effectively than just knowing something is wrong. Maria didn't realize her shortcuts were creating real risks. When Rebecca explained that skipped review steps had resulted in errors reaching clients and created cleanup work for others, Maria understood why the issue was serious.

Feedback should be two-way. Don't just deliver information; invite perspective. Ask questions: "Help me understand why the review step was skipped. Were you unclear about the process? Was there time pressure? What got in the way?" This dialogue often reveals system issues or obstacles you didn't know about.

When Rebecca finally asked about Maria's perspective, she learned that Maria felt overwhelmed by volume and thought the review steps were overkill for simple documents. This explained the behavior and pointed to solutions—either reducing Maria's workload or clarifying which documents genuinely required full review and which could be streamlined.

Feedback should be forward-focused. Don't dwell on past failures; focus on future improvement. After acknowledging an issue and understanding its causes, shift to "Here's what I need going forward" and "How can we ensure this doesn't happen again?"

Rebecca's most effective feedback included clear forward expectations: "Going forward, every document must go through the complete review process before being marked complete. No exceptions. If volume is creating time pressure, we'll discuss workload adjustment. But the quality process is non-negotiable."

Feedback should include support. Don't just identify problems and walk away. Ask what help the person needs to improve. Offer resources, training, or guidance. Make it clear you're invested in their success.

Rebecca asked: "What support do you need to ensure you can complete the full review process? Do you need time management help? Should we clarify which documents require which level of review? Do you need additional training on any aspect of the process?" This positioned Rebecca as a partner in Maria's success, not just a critic of her performance.

Feedback should be documented for significant issues. Verbal feedback is fine for minor course corrections. But significant performance issues should be documented—not for punitive reasons, but to create clear record of expectations, ensure shared understanding, and provide reference for tracking improvement.

After her conversation with Maria, Rebecca sent a follow-up email: "Thanks for our conversation today. To summarize what we discussed: [specific issues], [impact of those issues], [expectations going forward], [support being provided]. I'm confident you'll address these issues. Let's check in two weeks from now to assess progress."

This documentation ensured Maria knew exactly what was expected, created accountability for improvement, and protected Rebecca if the issues persisted and required stronger action.

Creating Accountability Without Micromanagement

Accountability and micromanagement are not the same thing, but many attorneys conflate them. Micromanagement is controlling how work is done. Accountability is ensuring work meets agreed standards. You can have strong accountability without micromanaging.

Accountability starts with clear expectations. People can't be accountable to undefined standards. If you haven't clearly communicated what quality looks like, what deadlines apply, and what process should be followed, you can't hold people accountable for failing to meet those expectations.

Rebecca realized she'd never clearly communicated her review process expectations. She assumed Maria knew the standards because Maria had been there for years. But assumptions aren't communication. Once Rebecca explicitly stated: "Every document must go through these five review steps before client delivery. This applies to all documents, regardless of complexity or time pressure," accountability became possible.

Clear expectations require specificity. "High-quality work" is too vague. "Documents with no substantive errors, consistent formatting, complete legal citations, and thorough review using our five-step process" is specific enough to create accountability.

The second element of accountability is measurement. You can't hold people accountable for what you don't measure. Identify the key indicators of success for delegated work and track them systematically.

Rebecca implemented simple tracking: completion rate of the full review process, error rate in client deliverables, client feedback on document quality, and timeline adherence. These metrics made performance visible and created objective accountability.

Measurement doesn't mean constant oversight. It means having systems that show you whether expectations are being met without requiring you to check every detail. Dashboard metrics, spot-check sampling, and periodic review are measurement approaches that create accountability without micromanagement.

The third element is regular check-ins. Scheduled accountability conversations—weekly, biweekly, or monthly depending on the situation—create structured opportunities to discuss performance without constant interruption.

Rebecca implemented biweekly check-ins with Maria focused on quality metrics and process adherence. These structured conversations replaced the previous pattern of either silence or crisis-driven discussions. Maria knew when feedback conversations would happen, could prepare for them, and received consistent information about her performance.

The fourth element is consequences—both positive and negative. Accountability without consequences is just wishful thinking. When performance meets or exceeds expectations, acknowledge it. When performance falls short, there should be clear consequences.

Positive consequences for meeting expectations might include praise, increased responsibility, professional development opportunities, or financial rewards. Negative consequences for failing to meet expectations might include additional oversight, reduced autonomy, formal performance improvement plans, or ultimately separation.

Rebecca established clear consequences: "If you consistently meet our review process standards for the next month, we'll discuss giving you more complex matters to handle. If the issues continue, we'll implement a formal performance improvement plan with daily oversight until quality is consistent."

The fifth element is follow-through. Accountability dies when leaders don't follow through on stated consequences. If you say performance will be reviewed weekly and then skip reviews, you've communicated that accountability doesn't really matter. If you establish consequences and then don't apply them, you've undermined the entire system.

Rebecca had to hold herself accountable for following through. She kept every scheduled check-in. She documented what she said she'd document. She provided the support she promised. And when Maria's performance improved, Rebecca acknowledged it and expanded her responsibilities as promised.

The distinction between accountability and micromanagement is this: Micromanagement focuses on controlling how work is done. Accountability focuses on ensuring results meet standards, regardless of how those results are achieved.

Rebecca didn't tell Maria exactly how to conduct reviews or stand over her shoulder during document preparation. That would be micromanagement. Instead, Rebecca defined the quality standards, provided the review process framework, measured adherence and outcomes, had regular accountability conversations, and applied consequences. That's accountability.

Team members actually appreciate clear accountability. They want to know where they stand. They want to understand expectations. They want feedback on their performance. What they don't want is arbitrary oversight, unclear standards, or being left to guess whether they're meeting expectations.

When Rebecca established clear accountability systems, Maria initially bristled—it felt like increased oversight. But within a month, Maria admitted the clarity was helpful: "I know exactly what's expected now. I know when we'll discuss my performance. I'm not wondering if you're secretly unhappy with my work. It's actually less stressful than before."

That's the paradox of accountability. It feels like more structure and oversight, but it actually reduces anxiety and improves performance because everyone knows the standards and where they stand.

Coaching for Capability Development

Feedback addresses current performance. Coaching develops future capability. Both are essential for effective delegation, but they serve different purposes and require different approaches.

Coaching is about building skills, developing judgment, expanding capacity, and preparing people for greater responsibility. It's forward-looking and developmental, not backward-looking and corrective.

Rebecca discovered the difference when she shifted from just giving Maria feedback on errors to actively coaching her toward better judgment. Instead of "You made an error in the distribution provision," Rebecca would ask: "Walk me through how you determined the distribution percentages. What factors did you consider? What might you look at differently next time?"

This coaching approach helped Maria develop better analytical skills, not just correct a single error. It built capability rather than just fixing problems.

Effective coaching follows the Socratic method—asking questions that guide people to insights rather than just telling them answers.

"What do you think the issue is here?" is more powerful than "Here's the issue." "How would you approach this differently?" builds judgment better than "Here's how to do it."

Rebecca's coaching conversations became question-driven:

- "What factors should we consider in this client's situation?"
- "How would you analyze the trade-offs between these two approaches?"
- "What concerns should we anticipate with this strategy?"
- "If you were handling this independently, what would be your next step and why?"

These questions forced Maria to think strategically, not just execute tasks. Over time, her judgment improved because she was exercising it regularly with Rebecca's guidance.

Coaching also involves sharing your thinking process. When you make a decision or solve a problem, articulate your reasoning so team members learn your approach. "Here's how I'm thinking about this..." or "The factors I'm weighing are..." teaches decision-making frameworks.

Rebecca started doing this deliberately: "I'm recommending this trust structure for the client because of three factors: their business succession goals, the tax implications of the alternatives, and their family dynamics. Let me explain how I weighted each factor..." Maria learned not just the decision but the process of reaching good decisions.

Coaching should be progressive—building toward increasing complexity and responsibility. Start with simpler challenges, provide support, gradually increase difficulty, reduce support as capability grows. This scaffolding approach develops confidence alongside competence.

Rebecca created a coaching progression for Maria:

- Month 1: Rebecca explains her analysis, Maria observes
- Month 2: Rebecca and Maria analyze together, discussing reasoning
- Month 3: Maria analyzes first, Rebecca provides input and refinement
- Month 4: Maria analyzes independently, Rebecca spot-checks and coaches
- Month 5: Maria handles independently, Rebecca available if needed

This progression built Maria's capability systematically while maintaining quality through graduated support.

Coaching requires time investment upfront that pays dividends later. Taking fifteen minutes to coach someone through a problem you could have solved for them in three minutes feels inefficient. But it's not. The fifteen minutes develops capability that prevents future three-minute problems.

Rebecca had to overcome her instinct to just solve problems quickly. When Maria brought issues, Rebecca's default was to quickly provide the answer and move on. Coaching required her to slow down, ask questions, guide Maria's thinking, and invest time in development. Initially this felt wasteful. Within two months, it paid off as Maria solved problems independently that she would have previously brought to Rebecca.

The coaching mindset is "develop capability" rather than "solve problems." Every interaction is an opportunity to build team member skills. The current problem is a teaching moment, not just an issue to resolve.

Create coaching time separate from crisis management. When you're putting out fires, you don't have time for developmental coaching. Schedule regular coaching sessions focused on skill building, not just problem-solving. This dedicated time allows for the thoughtful development that crisis moments don't permit.

Rebecca implemented monthly coaching sessions with each team member separate from their accountability check-ins. These sessions weren't about current performance issues; they were about capability development, career growth, and skill advancement. The dedicated focus on development accelerated team capability dramatically.

Celebrate growth and improvement. Coaching should include recognition when someone demonstrates new capability. "Last month you brought me this type of problem. Today you solved it independently. That's real growth." This acknowledgment reinforces progress and motivates continued development.

The goal of coaching is progressive independence. Each coaching interaction should move the person toward needing less support for that type of issue. If you're coaching someone on the same issue repeatedly without progress, either your coaching approach needs adjustment or you have a capability mismatch that coaching can't fix.

Rebecca tracked coaching topics over time. If she coached Maria on trust funding approaches three times without Maria developing independent capability, that signaled either a teaching problem (Rebecca's coaching wasn't effective) or a learning problem (Maria couldn't develop this particular skill). Either way, it required a different approach than continuing the same coaching.

Coaching transforms delegation from task assignment to capability building. When you coach effectively, you're not just getting work done today—you're building the team capability that allows increasingly complex delegation tomorrow.

Addressing Performance Issues Constructively

Despite good systems, clear expectations, and regular feedback, performance issues will arise. How you address them determines whether they're resolved or escalated into bigger problems.

The first principle in addressing performance issues is speed. Don't wait, don't hope the problem resolves itself, and don't accumulate examples. Address issues when you first notice a pattern—ideally after the second occurrence of the same problem.

Rebecca's mistake with Maria was waiting for months while accumulating examples. By the time they talked, Maria felt ambushed by a long list of issues she didn't know existed. Had Rebecca addressed the first instance of corner-cutting immediately, the pattern might never have developed.

The second principle is directness. Don't hint, imply, or hope the person figures out your concern. State the issue clearly and specifically. Indirect communication about performance problems creates confusion and resentment.

Rebecca learned to be direct: "Maria, I've noticed a pattern over the past two weeks of review steps being skipped. Yesterday it was the Smith file, and last Thursday it was the Henderson file. This is creating quality risks I need you to address." Clear, specific, direct.

The third principle is focusing on behavior and impact, not intentions or character. You can observe behavior and measure impact. You can't know intentions, and attacking character is counterproductive.

Poor approach: "You're being lazy about reviews." Better approach: "You've skipped review steps on three files this week, which has resulted in errors reaching clients."

The fourth principle is seeking to understand before demanding change. Ask why the performance issue is happening. There might be legitimate obstacles, misunderstandings, or system problems contributing to the issue.

When Rebecca finally asked Maria about the skipped reviews, she learned about overwhelming workload and Maria's belief that simple documents didn't need full review. These underlying causes pointed to solutions: workload adjustment and process clarification. Without understanding the causes, Rebecca would have just demanded compliance without addressing what made compliance difficult.

The fifth principle is collaborative problem-solving. After identifying the issue and understanding causes, work together on solutions. "How do we ensure this doesn't happen again? What needs to change? What support do you need?" This collaborative approach creates buy-in and often surfaces better solutions than you'd develop alone.

Maria proposed solutions Rebecca hadn't considered: "What if we create a simplified review checklist for routine documents so I can ensure quality without the time-intensive full process? And can we discuss which matters should be highest priority when I'm overwhelmed?" These solutions addressed the legitimate concerns while maintaining quality standards.

The sixth principle is setting clear expectations and timelines for improvement. Don't end a performance conversation without clarity about what needs to change, by when, and how success will be measured.

Rebecca was explicit: "For the next month, I need to see 100% completion of the full review process on all documents. We'll check in weekly to assess progress. After a month of consistent quality, we can revisit whether a streamlined process for simple documents makes sense."

The seventh principle is documenting significant performance issues. Verbal conversations are fine for minor issues. Significant or repeated problems should be documented to create record, ensure understanding, and support future actions if necessary.

Rebecca's documentation email summarized: the specific issues observed with dates and examples, the impact of those issues, their discussion of causes, agreed-upon solutions and support, clear expectations going forward, timeline for improvement, and consequences if improvement doesn't occur.

The eighth principle is appropriate escalation for persistent issues. If initial feedback doesn't resolve a performance problem, escalate the response. This might mean more frequent check-ins, written performance improvement plans, formal reviews, or involvement of HR or outside counsel for serious issues.

When Maria's performance didn't immediately improve after their first conversation, Rebecca implemented weekly check-ins instead of biweekly, created a written performance improvement plan with specific metrics, and made clear that continued issues could affect Maria's employment. This escalation communicated seriousness while still providing opportunity for improvement.

The ninth principle is distinguishing between skill gaps and will gaps. Skill gaps mean the person can't perform as expected—they lack the capability. Will gaps mean they won't perform as expected—they have the capability but aren't choosing to use it. These require different responses.

Rebecca realized Maria's issue was partly a will gap. Maria had the skills for thorough review but was choosing to skip steps. This required different conversation than if Maria didn't know how to conduct reviews properly. The response to a will gap is accountability and consequences. The response to a skill gap is training and support.

The tenth principle is recognizing when performance issues indicate a poor fit. Sometimes despite coaching, feedback, and support, someone simply isn't capable of meeting your standards or isn't willing to do so. Recognizing this and making tough staffing decisions is part of leadership.

If Maria's performance hadn't improved after a month of intensive support and clear accountability, Rebecca would have needed to consider whether Maria was the right fit for the role. Prolonging employment of someone who can't or won't meet standards serves neither the practice nor the individual.

Performance issue conversations are uncomfortable. But discomfort in addressing issues directly is far preferable to the dysfunction of letting problems persist. Your team deserves clarity about expectations and feedback on performance. Your practice deserves quality work. Both require willingness to address performance issues constructively when they arise.

Creating a Feedback Culture

Individual feedback conversations matter, but sustainable delegation requires a feedback culture—an environment where honest communication about performance is normal, expected, and valued.

Creating feedback culture starts with modeling. Give feedback regularly, receive feedback gracefully, and treat feedback as valuable information rather than criticism. Your behavior sets the tone for how feedback is perceived in your practice.

Rebecca started giving frequent positive feedback, not just corrective feedback. When Maria did excellent work, Rebecca acknowledged it specifically. When deadlines were met, she thanked people. When someone solved a problem well, she praised the approach. This regular positive feedback made occasional corrective feedback feel balanced rather than punitive.

She also started soliciting feedback on her own performance: "How can I support you better? What am I doing that's helpful? What am I doing that gets in your way?" This vulnerability modeled that feedback flows in all directions and that no one is above improvement.

Normalize feedback by making it routine. Don't reserve feedback for annual reviews or crisis situations. Build feedback into regular interactions. Weekly check-ins, project debriefs, and team meetings should include feedback exchanges.

Rebecca implemented "start, stop, continue" in weekly team meetings. Each person shared one thing they want someone to start doing, one thing to stop doing, and one thing to continue doing. This structure made feedback routine and reduced the stigma of critical input.

Create peer feedback mechanisms. Feedback doesn't only flow from leader to team. Team members should give each other feedback on collaboration, communication, and work quality. This distributes feedback responsibility and builds collective ownership of standards.

Rebecca implemented peer review for significant documents. Team members reviewed each other's work and provided feedback before final attorney review. This created a culture where feedback was part of quality assurance, not just a leadership function.

Teach feedback skills explicitly. Don't assume people know how to give or receive feedback effectively. Provide training on feedback frameworks, communication skills, and how to have difficult conversations.

Rebecca brought in a coach to teach the team feedback skills: how to deliver critical feedback constructively, how to receive feedback without defensiveness, how to ask for feedback effectively, and how to use feedback for improvement. These skills transformed feedback from an uncomfortable necessity to a valued practice tool.

Distinguish between public and private feedback. Praise publicly, correct privately. Public recognition amplifies positive feedback's impact. Public criticism humiliates and damages relationships. Keep corrective feedback in one-on-one settings.

Rebecca made a point of acknowledging excellent work in team meetings: "Maria's thoroughness on the Johnson matter prevented a significant issue. That's the quality standard we're aiming for." But performance issues were always addressed privately in scheduled conversations.

Create psychological safety for honest feedback. People won't give or receive feedback openly if they fear punishment, retaliation, or judgment. Make it safe to acknowledge mistakes, ask for help, and point out problems.

Rebecca explicitly told her team: "I want to hear about problems early when we can fix them. Hiding issues or mistakes only makes them worse. There's no punishment for bringing me bad news or acknowledging errors. There is a problem with hiding issues. If something's wrong, I want to know immediately."

Celebrate feedback-driven improvement. When someone receives feedback and demonstrably improves, acknowledge that growth. This reinforces that feedback leads to positive outcomes, not just uncomfortable conversations.

When Maria's quality dramatically improved after their feedback conversations, Rebecca acknowledged it: "Maria, your work quality over the past month has been exceptional. The feedback we discussed is clearly translating into better outcomes. That's exactly the kind of responsiveness to feedback that helps you grow professionally."

Use feedback for practice improvement, not just individual development. When feedback reveals system problems, unclear processes, or practice-level issues, address those systemically. This shows that feedback drives organizational learning, not just individual correction.

Maria's feedback about overwhelming workload led Rebecca to examine caseload distribution across the team. She discovered several team members felt similarly overwhelmed. This systemic issue required structural solutions—better workload tracking, clearer capacity management, and possibly additional hiring. Individual feedback surfaced a practice-level problem.

Make feedback expected, not exceptional. In a strong feedback culture, people ask for feedback proactively rather than waiting to receive it. "How could I have handled that better?" or "What should I work on?" become common questions.

Rebecca noticed this cultural shift when Maria started asking for feedback rather than just receiving it: "I tried a new approach on the Williams matter. Can you review it and let me know what worked and what didn't?" This proactive feedback-seeking showed the culture was changing.

Track whether feedback is actually given and received. Don't just assume feedback is happening. Verify it. Regular feedback should be documented in check-in notes, performance reviews, or feedback logs. If documentation shows no feedback for extended periods, the culture isn't as strong as you think.

Rebecca required managers to document feedback conversations in a simple log. Reviewing these logs quarterly showed whether feedback was flowing regularly or only in crisis moments. When patterns showed insufficient feedback, she coached managers on making it more routine.

A strong feedback culture transforms delegation effectiveness. When people regularly receive clear information about their performance, coaching to develop capability, and accountability for meeting standards, they perform better and grow faster. The practice benefits from higher quality work, and individuals benefit from accelerated professional development.

Rebecca's Feedback Transformation

A year after that difficult conversation with Maria about quality issues, Rebecca's practice had fundamentally changed. Not just in processes or systems, but in how people communicated about performance and accountability.

Maria had become one of Rebecca's strongest team members. The quality issues were completely resolved. More than that, Maria had developed into a coach for junior paralegals, using many of the feedback approaches Rebecca had learned to use with her.

The transformation required Rebecca to overcome her deep discomfort with feedback conversations. She'd had to learn that avoiding feedback wasn't kindness—it was actually unfair to team members who deserved to know how they were performing. She'd had to practice being direct, specific, and timely with both positive and corrective feedback.

She'd learned to create accountability without micromanagement by establishing clear expectations, measuring outcomes, having regular check-ins, and following through on consequences. Her team knew exactly what was expected and where they stood, which reduced anxiety and improved performance.

She'd learned to coach for capability development, not just correct current problems. By asking questions that guided people to insights, sharing her thinking process, and creating progressive challenges, she'd built team capability that allowed increasingly complex delegation.

She'd learned to address performance issues constructively by being direct about problems, seeking to understand causes, collaborating on solutions, and escalating appropriately when issues persisted. The uncomfortable conversations she'd avoided for so long became routine once she developed a framework for handling them.

Most importantly, she'd created a feedback culture where honest communication about performance was normal and valued. Her team gave each other feedback regularly. They asked for feedback proactively. They used feedback to improve rather than taking it as personal criticism. And the practice benefited from the continuous improvement this culture enabled.

The financial impact was substantial. Higher quality work meant fewer errors, less rework, and better client satisfaction. Better team capability meant Rebecca could delegate more complex work, freeing her time for highest-value activities. Clearer accountability meant problems were caught and addressed quickly rather than festering into crises.

But the most meaningful change was in relationships. Rebecca had feared that giving direct feedback would damage her relationships with team members. The opposite happened. People appreciated clarity about expectations and honest communication about performance. They felt respected when given direct feedback rather than patronized by vague hints.

Maria told Rebecca months later: "Those first feedback conversations were hard. I was defensive and upset. But looking back, that's when you started treating me like a professional instead of just being nice to me. The direct feedback and clear accountability showed you believed I could improve and held me to higher standards. That was more respectful than staying quiet about the issues."

Rebecca reflected on what she'd learned about feedback and accountability in delegation:

Feedback is essential, not optional. You can't delegate effectively without regular communication about how delegated work is being done. Feedback is how you maintain quality, develop capability, and ensure accountability.

Avoiding feedback is unkind, not kind. Silence about performance issues prevents improvement and leaves people wondering where they stand. Direct, timely feedback is a gift that enables growth.

Accountability and micromanagement are different. Clear standards, measurement, regular check-ins, and consequences create accountability. Controlling how every task is done is micromanagement. You need the former, not the latter.

Coaching builds capability. Asking questions, sharing reasoning, and providing progressive challenges develops team members' skills and judgment. This investment pays off through increasing delegation possibilities.

Performance issues require direct address. Hoping problems will resolve themselves is fantasy. Early, direct intervention resolves issues before they become crises.

Culture matters more than individual conversations. Creating an environment where feedback is normal, expected, and valued transforms how your entire practice operates.

Rebecca's advice to other attorneys struggling with feedback and accountability was straightforward: "Get comfortable being uncomfortable. Feedback conversations will always be somewhat awkward. But they get easier with practice, and they're absolutely essential for effective delegation. Your team deserves honest communication about their performance. Your practice deserves quality accountability. Both require you to give feedback you'd rather avoid."

The transformation from feedback avoidance to feedback culture was one of the most valuable changes Rebecca made to her practice. It enabled sustainable delegation, continuous improvement, and professional development that benefited everyone—the practice, the team, and Rebecca herself.

Action Items for This Chapter

1. Give Specific Positive Feedback This Week

Identify three instances of excellent work from team members this week and provide specific, timely positive feedback. Practice the feedback elements: specific behavior, impact explanation, and genuine appreciation.

Positive feedback given:

1. _____ (person/situation)
2. _____ (person/situation)
3. _____ (person/situation)

2. Address One Performance Issue Directly

Identify one performance issue you've been avoiding and schedule a direct conversation to address it within the next five days. Use the framework: specific behavior observed, impact of that behavior, seek to understand causes, collaborate on solutions, set clear expectations.

Issue to address: _____

Conversation scheduled for: _____

Outcome: _____

3. Implement Regular Check-Ins

Schedule recurring check-in meetings (weekly or biweekly) with each team member who receives significant delegated work. Use these for feedback, accountability, coaching, and addressing issues before they become problems.

Check-ins scheduled: Yes / No

Frequency: _____

First meeting date: _____

Before Moving to Chapter 14:

Feedback, coaching, and accountability are the communication infrastructure that makes delegation sustainable. Without honest performance communication, delegation devolves into either micromanagement or abdication. With effective feedback systems, delegation creates continuous improvement and capability development.

You now understand why feedback avoidance undermines delegation, how to structure effective feedback conversations, how to create accountability without micromanaging, how to coach for capability development, how to address performance issues constructively, and how to build a feedback culture that supports sustainable delegation.

The next and final chapter addresses scaling delegation as your practice grows. How do you maintain delegation effectiveness as you add team members? How do you delegate to managers who delegate to others? How do you create systems that scale beyond your direct involvement?

Chapter 14 shows you how to build a practice where effective delegation is embedded in your culture and systems, enabling growth without requiring your constant oversight.

One commitment before moving forward:

Think about the one feedback conversation you've been avoiding. Commit to having that conversation within the next week using the frameworks from this chapter.

Feedback conversation I've been avoiding: _____

When I'll have it: _____

Framework I'll use: _____

CHAPTER 12:

Scaling Delegation as You Grow

Thomas stood in his conference room looking at the organizational chart on the whiteboard. Five years ago, his criminal defense practice had been just him and one paralegal. Now he had twelve team members: four attorneys, five paralegals, an intake coordinator, an office manager, and a marketing director.

By most measures, his practice was a success. Revenue had grown from $400,000 to $2.8 million. The team was capable. Systems were in place. Delegation worked reasonably well at the individual level.

But Thomas felt like he was drowning again. The same bottleneck problems he'd experienced as a solo practitioner were back, just at a different scale. Instead of being involved in every client matter, he was now involved in every team decision. Instead of reviewing every document, he was reviewing every process. Instead of managing two people, he was managing twelve—and the complexity of those relationships had grown exponentially.

He'd successfully learned to delegate tasks and decisions to individuals. But he hadn't learned to scale delegation as the practice grew. His delegation approaches that worked beautifully with three people were breaking down with twelve. And he had ambitions to grow to twenty-five team members, which felt impossible with his current approach.

Thomas's challenge is common among growing practices. The delegation skills that work in a small practice don't automatically scale. Moving from solo to small team requires one set of delegation capabilities. Growing from small team to larger organization requires additional skills around organizational structure, management layers, cultural reinforcement, and systems that work without your direct involvement.

This chapter shows you how to scale delegation effectively as your practice grows. You'll learn how to create organizational structure that enables delegation at scale, develop managers who can delegate as effectively as you do, build systems and culture that maintain quality without your constant oversight, and transition from hands-on delegator to architect of a delegation-capable organization.

The Scaling Inflection Points

Practices experience predictable inflection points as they grow. Each inflection point requires different delegation approaches and creates new challenges that your previous methods can't solve.

The Solo to Team transition (1-5 people) is the first inflection point. You're learning basic delegation—task assignment, process documentation, quality standards, and direct oversight. Your delegation is one-to-one. You know everyone's work intimately because you're directly involved with each person.

Thomas navigated this transition successfully. He learned to delegate client work to his first paralegal, then to his first associate attorney. He developed systems, created standards, and built basic infrastructure. His hands-on delegation approach worked because he could personally oversee everything.

The Team to Organization transition (6-15 people) is the second inflection point and where Thomas currently struggled. You can't personally oversee everyone anymore. You need management layers, delegation through others, and systems that work without your direct involvement. The practice becomes too complex for one person to manage all relationships and decisions.

This is where many practices stall. The owner tries to maintain the same hands-on delegation approach that worked with five people. With twelve people, it's overwhelming. The owner becomes the bottleneck again, but now at organizational level rather than task level.

The Organization to Enterprise transition (16-50+ people) is the third inflection point. Multiple management layers become necessary. You're several steps removed from front-line work. Culture and systems must maintain quality and alignment without your personal involvement in most decisions. You're delegating not just to individuals or teams, but building an organization capable of self-management.

Thomas aspired to this level but couldn't see how to get there. His current approach wasn't scalable beyond his current size, let alone to fifty people.

Each inflection point requires letting go of what worked previously and adopting new approaches. The hands-on oversight that's essential early becomes micromanagement later. The personal relationships that drive small team performance must be supplemented with structure and systems in larger organizations. The direct delegation that works at small scale must evolve into delegation through managers at larger scale.

Thomas's realization was that he needed fundamentally different delegation approaches for his current size. The skills that got him to twelve people wouldn't get him to twenty-five. He needed to evolve from delegator to delegation architect—building an organization where effective delegation happened at every level, not just from him to his direct reports.

Creating Organizational Structure for Scaled Delegation

Structure enables delegation at scale. Without clear organizational design, growing practices devolve into chaos where everyone reports to the owner and nothing gets done without the owner's involvement.

The first structural principle is limiting span of control. Research suggests 5-7 direct reports is optimal for most managers. Beyond that, relationship complexity overwhelms and quality of oversight deteriorates. If you have twelve team members all reporting directly to you, you've exceeded effective span of control.

Thomas had all twelve team members reporting to him. This created bottlenecks because everything flowed through him. His solution was creating a clear organizational structure with appropriate reporting relationships.

He organized his practice into three functional areas, each with a leader:

- **Legal Operations** (led by senior attorney Sarah): All attorneys and case-related paralegals reported to Sarah
- **Business Operations** (led by office manager Jennifer): Intake, administration, and operational staff reported to Jennifer
- **Client Development** (led by marketing director Kevin): Marketing and business development activities reported to Kevin

This structure reduced Thomas's direct reports from twelve to three. Sarah, Jennifer, and Kevin each managed 3-4 people—well within optimal span of control. Thomas could focus on leading these three managers rather than trying to manage everyone.

The second structural principle is clear role definition. Every position should have defined responsibilities, decision authority, and accountability. Vague roles create confusion about who should do what and who has authority to make decisions.

Thomas created position descriptions for each role that specified:

- Primary responsibilities
- Key performance indicators
- Decision authority (what they could decide independently, what required consultation, what required approval)
- Reporting relationships
- Collaboration expectations with other roles

These clear definitions eliminated much of the "who should do this?" confusion that had created bottlenecks.

The third structural principle is appropriate management layers. Flat organizations work well at small scale. As organizations grow, management layers become necessary for effective delegation and oversight.

Thomas recognized he needed a management layer between himself and front-line staff. Sarah, Jennifer, and Kevin became true managers with responsibility for their functional areas, not just senior individual contributors. This layer allowed delegation to scale—Thomas delegated to managers who delegated to their teams.

The fourth structural principle is cross-functional coordination mechanisms. As organizations grow and specialize, silos develop. Coordination mechanisms ensure different parts of the organization work together effectively.

Thomas implemented weekly leadership team meetings where Sarah, Jennifer, and Kevin coordinated their areas. He created standard processes for how legal operations would hand off to intake, how marketing would support business development, and how operations would support legal delivery. These coordination mechanisms prevented silos from undermining organizational effectiveness.

The fifth structural principle is progressive specialization. Early-stage practices need generalists who can do many things. As practices grow, specialization increases effectiveness. But specialization must be introduced deliberately to avoid rigidity.

Thomas created specialized roles as the practice grew:

- Paralegals specialized by case type (DUI, violent crimes, drug offenses)
- Attorneys developed practice area focus while maintaining some breadth
- Administrative functions specialized (intake, scheduling, billing, operations)

This specialization increased expertise and efficiency. But Thomas maintained some cross-training to prevent over-specialization that would make the organization fragile.

Organizational structure isn't about control—it's about enabling effective delegation. Good structure clarifies who's responsible for what, creates appropriate oversight relationships, limits complexity for any individual manager, and provides coordination across the organization. Without structure, delegation at scale is impossible.

Developing Managers Who Delegate

The transition from hands-on delegator to organizational leader requires developing managers who delegate as effectively as you do. Your personal delegation skills must be replicated across your management team.

Thomas realized that Sarah, Jennifer, and Kevin were promoted because of their individual competence, not management capability. Sarah was an excellent attorney. Jennifer was a highly organized administrator. Kevin was a creative marketer. But none had formal management training or experience leading teams.

Promoting individual contributors to management without developing their leadership capabilities is a common failure mode in growing practices. The best attorney doesn't automatically become a good legal operations manager. The most organized person doesn't automatically know how to lead an operations team.

Thomas's first step was explicit training in delegation and management skills. He brought in outside consultants to teach his management team:

1. How to delegate effectively (the frameworks and skills from this book)
2. How to give feedback and coach team members
3. How to create accountability without micromanaging
4. How to make decisions and empower team decision-making
5. How to manage performance and address issues

This formal training gave them frameworks and skills they wouldn't develop through trial and error alone.

The second step was modeling and coaching. Thomas shared his delegation approaches with his managers. He involved them in his delegation decisions so they could see his thinking. He coached them when their delegation attempts struggled.

When Sarah struggled with delegating case strategy decisions to her associate attorneys, Thomas coached her: "You're holding onto decisions they're capable of making. Use the 1-3-1 framework— have them bring you problem definition, three options, and a recommendation. Often you'll approve their recommendation. When you don't, you're teaching them better judgment."

The third step was creating management processes and rituals. Thomas implemented:

- Weekly manager check-ins where each manager discussed their team's performance and delegation challenges
- Monthly management team meetings for cross-functional coordination and shared learning
- Quarterly management retreats for strategic planning and skill development
- Performance review processes that assessed both individual results and team development

These processes created structure for management excellence and continuous improvement.

The fourth step was establishing management standards. Thomas defined what good management looked like in his practice:

- Managers must hold regular one-on-ones with each team member
- Managers must provide regular feedback (both positive and corrective)
- Managers must delegate progressively, building team capability
- Managers must create accountability while avoiding micromanagement
- Managers must develop succession plans within their teams

These standards created clear expectations for management performance.

The fifth step was accountability for management effectiveness. Thomas measured his managers not just on their functional area results, but on team development. Sarah was assessed on both case outcomes and attorney development. Jennifer was evaluated on operational efficiency and team capability. Kevin was measured on marketing results and team growth.

When Sarah's team consistently needed her personal involvement in routine decisions, Thomas addressed it: "Your team isn't developing decision-making capability. They're too dependent on you. That's preventing your scaling. Let's work on your delegation and their empowerment."

This accountability reinforced that management and delegation were core responsibilities, not optional add-ons to functional expertise.

The sixth step was creating peer learning among managers. Thomas facilitated sharing of delegation approaches, challenges, and solutions. When Jennifer successfully implemented a new delegation framework with her team, Thomas had her share the approach with Sarah and Kevin. When Sarah struggled with a performance issue, the management team problem-solved together.

This peer learning accelerated management capability development faster than Thomas teaching each manager individually.

The critical insight is that management skills must be deliberately developed. Hoping that capable individual contributors will figure out how to manage and delegate is organizational malpractice. Growing practices require investment in management development or they'll be led by frustrated, ineffective managers who become bottlenecks themselves.

Building Systems That Scale Without You

Personal delegation has limits. As organizations grow, systems and processes must carry the delegation load. You can't personally teach every new hire. You can't personally ensure every process is followed. You can't personally maintain quality on every deliverable.

Systems are how delegation scales beyond your direct involvement. They embed your standards, processes, and decision frameworks into organizational infrastructure that works whether you're present or not.

Thomas realized his practice was too dependent on his personal involvement. When he was gone, decision-making slowed. When new people joined, they had to learn everything from individual instruction. When quality issues arose, they required his personal intervention.

His solution was building systems that maintained delegation effectiveness without his constant oversight.

Documentation systems were Thomas's first priority. He created comprehensive documentation of:

- Standard processes for every recurring task type
- Decision frameworks for common decision categories
- Quality standards and review processes
- Role expectations and performance standards
- Training materials for all positions

This documentation meant new team members could learn from written materials instead of requiring his personal instruction. It meant standards were clear and consistent regardless of who was managing. It meant the "how we do things here" knowledge wasn't locked in people's heads.

Workflow systems were second. Thomas implemented practice management software that embedded processes and standards into daily work:

- Case management workflows that guided attorneys and paralegals through standard case progressions
- Document automation that ensured consistent quality and completeness
- Task management that made delegation and accountability visible

- Communication templates that maintained brand and quality standards

These workflow systems meant proper process was the path of least resistance. Following standards was easier than deviating from them.

Quality assurance systems were third. Thomas built quality checks into work processes:

- Peer review requirements for significant work products
- Automated quality checklists for document preparation
- Random sampling and review of completed work
- Client feedback collection and analysis

These quality systems caught issues without requiring Thomas's personal review. They created multiple quality checkpoints distributed across the organization.

Knowledge management systems were fourth. Thomas created repositories of organizational knowledge:

- Template library of excellent work products
- Case law research database organized by issue
- Client situation scenarios with recommended approaches
- Lessons learned documentation from past matters

These knowledge systems made organizational wisdom accessible to everyone, not just those who worked with Thomas directly.

Communication systems were fifth. Thomas implemented structured communication that kept information flowing without his personal involvement:

- Regular team meetings with standard agendas
- Cross-functional huddles for coordination
- Performance dashboards visible to all relevant parties
- Automated reporting and alerts

These communication systems meant people had the information they needed when they needed it, without waiting for Thomas to relay it.

Decision support systems were sixth. Thomas embedded decision frameworks into tools and processes:

- Decision trees for common client situations
- Authority matrices showing who decides what
- Risk assessment frameworks for case evaluation
- Pricing calculators for fee quotes

These decision support systems guided good decisions without requiring Thomas's involvement in each one.

The power of systems is that they scale infinitely. Documentation teaches the hundredth employee as effectively as the first. Workflows guide the thousandth case as reliably as the tenth. Quality systems catch errors whether Thomas is present or on vacation.

Building systems requires upfront investment. Creating documentation, implementing software, designing workflows, and building knowledge repositories takes time. But that investment pays returns forever as the systems enable scaled delegation without scaled personal involvement.

Thomas tracked the impact: Before systems, onboarding a new team member required forty hours of his personal time. After systems, onboarding required five hours of his time with the rest handled by documentation, training materials, and structured shadowing. That 35-hour savings per new hire accumulated quickly as the practice grew.

Embedding Delegation in Culture

Systems enable scaled delegation. Culture sustains it. The values, norms, and behaviors that constitute your practice culture either reinforce effective delegation or undermine it.

Thomas realized his practice had no deliberate culture around delegation. Some managers delegated well, others didn't. Some team members took initiative, others waited for direction. Some decisions were made at appropriate levels, others escalated unnecessarily. This inconsistency reflected lack of cultural clarity about delegation expectations.

His solution was embedding delegation principles into practice culture deliberately and explicitly.

Core values alignment was first. Thomas identified that effective delegation required certain values:

- Trust (believing team members are capable)
- Accountability (holding people to standards)
- Growth mindset (believing capabilities can be developed)
- Empowerment (giving people authority to act)
- Learning orientation (viewing mistakes as development opportunities)

He made these values explicit and connected them to delegation: "We value trust, which means we delegate meaningfully and believe our team can handle it. We value accountability, which means we give clear expectations and measure results. We value growth, which means we develop capability through progressive delegation."

Behavioral norms were second. Thomas defined specific behaviors that reflected delegation culture:

- Managers should delegate to the lowest capable level
- Team members should solve problems before escalating

- Everyone should use decision frameworks for empowered decisions
- Feedback should be regular, specific, and developmental
- Mistakes should be learning opportunities, not sources of blame

These behavioral norms gave concrete guidance about how delegation culture manifested in daily work.

Recognition and rewards were third. Thomas recognized and rewarded delegation-consistent behaviors:

- Managers who developed team capability were promoted and praised
- Team members who demonstrated good judgment in delegated work were acknowledged
- Successful delegation examples were shared in team meetings
- Annual awards included "best developing manager" and "most empowered team member"

What gets recognized gets repeated. By celebrating effective delegation, Thomas reinforced cultural expectations.

Stories and symbols were fourth. Thomas used stories to reinforce delegation culture:

- He shared examples of successful delegation creating great outcomes
- He told stories of team members who grew through progressive responsibility
- He acknowledged his own delegation mistakes and learning
- He celebrated instances where appropriate decision-making prevented problems

These stories created cultural mythology around delegation that guided behavior more powerfully than policies alone.

Hiring for culture fit was fifth. Thomas added delegation-readiness to hiring criteria:

- Interview questions assessed candidates' comfort with autonomy
- Reference checks asked about decision-making and initiative
- Trial projects evaluated how candidates handled delegated responsibility

Hiring people who fit delegation culture was easier than trying to change people who didn't.

Onboarding for culture was sixth. Thomas's onboarding process explicitly taught delegation expectations:

- New hires learned the decision frameworks and authority levels
- Orientation covered delegation principles and cultural norms
- Early assignments progressively tested delegation readiness
- New hire feedback included assessment of delegation cultural fit

This early cultural immersion set expectations from day one.

Leadership modeling was most important. Thomas recognized that culture flows from leadership behavior. His actions mattered more than his words.

He deliberately modeled delegation culture:

- He delegated meaningfully to his managers and didn't second-guess them
- He acknowledged when he was holding onto decisions he should delegate
- He celebrated team member initiative even when outcomes weren't perfect

- He gave his managers authority and backed their decisions publicly
- He admitted his own delegation mistakes and shared what he learned

His team watched how he delegated more than they listened to what he said about delegation. His modeling set cultural tone.

Culture change is slow but powerful. Thomas didn't transform practice culture overnight. But consistent reinforcement of delegation values, norms, and behaviors gradually shifted how everyone thought about delegation.

Within eighteen months, the cultural shift was evident. New team members internalized delegation expectations quickly because everyone around them modeled it. Managers competed to be recognized for team development. Team members took initiative without being asked. Decisions happened at appropriate levels without escalation.

The practice had developed a delegation culture that reinforced and sustained effective delegation without Thomas's constant attention.

Measuring Delegation Effectiveness at Scale

As organizations grow, what gets measured gets managed. Delegation effectiveness must be measured systematically or it will deteriorate invisibly until crisis forces attention.

Thomas recognized he had no systematic measurement of delegation effectiveness. He had vague sense of whether delegation was working based on how busy he felt and whether crises emerged. That's not measurement—that's intuition. And intuition doesn't scale.

His solution was implementing delegation metrics at multiple levels.

Individual level metrics measured how well each team member received and executed delegated work:

- Percentage of delegated tasks completed on time
- Quality scores on delegated work (through spot checks and reviews)
- Number of escalations (distinguishing appropriate from unnecessary)
- Growth in scope of work successfully handled
- Feedback scores from those delegating to them

These individual metrics showed who was succeeding with delegation and who needed additional development.

Manager level metrics measured how well managers delegated to their teams:

- Team member capability development (measured through skills assessments)
- Distribution of decision-making (what percentage of decisions made at team level vs. requiring manager)
- Team member autonomy scores (from surveys and observations)
- Time managers spent on manager-level work vs. doing team member work themselves
- Team member retention and satisfaction

These manager metrics revealed whether managers were building capable teams or creating dependent ones.

Organizational level metrics measured overall delegation effectiveness:

- Decision velocity (time from issue identification to decision)
- Percentage of decisions requiring owner involvement
- Scalability indicators (whether growth in team size enables proportional revenue growth)

- Quality maintenance as work scales (whether quality deteriorates with growth)
- Owner time allocation (percentage on strategic work vs. operational involvement)

These organizational metrics showed whether delegation was scaling effectively or breaking down.

Thomas implemented regular delegation reviews:

- Monthly manager reviews of individual team member delegation metrics
- Quarterly leadership reviews of manager-level delegation metrics
- Annual organizational assessment of delegation system effectiveness

These reviews made delegation performance visible and created accountability for improvement.

The metrics revealed issues Thomas hadn't recognized. One manager's team showed high escalation rates and low autonomy scores—the manager was micromanaging. Another manager's team showed capability stagnation—insufficient delegation of developmental work. The organization showed that Thomas's involvement in decisions had actually increased as the practice grew—he was becoming a bigger bottleneck, not smaller.

Each issue identified through metrics led to targeted intervention. The micromanaging manager received coaching on empowerment. The manager not developing team capability got training on progressive delegation. Thomas himself committed to reducing decision involvement by 50% over six months.

Within a year, metrics showed dramatic improvement:

- Team member autonomy scores increased 40%
- Decision velocity (time to decision) decreased 35%
- Owner involvement in decisions decreased 60%

- Quality scores maintained or improved despite delegation increases
- Revenue per team member increased as delegation improved

The metrics confirmed that systematic focus on delegation was working. They also revealed that delegation effectiveness required ongoing attention. When quarterly reviews showed delegation metrics declining, Thomas investigated and addressed root causes before problems became serious.

Measurement transforms delegation from aspiration to accountability. When delegation effectiveness is measured, it improves. When it's not measured, it deteriorates invisibly.

Thomas's Scaling Success

Two years after standing in his conference room feeling overwhelmed by organizational complexity, Thomas stood in the same room with a very different feeling. The practice had grown to twenty-two team members. Revenue had reached $4.2 million. And Thomas felt less busy than he had when the practice was half the current size.

The transformation came from learning to scale delegation effectively. He'd moved beyond personal delegation to building an organization where effective delegation was embedded in structure, systems, culture, and management capability.

The organizational structure transformation was fundamental. Clear reporting relationships, appropriate span of control, and well-defined roles eliminated the chaos of everyone reporting to Thomas. The three-leader structure (Legal Operations, Business Operations, Client Development) created manageable complexity and enabled delegation through management layers.

The management development investment paid enormous dividends. Sarah, Jennifer, and Kevin had evolved from individual contributors into capable managers who delegated as effectively as Thomas. They built capability in their teams, made good decisions about what to delegate, and created accountability without micromanagement. Thomas could delegate to them with confidence because they had the skills to delegate further.

The systems transformation was perhaps most impactful. Documentation, workflows, quality assurance, knowledge management, communication systems, and decision support tools carried the delegation load. The practice could onboard new people, maintain quality, make good decisions, and execute effectively without Thomas's personal involvement in every detail.

The cultural transformation sustained everything else. Delegation values, behavioral norms, recognition systems, and leadership modeling created an environment where effective delegation was simply "how we do things here." New team members absorbed delegation expectations from the culture itself.

The measurement transformation created continuous improvement. Regular tracking of delegation metrics revealed issues early and confirmed that interventions were working. Delegation improved because it was measured, reviewed, and actively managed.

The financial impact was substantial. Revenue per team member increased because delegation enabled higher productivity. Thomas's own earning increased because his time was deployed on highest-value activities. Profitability improved because well-delegated work was executed more efficiently.

But the personal impact mattered most to Thomas. He'd built a practice that could grow without consuming him. He could take real vacations without the practice stumbling. He could focus on strategy, major client relationships, and business development while confident that operations ran smoothly. He'd transformed from bottleneck to architect of an organization that worked.

Thomas reflected on the critical lessons of scaling delegation:

Structure enables scale. Without organizational design that limits span of control and creates appropriate management layers, delegation can't scale beyond a handful of people.

Management capability must be developed. Individual contributors promoted to management need delegation and leadership training. Hoping they'll figure it out is organizational malpractice.

Systems carry the load. Personal delegation has limits. Systems embed processes, standards, and decision frameworks that work without personal involvement.

Culture sustains delegation. Values, norms, and behaviors that reinforce delegation create self-sustaining effectiveness.

Measurement drives improvement. What gets measured gets managed. Systematic delegation metrics reveal issues and confirm progress.

Letting go is essential. Scaling requires releasing control over details and trusting the organization you've built. The hardest part of scaling delegation is psychological—accepting that you can't personally oversee everything.

His advice to other attorneys approaching scaling challenges was direct: "Everything that works at small scale needs to evolve for larger scale. Your hands-on delegation must become structural delegation through managers, systems, and culture. You must shift from doing and directing to designing and developing. That shift is uncomfortable but essential for growth."

The practice Thomas envisioned—twenty-five people, $5 million in revenue, running smoothly without his constant involvement—was no longer a distant dream. It was an achievable reality because he'd learned to scale delegation effectively.

He stood in the conference room looking at the updated organizational chart. Twenty-two people, organized into clear structures, led by capable managers, supported by robust systems, operating within a strong delegation culture.

And he smiled, knowing that the chart would soon show twenty-five people, then thirty, then more. Because he'd built an organization capable of growth. An organization where delegation scaled as effectively as the practice itself.

Action Items for This Chapter

1. Assess Your Current Organizational Structure

If you have more than 5-7 direct reports, create an organizational structure with appropriate management layers. Define reporting relationships, role clarity, and span of control limits. Implement within 30 days.

Current direct reports: _____

New structure needed: Yes / No

Implementation deadline: _____

2. Develop One Manager's Delegation Skills

Select one manager (or future manager) and invest in developing their delegation capability. Provide training, coaching, and clear expectations for how they should delegate to their team.

Manager selected: _____

Development plan: _____

First development session: _____

3. Build One Scalable System

Identify one area where personal involvement is bottlenecking scale. Create a system (documentation, workflow, quality process, decision framework) that works without your constant involvement.

Bottleneck area: _____

System to build: _____

Completion target: _____

Conclusion: From Bottleneck to Builder

You picked up this book because you were stuck. Your practice had grown to the point where you couldn't personally handle everything, but you hadn't figured out how to let go without losing control. You were working harder than ever but seeing diminishing returns. You'd become your own bottleneck.

If you've implemented even a fraction of what this book teaches, you're no longer stuck. You understand that the problem wasn't your workload or your team—it was your delegation approach. And you have frameworks, systems, and skills to delegate effectively.

You've learned to recognize bottleneck syndrome and understand its real costs. You know the legal landscape for delegation and how to navigate it safely. You can identify what to delegate and what to keep. You know how to find and develop people capable of receiving meaningful delegation.

You've learned to introduce team members to clients in ways that build confidence rather than resistance. You can maintain client relationships while delegating substantially. You have decision frameworks that empower your team. You've developed feedback and accountability skills that sustain delegation. And you understand how to scale delegation as your practice grows.

The transformation from bottleneck to builder isn't instantaneous. It requires commitment to changing how you work, discomfort with letting go of control, and patience as you develop new capabilities in yourself and your team. But the transformation is possible. The practices and people profiled in this book are real examples of attorneys who made this journey successfully.

Your next steps are clear:

This week: Implement the 1-3-1 decision framework. Stop making decisions that your team should make with guidance.

This month: Delegate one significant responsibility you've been holding. Use the frameworks from Chapter 4 to choose wisely and Chapter 5 to ensure the right person receives it.

This quarter: Build one system that enables delegation to scale without your constant involvement. Documentation, workflow, or quality assurance—choose what your practice needs most.

This year: Transform your practice culture to reinforce effective delegation at every level. Values, norms, recognition, and modeling that embed delegation into how your practice operates.

The goal isn't perfection. The goal is progress. Each small improvement in delegation effectiveness compounds over time. The motion you delegate this week frees an hour. That hour enables strategy work that improves the practice. The improved practice creates capacity to delegate more work. The cycle accelerates.

Within a year of committed delegation development, your practice will be unrecognizable. Work you once handled personally will flow smoothly through your team. Decisions you once made will be made confidently at appropriate levels. Client relationships you once maintained personally will be strengthened by team member involvement. Growth you once thought impossible will become sustainable.

You'll reclaim your time for the work only you can do—strategy, key relationships, practice development, and leadership. You'll build a practice that serves you instead of consuming you. You'll create a team that grows in capability and engagement. You'll achieve the professional success and personal freedom that brought you to law in the first place.

The bottleneck syndrome that once defined your practice will become a distant memory. In its place will be a well-delegated, highly capable practice that grows sustainably and serves clients excellently without requiring your involvement in every detail.

That's the promise of mastering delegation. That's what's possible when you get out of your own damn way.

Now stop reading and start delegating.

Your practice—and your life—will thank you.

ABOUT THE AUTHOR

Jay Ruane is the founder and CEO of Ruane Attorneys at Law, a criminal defense firm that has grown from a solo practice to a multi-million-dollar operation serving clients throughout Connecticut. Since 1998, Jay has represented thousands of clients facing criminal charges while developing systematic approaches to practice management and client acquisition that have transformed his firm into one of the most successful criminal defense practices in the state.

Recognizing that most attorneys struggle with the business side of law practice, Jay founded The Criminal Mastermind in 2023—the only coaching community focused exclusively on criminal defense attorneys. Through this platform, he teaches practice management, marketing strategies, and systematic client conversion techniques to criminal defense lawyers across the nation.

Jay is a frequent speaker at criminal defense conferences and contributes regularly to The Champion, the magazine of the National Association of Criminal Defense Lawyers, where he writes about firm management and business development.

A graduate of law school with nearly three decades of criminal defense experience, Jay has been recognized by his peers for both his legal advocacy and his leadership in advancing the criminal defense bar. He is admitted to practice in Connecticut and New York and the United States Supreme Court..

Jay lives in Connecticut with his wife Jill and their four children. When not working with clients or coaching attorneys, he enjoys golf, learning guitar, and supporting local charities focused on justice and community development.

For more information about Jay's work with criminal defense attorneys, visit thecriminalmastermind.com.